The United Way Scandal

Other Titles in the Nonprofit Law, Finance, and Management Series

The United Way Scandal

AN INSIDER'S ACCOUNT OF WHAT WENT WRONG AND WHY

John S. Glaser

John Wiley & Sons Inc.
New York • Chichester • Brisbane • Toronto • Singapore

Copyright © 1994 by John Wiley & Sons, Inc.

Library of Congress Cataloging in Publication Data
Glaser, John S., 1939–
    The United Way scandal : an insider's account of what went wrong and why / by John S. Glaser.
        p.   cm. — (Nonprofit law, finance, and management professional series)
    Includes Index.
      ISBN 0-471-59114-9 (cloth : acid-free paper)
      1. United Way of America—Management.   2. Charities—United States—Management—Corrupt practices.   3. Aramony, William.   I. Title.   II. Series.
    HV97.U553G53   1993
    361.8'0973—dc20   93-13207
                                                                                         CIP

Printed in the United States of America

10 9 8 7 6 5 4 3 2 1

Dedicated to the future volunteer and professional
leaders of the United Way movement and of all
charities which serve the people of our nation.

ACKNOWLEDGMENTS

This book owes debts of gratitude to many who must remain nameless. They provided me with very valuable information. Without them, this book would not have been possible.

Staff at United Way of America at all levels were most open and cooperative. The interim president of United Way of America, Ken Dam, made himself available as he was rushing to leave the organization he had tried to make right again; Jon Powers, on loan from IBM, who briefly succeeded Dam, was forthright and helpful.

To my editor at John Wiley & Sons, Marla Bobowick, who saw a good story and asked me to write a book which would help those who work in the voluntary sector to learn from the mistakes made at United Way . . . in some small measure, I hope this effort has achieved that goal. And to Rose Kernan, my copy editor, who toiled laboriously over my prose . . . thank you for making it a "better read."

To my friends and relatives who provided me with essential emotional support and practical advice . . . you stayed with me during a most difficult year. Finally, to my family, Rochelle, Matthew, and Leah, who bore the burden as much as me . . . as always, you were there when I needed you the most. Also, a special thanks to Jill Schoenhaut, Elizabeth Costales, and Paul C. Wells for their patience and understanding during the production process. I am also deeply appreciative of the help provided by Bruce R. Hopkins and W. Mallory Rintoul whose professional criticisms and comments served this project so well.

CONTENTS

FOREWORD

I t is a pleasure and an honor to be able to write both a Foreword and an Afterword to John Glaser's very interesting, important, and challenging book on the fall and near-extinction of one of the nation's most prestigious charities. As editor of the series of which this book is a part, a practicing lawyer, and a long-time colleague of John's, I have closely observed the events leading up to and following this crisis at the United Way of America.

In my law practice, I specialize in representing charitable and other types of nonprofit organizations. Over the 25 years I have been doing this, I have been concerned about many of the practices John details in this book. This country's charitable sector has troubles—sometimes big troubles—when it comes to the composition and functioning of boards of directors, payment of compensation, and transactions between the organizations and those that are supposed to serve them. Do not assume that what you are about to read concerning the adventures of Bill Aramony and the United Way is singularly unique. These things and worse take place all too frequently, though they do not necessarily involve law-breaking; more will be said about this subject later, here and in the Afterword.

I have known John for over twenty years. During this period, he and I have toiled together in Washington, D.C., on behalf of charitable organizations; he for United Way of America and I as a lawyer. During this period, I came to know John quite well, and we have worked together on various task forces and other projects concerning nonprofit organizations in this country and around the world.

I have the highest regard for John Glaser. He exemplifies the best of those who devote their professional lives to service in the nonprofit world. This man is as generous to this cause as any, selflessly working year in and year out to improve society and benefit those who need society's assistance. I admire John, and therefore the tragedy that affected him so deeply, both professionally and personally—that is, the United Way scandal—is a matter for me of great sorrow and sympathy for what he has endured. And yet, in the spirit that something good comes out of everything, had John not labored and suffered as he did, he could not have offered up this book that is so timely and meaningful to every nonprofit organization in the land—and those who work for them.

I recall being on a business trip, eating breakfast in some hotel's coffee shop, and reading the *New York Times*. I came upon an article about the investigations of the doings at the United Way and read of a visit to John's home by federal authorities, who subpoenaed various documents. At that point, John was on administrative leave from the United Way (which would turn out to be permanent), had hired a lawyer, and was struggling with this crisis in his life. I could not help but be saddened by this terrible end of a career that had benefited this country so much.

The only good to come out of this saga are lessons for all of us. For the sake of many, let us hope that the learnings from this important contribution to the literature about the nonprofit field will prevent another such "scandal."

I also know Bill Aramony, although not nearly as well as John. While I generally knew of Bill's management style and his—if you will—flamboyance, I always regarded him as one of the giants of the world of organized charity. He, too, seemed tireless in his drive to improve American society by revamping and expanding the United Way. Sure, he was aggressive and self-promoting, and sometimes downright embarrassing, but he was also a bright star in a field where blandness can be so prevalent. Before the details of this "scandal" came to light, I often said that this nation's nonprofit sector needed more Bill Aramonys. Admittedly, while I still feel this way generally, except for this writing, I keep this thought to myself these days.

Although I know these men, I was not (and am not) an "insider" when it comes to the United Way of America. My impression of the United Way "scandal," before reading this book, was derived from media reports and what I heard throughout the network of nonprofit organizations in this country. I followed this tale voraciously, reading and listening to whatever I could dredge up on the subject—and, in Washington, D.C., there were ample ways to assuage this hunger.

Tax-exempt, mostly charitable organizations are predominantly mentioned in the media these days—and the accounts are none too positive. If you make the slightest point of it, you can find reports of real and ostensible wrongdoings on a regular basis on television and radio, and in magazines and newspapers. These accounts are, inevitably, of a negative task.

My favorite of these media yarns (admittedly, in some kind of morbid sense) is the one concerning the United Way. But I cannot resist briefly sharing with you my second-favorite of these tales.

There is an organization called the America 3 Foundation. It was established by a wealthy man named William I. Koch, who is its president. He was the winner of the America's Cup, prevailing over the Italians in May of 1992. Mr. Koch contributed $10 million to the Foundation, out of $68.5 million raised.

The *Washington Post,* on May 26, 1992, contained a long story about the Foundation. The article did not dwell much on the purposes of the Foundation, except to note that its function is to promote amateur athletics in international competition. The America's Cup campaign was a program of the Foundation. The newspaper account stated that the Foundation "plans to support sailors in other amateur competitions, such as the Olympics."

The *Post* account was steeped in offense that a wealthy individual could engage in his favorite sport and do so by means of a tax-exempt, charitable organization. While admittedly that cannot often be done, in this case the law allowed it; even the IRS thought so. The article did not attack Congress for writing the law or the IRS for the way that agency interpreted it, but lampooned Mr. Koch for utilizing it.

Mr. Koch and his practices in this regard were excoriated. He was portrayed as becoming "eligible for millions of dollars of federal income tax deductions by obtaining tax-exempt status" for the Foundation and "then contributing heavily to it." The size of Mr. Koch's tax benefits (not described) were said to be "unusual." The article said that "U.S. taxpayers subsidized" Mr. Koch's "personal triumph" because "the money sheltered from taxes would be lost to the U.S. Treasury." The Foundation was described as Mr. Koch's "nautical shelter." A donor to the Foundation was quoted as saying that the "tax-exempt financing of his [Mr. Koch's] racing campaign" is "immoral." An unidentified lawyer was quoted as saying that the Foundation's charitable status "doesn't pass the smell test."

Why this account? Was it just to roil the emotions of the majority of the population because one individual is so wealthy that he can use "sophisticated legal advice" (wrote the *Post*) to take advantage of the "U.S. tax code's vagaries" (again, the *Post*)? What these articles do, of course, is taint the population's view of charity in general.

Then came the United Way of America story.

John has provided all of the details, but I will pick up my remembrance of the story (before I read this book) when the federal authorities stepped into the fray. The *New York Times* of May 28, 1992, reported that two days before, the Department of Justice "subpoenaed extensive records from the United Way of America and several organizations it controls to determine if any federal criminal law was violated by the

charity's transfer of millions of dollars to the spinoff organizations."
The general impression created by the media was that Mr. Aramony
and his colleagues engaged in practices that were "wrong." Some individuals concluded that some practices were "unethical." Probably
quite a few individuals believe, consciously or subconsciously, that
laws were broken.

But wait. Just what lawbreaking took place? The federal tax laws, for
example, are the principal base of regulation of charitable organizations
in this country. How about those laws?

One of the most publicized of the sets of charges is that United Way
established what many people like to call "spinoffs." (See the above
quote, for example.) John uses this term, too, without boring the reader
with the details of all of the ins and outs of the law on the subject.
Simply stated, a "spinoff" is a "subsidiary organization" created by,
and usually controlled by, another organization.

The media loves to imply that there is something wrong with this
practice. However, the fact is that this practice is quite lawful and quite
common—and usually quite appropriate and, in some instances, necessary. To be more specific, there is nothing unlawful about a tax-exempt organization establishing either or both tax-exempt and for-profit
subsidiaries, using money and/or property of the exempt organization,
by "spinning off" those items to one or more subsidiaries. Congress in
many places in the Internal Revenue Code has specifically authorized
the practice. (I advise organizations on a regular basis to use "spinoffs.")

Thus, as to the establishment of for-profit subsidiaries by tax-exempt
organizations, the federal law specifically contemplates the practice by:

- Providing for the tax treatment of income flowing from a taxable subsidiary to a tax-exempt parent, and
- Providing for the tax consequences of liquidation of a taxable
  subsidiary into a tax-exempt parent.

Thus, it is crystal clear that a tax-exempt organization (including charities like United Way) can create and utilize one or more for-profit
subsidiaries. The IRS has issued many private letter rulings reflecting
and approving this technique.

So, too, can a tax-exempt organization establish tax-exempt subsidiaries. Congress has legislated extensively on this subject as well, creating rules that provide for the non-private foundation status of these

tax-exempt subsidiaries. Court opinions, including those from the Supreme Court, expressly approve this practice, such as the use of a tax-exempt lobbying subsidiary by a tax-exempt charitable parent. Thus, it is also amply clear that a tax-exempt organization can create and utilize one or more tax-exempt subsidiaries. Again, there are dozens of IRS private letter rulings condoning this practice.

The rule of law, then, is not that subsidiaries of tax-exempt organizations are illegal or otherwise wrong. Yet the media has portrayed this practice as somehow insidious, a violation of "charity law." Thus, the *New York Times* article stated that the "spinoff" organizations were created by Mr. Aramony, which, of course, is clearly untrue. They were created by the United Way of America.

As indicated in the above quote from the *New York Times,* the media reported that United Way spun off "millions of dollars" to the subsidiaries. Initially, that may strike some as plumbing the depths of evil. However, one has to look to see why the transfers were made and how the funds were used. As to the tax-exempt "spinoffs," if the funds were used for program purposes, the practice carries with it no violations of law whatsoever. As to the for-profit organizations, the test is the appropriate amounts needed to capitalize the operations and to get them operational, as well as ultimate use of the funds. If funds were misused, that is one thing. But it is unfair to portray the transfers themselves as evidence of wrongdoing.

A correlative charge is that Mr. Aramony was a member of the board of directors of most of the "spinoff" corporations. But this too is a common practice. It is responsible behavior for a tax-exempt parent to monitor the activities of its subsidiaries and to do this by the mechanism of overlapping directorates. This, as well, is being portrayed as some form of inappropriate practice.

Not satisfied with making the subsidiaries and the overlapping boards seem something that a legitimate charitable organization would not do, the media focused on what the *New York Times* article darkly called a "web of transactions" between the United Way and the subsidiaries. What is a "web of transactions"? It should not be surprising that there were transactions between the entities; how could it be otherwise? The United Way of America and its affiliates were a major, sophisticated, and complicated set of organizations—and properly so, given the wide range of its programs and purposes.

What is a "web' in this context? Mere complexity? The word suggests—I will submit, when used in these media accounts, deliberately—

dark corners where strange forces are at play and deadly spiders cavort. But "webs" or not, intricate corporate structures are no crime, not even in the nonprofit organization setting.

The ultimate resolution of this matter of the spinoffs, as a point of law, will turn on whether there was a suitable rationale for the creation of the "spinoff" corporations. If the rationale exists (and for United Way International, Charities Funds Transfer, and Partnership Umbrella, at least, that rationale was amply apparent), it will become a question as to the appropriate use of each of the seven subsidiaries. The *creation* of them, as such, should not be an issue.

Then, of course, there is the matter of United Way of America's compensation of Mr. Aramony. This involves another term that John uses throughout his book: "private inurement" (or sometimes "private benefit"). These words—much like "spinoff"—are frequently misunderstood. I will address this concept of private inurement more fully in the Afterword, because it concerns one of the most significant elements of law underlying the United Way "scandal." At this point, I will simply say that private inurement takes place when the income, assets, or other resources of a charitable organization are impermissibly used for the benefit of someone like a director, trustee, officer, or key employee of the organization. If there is private inurement, the IRS is supposed to revoke the tax-exempt status of the offending organization, as well as its ability to receive tax-deductible contributions.

Bill Aramony's annual compensation was $390,000 plus benefits. In law, the test is superficially simple: Is that level of compensation "reasonable" under the circumstances? If it is, then, as a matter of law, that is the end of the issue for United Way. If it is not—that is, if the compensation is "unreasonable" or "excessive"—then United Way's tax exemption could be at stake because excessive compensation to an insider is a form of private inurement, which is impermissible under the federal tax law. The reasonableness of Mr. Aramony's compensation is a question of fact—to be judged on the basis of his competence, expertise, experience, responsibility, achievements, and time devoted to the position.

The media also focused on Mr. Aramony's pension. There is nothing illegal about a tax-exempt organization providing pensions to its employees. Pensions can also be provided by subsidiary corporations. Again, the test is whether the benefit levels are reasonable. Yet all too many accounts suggest that his pension(s) are somehow per se inappropriate.

Then there is the charge that Mr. Aramony placed his son and some "cronies" in key employment positions with United Way. This, too, is not a violation of law. It is—for better or worse—a rather common practice in the worlds of nonprofit and for-profit organizations. The questions are: Was their compensation reasonable; and did they do anything illegal while in the employ of United Way or one of the subsidiaries? This, as well, is a matter more of appearances than law.

There were even more charges against United Way of America and Mr. Aramony. There is the charge that he traveled on the supersonic Concorde at United Way's expense. Is this a violation of law? The answer is no. This, like nearly everything in this unfortunate tale, is about appearances, about propriety. Probably most people in this country believe that charitable dollars should not be used for Concorde tickets—under any circumstances. But this "issue" will be resolved on the basis of the circumstances.

In one of the early newspaper stories about this "scandal," one representative of a local United Way was quoted as saying that Mr. Aramony's use of the Concorde was "unethical." No one has ever indicated what code of ethics was being referenced.

Is it inappropriate for charitable dollars to be used for first-class air travel? Business class? Air travel at all? The very questions generate the obvious answers. Again, there is no law violation, assuming the trips were primarily for the pursuit of United Way matters. It becomes a matter of propriety, of appearances. The same is true for the chauffeured car travel.

It is hard to avoid the conclusion that this matter has been unfairly handled by the media. The defense from that quarter will be that the media only reported the facts. That, concededly, is basically true. But the facts have been reported in ways to suggest wrongdoing—not just in the sense of appearances or ethics, but of law. At this stage, nothing that I know of has surfaced that, on its face, constitutes a violation of federal law. Let me state this more starkly: I have reviewed all of the public facts in this case and have concluded that neither the United Way of America nor William Aramony violated any federal laws. (John suggests one or two technical violations of New York law; I have not looked into this.) That is why I repeatedly place the word "scandal" in quotes.

I realize that it is not realistic to expect the popular media to stop at points along the way in a story and dwell on the fine details of the law. That is unrealistic if only because it would detract from the drama and the sweep of the story. But if there has been publication, in the popular or technical press, of an objective analysis of the law aspects of this story, I have not seen it.

These words are not a defense of the organizations or the individuals involved in this affair. They are an attempt to show that the popular telling of this and similar tales has amounted to a massive (almost to the point of deception) "spin" on the facts, to make it seem that lawbreaking was rampant. I will leave to others to debate the proprieties of what was done—including the role of the boards of directors.

There is a trend in the land to regard with suspicion acts or structures of nonprofit organizations that are, or appear to be, "sophisticated." This is the case, whether new forms of compensation, new approaches to programming or fund-raising, or the use of subsidiaries, partnerships, and joint ventures are involved. This suspicion is grounded in ignorance of contemporary management and fiscal practices and a yearning for simpler days when charities were operating in the red with the assistance of volunteers or staff paid at bare subsistence levels. The benefits of these practices to the charities involved and their beneficiaries are usually overlooked.

There are many tragedies associated with the United Way "scandal" and its counterparts, and the furthering of this suspicion is one of them.

Please read this fine book. For me personally, I was particularly interested to learn how my perceptions correlated to John's insights. Perhaps you, as well, will read on to see how your views as to what happened—shaped by what you may have already seen, heard, and read—compare to John's.

You are in for a fascinating, albeit tragic, tale. It ends on a positive note, however: John has provided some sound recommendations for avoiding repeat performances.

Bruce R. Hopkins
Washington, D.C.
August 1993

P R E F A C E

Respice post te hominem te esse memento.

from "Triumphus" in *Der Kleine Pauly*

O my son!
These are no trifles! Think: all men make mistakes,
But a good man yields when he knows his course
  is wrong,
And repairs the evil. The only crime is pride.

from Antigone by Sophocles

I have always wanted to write a book about a great charitable, uniquely American institution which has contributed so much to the well-being of this nation for over a hundred years; whose roots began in the backwash created by the industrial revolution and the rebuilding and resettlement of the nation after the Civil War. With the help of the United Way, communities across the nation had succeeded in creating an effective system of social services to meet the needs of millions of people. Regrettably, what follows is not that story.

In 1991, and even before, allegations had surfaced regarding various management practices at United Way of America under the leadership of William Aramony, for whom I had worked for 23 years. *The Washington Post* had begun to raise questions about United Way of America based on information it had received regarding Aramony's salary and benefits, lifestyle, and the establishment of questionable "spinoff" organizations. With the concurrence of the Board of Governors of United Way of America, investigators were hired to look into the charges and report their findings to Aramony and the Board. On Monday, February 3, 1992, following a preliminary report, Aramony received a "resounding vote of confidence" from the Board.

On February 12, a column by Jack Anderson and Michael Binstein appeared in newspapers across the country discussing many of these charges. Four days later, a major article regarding Aramony's lifestyle and management practices hit the front pages of *The Washington Post*. Within a week, *Regardies*, a now defunct local magazine that covered the Washington area business scene with lively, gossipy articles, conducted its own investigation and published a story articulating many of the same issues raised by *The Post*. On February 24, another front-page story in *The Post* focused on several of the United Way spinoffs and their interlocking Boards and financial practices.

Finally, on February 27, at a closed-circuit teleconference for United Way organizations throughout the country, Dr. LaSalle D. Leffall, Jr., the chairman of United Way of America's Executive Committee, reported that Aramony was "retiring" but would stay on until a successor could be found. Outrage over the news that he was not retiring immediately was so great that he resigned the next day. On March 5, at a second teleconference, John F. Akers, chairman of IBM and chairman of the Board of Governors of United Way of America, announced the "loan" of interim president Kenneth W. Dam, an IBM vice president who would oversee the transition of the United Way organization to new leadership.

This book will explore what went wrong and why with the United Way. It will show how the line became blurred between the shared goals of its advocates and the often dubious means used to achieve them. It will describe how an institution which gained its strength by building consensus lost sight of the process designed to create that consensus. It will show that the resulting crisis was caused as much by the failure of the United Way to keep faith with its historic and democratic traditions as it was by the excesses of its leader, Bill Aramony.

I first began working for Bill Aramony in 1969 when I moved my young family to Miami, Florida. Years before, I had cut my teeth as a volunteer in rural Haiti where I helped build a school and taught literacy and basic agricultural techniques for the American Friends Service Committee. There, I was deeply influenced by Dr. Larimer Mellon, a relative of the Pittsburgh Mellons, who gave up a life of luxury to establish the Albert Schweitzer Hospital in the Artibonite Valley—a location said to have the greatest concentration of disease in the Western hemisphere. Mellon had studied with Schweitzer in a town called Lambaréné in French West Africa. He was the closest human being to a saint I had ever met before or since. He was motivated not by religious zeal but by a compelling humanism. He would trudge for days on horseback into the countryside to convince even one fearful person to come to his hospital and experience the lifesaving benefits of modern medicine.

But these were the years of "Papa Doc" Duvalier, Haiti's notorious dictator. When President Kennedy cut off aid to Haiti in the summer of 1963, local government officials unleashed a barrage of anti-American invective. When my Haitian colleagues started packing sidearms, I knew it was time to leave.

Following my graduation from the Boston University School of Social Work, I spent four years organizing public housing tenants in Somerville, Massachusetts, a low-income suburb of Boston. I was again blessed to work with a very special person, Tom Vassil, now a professor of social work and a deeply committed and caring social group worker. Nearly twenty years after he left his work there, the kids he saved, now adults with families and jobs, called him back to the old neighborhood to honor him with a banquet and speeches. They wanted to thank him for giving them back their lives.

This was an exciting time. It was late in the 1960s, and the vision of the New Frontier gave the promise of a national commitment to ameliorating poverty through the empowerment of citizens. We were all caught up in the "good fight." I, like so many of my generation, had marched in Selma, picketed George Wallace, passed out leaflets at the Justice Department supporting civil rights, and helped in the effort to boycott grapes for Cesar Chavez' *La Causa*. The idealism of these times made a stark contrast with the gross materialism of the 1980s.

Eventually, I burned out. The constant battles with bureaucrats and politicians, the endless search for human and financial resources, the realization that even with so much effort, little could be accomplished—all this took its toll.

Bill Aramony offered me a new vision of the future. When I joined the United Way, he told me that I would be in a position to make a much greater impact on the lives of people through the United Way than I could doing anything else. He cited the numerous examples from his own experience which had made him a maverick hero among his peers in the United Way.

"Your resume is full of shit, Glaser," he said, throwing it into the wastepaper basket, "but I like your eyeballs." At that moment I began a career in the United Way that would span nearly half my life and take me to dozens of countries.

I was honored to have had the opportunity to serve the United Way for so many years. I saw how the United Way process of helping people could be easily transferred to other countries and other cultures. All it took was a little humility and a bit of creative listening. Often what seems trivial is in fact a profound truism; namely, that there are highly motivated and good people everywhere and in every community who deeply care about the well-being of their fellow countrymen. They seek no reward, they seek no glory . . . save only that of doing good.

Some will criticize many of the comments in this book with regards to the players at the United Way in general and to Bill Aramony in particular. My only response is that I have described events and situations as I heard and witnessed them. I have included only those I believe to be important in order to understand what went wrong and why. Others will say that I am compromised because of my long and close association with Aramony, longer than anyone had ever worked for him on a continuous basis (the last 18½ of those years, I reported to him directly). Few were privy to as much information as I was, some of which I personally observed; other information was provided by friends and colleagues who were close to the situation in other ways and confided in me what they knew and observed. In my search for the truth, I was in contact with nearly 50 people. Since much of what went wrong was due to Aramony's personality and leadership, I am one of the handful of people who were actually present and in a position to know what happened over the long haul.

Unfortunately, Aramony was not a Larimer Mellon or a Tom Vassil. This preface opens with the Latin phrase *respice post te hominem te esse memento*. These words were whispered in the ear of a victorious general during his triumphant victory procession through the cheering streets of ancient Rome by a slave who stood close to him in his chariot. "Look behind you and remember that you are but a man," he would say repeatedly. Perhaps if Aramony had listened to such advice, his tenure may have had a different ending.

The Greeks also knew much about the fatal flaw of **hubris**, a term meaning "insolence" or "excessive pride." Today, we might call it the "arrogance of power." Hubris was often a fatal human quality against which the ancients believed one must be ever vigilant or it would inevitably lead to one's downfall.

The signs of what went wrong were everywhere, strewn like so many grape leaves over a long meandering trellis. The fault rests not only with the hubris that was so much a part of Bill Aramony's psyche, but also with the hundreds of volunteers and professionals who ignored the warning signs. Yet, they were always around to drink the wine and eat the fruit served to them by a leader they loved and respected for over two decades. He had created a modern and, until recently, an enormously successful charity movement entirely from the force of his own considerable will.

My desire to write a positive account about that very special means of helping people—the United Way—will have to await another day or another write. However, perhaps the observations of a social worker who has served the United Way movement in America and abroad for nearly a quarter of a century will keep the recent past from repeating itself. Hopefully, the United Way and all charities in America will be able to better serve the people in the years ahead as a result of this effort.

John S. Glaser
Alexandria, Virginia

NOTES ON UNITED WAY TERMINOLOGY

It is important for the reader to understand that the "United Way" is a group of separately incorporated, independent, and autonomous organizations which are based in approximately 2,300 communities throughout the United States (as well as Canada and other countries). Of this number, about 1,400 are members, or affiliates, of the national association known since 1970 as United Way of America. Each of the members is commonly known as "The United Way of (name of city, count(ies), or region)." As members, they pay a small percentage of what they raise locally to support the national association in return for a number of services. Therefore, almost all of the money raised in local communities is distributed to charities within those communities based upon criteria determined by their individual boards of directors. Virtually every major and minor city is a member. The total amount of money raised nationwide (currently over $3 billion) is the total of all of the local fund-raising campaigns added together.

United Way of America has no control over United Way organizations, other than the force of persuasion, since each has its own board of directors as well as its own policies and procedures. Those who pay what are termed fair share dues to the national association receive certain benefits over those who don't pay the full amount or nothing at all.

This book uses a number of terms interchangeably. When *national office* or *national association* is used, it refers to United Way of America. The terms *the United Way, the United Way movement,* and *the United Way system* generally refer to both the national association and local members. When the terms *United Ways* or *local United Ways* are used, they refer to the members only. The word *field* has also been used to describe United Way paid professionals who lead the local organizations.

The word *volunteer* is used throughout this book. It refers to those individuals who are trustees of either local United Ways or United Way of America. Unless otherwise specified, the term does not refer to the volunteer who provides direct services to those in need. Volunteers receive no pay or compensation, whereas professionals receive salaries and benefits.

Finally, I have used what some would consider the archaic word *charity* to describe what most professionals in the field refer to as agencies, that is, those places where beneficiaries or clients go to receive services. Since agencies can also be government entities, the word *charity* hopefully makes the distinction clearer.

CHAPTER 1

The Crisis Begins

Every institution, business, government, academia, charitable organization, every individual, you and me, and all of us have frailties. All of us. Frailties here at United Way of America have caused us to stumble.

John F. Akers, (former) Chairman of the Board,
IBM Corporation, March 5, 1992[1]

"**C**an you believe it?" said Bill Aramony the day after he resigned as president of United Way of America. We were walking with his son through a building housing two of the spinoff organizations. His eyes became bigger and his voice grew louder and the index finger of his right hand began stabbing the air. "I made the front page of four major papers today! Ten years ago they wouldn't have even known who I was."[2]

With his support from all quarters eroding dramatically, Bill Aramony resigned on February 28, 1992 after 22 years as president of the organization he had largely created in his own image. He had officially "retired" the day before during a nationwide teleconference. He was to stay until a successor could be found. Because of tremendous pressure from volunteers and professionals throughout the country, however, he left the next day.

HOW THE STORY BROKE

Rumblings concerning a possible article by *The Washington Post* were first heard around Thanksgiving of 1991, according to Sunshine Overcamp, United Way of America's senior vice president for Corporate

Communications. On the advice of in-house counsel, Aramony hired a team of lawyers and investigators to look into the allegations as well as areas of United Way of America's operations and procedures that might have been vulnerable to exploitation by the media. From November 1991 until Sunday, February 16, 1992 when the first of two articles appeared, every attempt was made by United Way of America to provide Charles E. Shepard, the Pulitzer prize–winning writer of the story, with all the information he sought on the organization. On February 3, the executive committee, after having received a report of the ongoing inquiry, reportedly had given Aramony a "resounding vote of confidence." Some sources have since indicated that it was not a resounding vote of confidence, an interpretation preferred by Aramony, but more of an attitude of giving him the benefit of the doubt until any irregularities uncovered by the investigation could be explained.

During this time, Alicia Mundy, a reporter for *Regardies*, a popular "chronicle of the 1980s Washington land and power frenzy," was also ready to publish a story. And on February 12, a few days before the Shepard article was published, a column by Jack Anderson and Michael Binstein entitled "Charity Begins at Home for United Way" appeared through syndication in newspapers throughout the country.[3] I was attending a regional meeting of United Ways of the Asia and Pacific Rim nations when I received a copy of the Anderson/Binstein article. I knew it was only the beginning of more to come. The column alluded to many of the allegations that were discussed in much greater detail in subsequent articles by *The Washington Post*.

THE ACCUSATIONS AND THE COUNTERS

United Way of America had received an advance copy of the Anderson/Binstein article. In a letter dated February 11 to Andy BeDell, senior editor of United Features Syndicate, Dr. Lasalle D. Leffall, Jr., chairman of the executive committee of the board of United Way of America, discussed the many errors in the column and requested that BeDell reconsider any decision to print it. Since this newspaper story was the first public accounting regarding the allegations that eventually led to Aramony's downfall, I think it would be useful to discuss them and United Way of America's written responses. The points in the article that Leffall specifically disputed were as follows:

1. *Accountability*—Anderson referred to United Way of America's "consistent refusal to be anything but superficially accountable to contributors." Leffall countered that IRS Form 990, audits, and other records are routinely made available to the public, including reporters.

2. *Coercion*—Anderson stated that "hardly a worker in America hasn't had his or her arm twisted on the job for United Way." Leffall stated that coercion has never been acceptable to United Way organizations and that giving is a personal matter.

3. *Spinoffs*—Anderson said, "The most questionable of these spinoffs is Charities Funds Transfer (CFT), the electronic banking function of United Way that collects the money and distributes it to charities" and that interest from funds in transit "has brought in as much as half a million dollars a year to CFT, some of which went back to United Way. . . ." Leffall's letter denied that any money reverted to United Way of America and stated that CFT simplifies and speeds the distribution of funds for corporate, employee, retiree, and foundation grants.

4. *United Way of America's "Burgeoning Headquarters Budget"*—Leffall claimed that the headquarters budget had in fact been reduced 2.9 percent between 1991 and 1992.

5. *Salaries and perks*—The article stated that "salaries and perks at United Way and its spinoffs are generous by other nonprofit standards." Leffall's letter claimed that salaries are set by the Board and are based on comparative and competitive information gathered from "a well-known leader in the field of compensation," Towers Perrin.

6. *Super Bowl*—The article claimed that Aramony took his key staff annually to the Super Bowl. Leffall countered that the NFL provides the United Way of America with $45 million of free advertising, and therefore, the tickets are an appropriate business expense.[4]

Many people have asked me if I know who started the media blitz ball rolling, as though they expected it to be one person. It seems clear to me that numerous groups, newspapers, and magazines had documents and personal testimonies relating to many areas of suspected abuse at United Way of America. They had been supplied by many different sources dating back many years. For example, the Board of Governors had received an anonymous letter concerning alleged unorthodox activities relating to a particularly lucrative contract of a former employee. The charges in the letter were investigated but proved to be frivolous. One Board member told me that she just threw it into the wastepaper basket because it was unsigned and, therefore, valueless. The charges were unfounded, but they probably helped to start the ball rolling.

Other allegations soon surfaced as a result of investigative reporters looking into information they had received indicating that Aramony had:

1. used United Way of America personnel, funds, and other resources for personal benefit;
2. installed friends in senior positions at United Way;
3. arranged for favored colleagues to receive similar benefits from their relationships to spinoffs;
4. used United Way of America resources to pay for activities that should have been charged to the spinoffs; and
5. [may have] interceded with one spinoff to hire his son.[5]

However, when he realized that these and other allegations could be harmful to the United Way if made public, Aramony determined that the best defense was a good offense and decided to have the allegations investigated. Dr. Lisle C. Carter, Jr., in-house counsel at United Way of America, sought the advice of his previous employers, Verner, Liipfert, Bernhard, McPherson and Hand. They recommended The Investigative Group, Inc. headed by Terry F. Lenzner, former assistant chief counsel to the Senate committee that investigated the Watergate break-in and subsequent cover-up that led to the 1973 resignation of former President Richard Nixon. Lenzner's initial role was to determine the legitimacy of the specific allegations that had surfaced in 1991 and those that were "relevant to the Executive Committee's stewardship of UWA."[6]

THE BIG BLOW—*THE WASHINGTON POST* ARTICLE

On February 16, the front page headline of *The Washington Post* accompanied by a picture of Aramony said it all:

Perks, Privileges and Power in a Nonprofit World
Head of United Way of America Praised, Criticized for
Running It Like a *Fortune 500* Company

The article was followed by a full page of text supporting the headline, including graphs showing fund-raising results and administrative costs and describing sources of income and expenses of the national association. Under the front page picture of Aramony the caption read, "$390,000 plus perks and benefits." In addition, there was another, positive article of two columns that included a picture of Aramony with a child. It is doubtful that many people read the second, very favorable, but much shorter article.

In addition to the content, a number of factors contributed to the negative impact of the primary article, including:

1. it appeared on the front page on a Sunday;
2. the headline was emotionally charged; and
3. the article covered more than an entire page of the newspaper.

The shock of these headlines contributed immensely to the initial and profound negative impact of the main story. If people had read no further than the headlines, the public perception would still have been catastrophic.

QUESTIONABLE POLICIES WERE BROUGHT TO THE FORE

The Washington Post article provided a description supporting the headlines. The content can be classified into three main categories.

Salary and Perks

The article indicated that Aramony's salary and benefits totaled $463,000. The salary figure ($390,000) had been published before and is easily available from Internal Revenue Service Form 990. It said that Aramony used "chauffered automobiles" at a cost of $20,000 for one year. The reader should note that the reporter never used the word "limousine." In fact, the vehicle was a Ford sedan—a far cry from a limousine. Aramony did use limousines during conferences when they had been hired for board members.

The article also said that he flew the Concorde on several occasions, had a rosewood table in his office, motorized blinds, and TV monitors trained in on his secretaries. In responding to why he needed a car and driver, Aramony is quoted as saying, "I can't afford to be waiting for cabs," explaining that he often had back-to-back appointments. The paper reported that in some years Aramony's personal travel budget was $100,000 over budget.

Friends and Relatives

In regard to Aramony hiring his friends and cronies, the article concentrated primarily on his chief financial officer, Thomas J. Merlo.

In the 1980s, according to *The Post*, United Way of America had paid Merlo a $15,000 yearly retainer. In 1988, Merlo's accounting firm received $44,715. In 1989, he was hired once again and received a contract worth $60,000 a year. By 1990, he was on staff at United Way of America earning $211,000 a year plus an apartment costing $1,050 per month. United Way of America also paid his weekly commuting expenses to his home in Florida.

Aramony said, "I didn't [check his background] because I knew him." (Aramony had known him for over three decades. In fact, he had socialized extensively with Merlo during his frequent visits to Florida.)

The February 16 article also mentioned the selection of Aramony's son, Robert, to head Sales Service/America. United Way of America provided Sales Service/America with a $1.5 million start-up loan. Robert had worked for three other spinoff companies before becoming president and chief executive officer of Sales Service/America. "I had nothing to do with his hiring," said the elder Aramony. O. Stanley Smith, Jr., who was a close colleague of Aramony from his days in Columbia, South Carolina, said the job was never advertised. He told *The Post*, "[B]ut I didn't really interview anybody and didn't feel that was really my responsibility. I would say it was Merlo's. He was the project manager to try to separate" Sales Service/America from United Way of America. Robert Aramony had also received a $3,000 consulting contract from Professional Travel Systems (PTS) to sell PTS services in Florida. The younger Aramony was living in Florida at the time. The contract was arranged by Stephen J. Paulachak, who in 1989 hired Robert Aramony as vice president of Partnership Umbrella, Inc. and Charities Fund Transfer, two other spinoffs.

The Washington Post article also cited the annual travel to Super Bowl games by Aramony and his aides in order to cultivate the National Football League (NFL). I was aware that very often those attending were friends and colleagues who had little to do with cultivating the NFL. Aramony received 15 to 20 tickets from Mario Pellegrini, who has produced the NFL spots for United Way of America for over two decades. The number of people going to the Superbowl in Minneapolis in January 1992 was drastically reduced because of the pending article. Aramony said he had sent members of the board of Partnership Umbrella in previous years to repay them for volunteering as board members. These board members were a handful of Aramony's closest friends and colleagues.

The article also cites the hiring of retired Marine Corps Col. Billy Duncan by United Way International. Duncan is the father of Rina Duncan, who had been Aramony's administrative assistant and is currently an employee of Partnership Umbrella. At his request, United Way International also agreed to pay Col. Duncan's wife's expenses because the couple had been away from each other for so many years as a result of his service duties, which included a long tour in Viet Nam.

Spinoffs

The Washington Post article focused extensively on Partnership Umbrella, the most controversial of the spinoffs. United Way of America, the article indicated, had provided $900,000 of seed money. With that money, Partnership Umbrella paid $430,000 for a New York condominium for Aramony. The rationale was that it was less expensive to buy an apartment than to pay for a hotel room. However, Aramony indicated in a later article that the condo was used only by Partnership Umbrella staff, which consists of just a few professionals. (It was not made available to the much larger United Way of America staff. Simple arithmetic suggests that if the cost of a New York hotel room averages $185 single occupancy per night that these three people would have had to spend about 2,324 nights in of hotel rooms to pay for the condo.) Partnership Umbrella also bought a condo in Florida from another spinoff for $125,000, which it then sold in April, 1991. In addition, it paid off a $200,000 loan to the then defunct Professional Travel Systems.

The article pointed out that United Way of America would not provide audited financial statements of Partnership Umbrella and Sales Service/America, or information related to Aramony's travels.[7]

United Way of America's communication staff says that the impact of the article was partly mitigated because it was published two days before the New Hampshire presidential primary. However, the fact that it appeared on a Sunday in Washington greatly contributed to the number of people who read and discussed it.

SENSATIONALISM—THE *REGARDIES* ARTICLE

About five days after the first article by Shepard appeared, *Regardies* published "It Works For All Of Them," subtitled, "For the Top Officials of America's Charity Empire, Charity Begins at Home," by Alicia Mundy. She raised many of the same issues Shepard mentioned, albeit in a much more sensationalized way and with considerable inaccuracies. Mundy wrote, "And some joke that the charity's famous slogan, 'Thanks to you, it works for all of us' should be reworked to say, 'Thanks to you, it works for him.' " Among the most egregious errors in the Mundy report is the reference to Mutual of America, the United Way's pension insurer, as a former "division" of United Way of America. In fact, Mutual of America began as the National Health and Welfare Retirement Association in 1947 by a predecessor to Aramony, Ralph Blanchard, and has always been independent.

Mundy quoted five Board members who told her in "almost the same words" that if Aramony had gone into private business, he'd be considered a genius and would have made a fortune.[8] This perception was aggravated by comments she attributed to Larry Horner, a certified public accountant and former chairman of United Way of America's audit committee. In response to the surprise among board members concerning the allegations, Horner is quoted as saying, "In business, you don't tell everyone everything," and in response to why Aramony wouldn't comment on the allegations, Horner stated (according to Mundy), "It's not unusual for an executive to not want to cooperate with a negative story."

A HEMORRHAGING OF NEGATIVE PUBLICITY

On February 20, *The Post* published an editorial that questioned Aramony's effectiveness in helping local United Ways raise money. It noted that in real terms, adjusted for inflation, UW's growth was only 17 percent (from $787 million in 1970 to $3.1 billion in 1990), while national income rose 60 percent and total philanthropic donations a little faster. It made an urgent plea to support the United Way of the National Capital Area (Washington, D.C.).[9] That same day, *The Post* printed an article that said that Washington, Chicago, and San Francisco were asking United Way of America for a further explanation of *The Post's* allegations. But until the publication of the editorial, United Way of America's communications staff had been routinely sending out the most relevant news stories that they felt were important. They delayed sending out this negative editorial because they had wanted to check with Aramony. However, another charity had sent the negative articles to several local United Way organizations to ask for a reaction. These United Way affiliates expressed tremendous irritation that they had not received it from United Way of America first. From then on, all releases were sent throughout the country. The communications staff reported that Aramony made no attempt to limit the distribution of press articles to the field. Some now blame this hemorrhage of negative publicity for exacerbating the crisis.

THE *COUP DE GRACE*

On Monday, February 24, *The Post* published its second and more devastating volley at Aramony and his management practices. It actually consisted of two articles, one entitled "United Way's For-Profit Offspring," subtitled "Spinoffs That Aim to Cut Charity Costs Collect Criticism." The second, shorter article, "Endowment Funds Bought Florida Condo," was subtitled "$1 million Centennial Gift, Honoring Aramony, Is Intended to Expand Voluntarism."

Whereas the February 16 article raised serious questions about Aramony's lifestyle and management practices, this second article was the *coup de grace*. It reiterated a number of the more sensational items of the earlier article. These included Aramony's inflated salary, chauffeured cars, and Merlo's financial and legal problems in Florida. It focused on two of the spinoffs—Professional Travel Systems, which went out of business in 1987, and Partnership Umbrella, Inc. These spinoffs, as well as Sales Service/America, had refused to provide financial data, claiming that:

1. it was unnecessary because they are not controlled by United Way of America; and
2. the release of the information would put them at a competitive disadvantage.

The National Charities Information Bureau, a voluntary nonprofit organization that which sets standards for other voluntary organizations, claims that the public should be given financial information about "related activities" when they raise money in the charity's name [more on this issue will be discussed later], reported *The Post*.

William J. Lehrfeld, a highly experienced lawyer in nonprofit activity, including six years with the exempt organizations division at the IRS, stated it somewhat differently when he was quoted by *The Chronicle of Philanthropy*, a popular trade journal serving charities. "The damage that can be done by non-disclosure by a charity or a related entity is far more serious than any actual money that could be involved," he declared. "Lack of disclosure brings distaste, and distaste brings lack of trust, and that could hurt donations to the main charity."[10]

The Post stated that Professional Travel Systems (PTS) began with a loan from United Way of America that eventually reached nearly $150,000. Aramony claimed it soon ran into trouble due to deregulation. (I was aware of major complaints about the inefficient service from across the country. In addition, local travel agencies serving United Ways simply reduced their costs below those of PTS in order to retain their clients.) Even though PTS lost $47,000 during the first six months of 1986, it spent $18,770, or almost half again as much, on travel for its own staff, its board members, and, according to the *Post*, for Aramony as well.

Among the other revelations mentioned was a review of PTS's accounting practices by Merlo. He reported that the books for the year 1985 showed a profit of $13,000 when the company actually had a loss of $21,000. At Merlo's suggestion, the article states, Paulachak was removed from the job. He had previously left his job as chief financial officer of United Way of America, a position he held from 1979 through 1983, stated *The Post*. It also stated that Paulachak handled Aramony's rental property in Alexandria and Fairfax County.

As for Partnership Umbrella, *The Post* stated that it began operations at the end of 1986 as an organization designed to obtain discounts for charitable organizations and was funded with an incentive payment from AT&T resulting from the sale of $25 million in phone equipment. Actually, by the time Partnership Umbrella had taken over the program, $8 million worth of equipment had already been sold.

In all, Partnership Umbrella received over $930,000 in incentive payments, despite the fact that United Way of America was going through a retrenchment due to budget problems. Partnership Umbrella used nearly $440,000 (this amount varies from the amount in the first Shepard article by about $8,000; the Investigative Report lists $394,000 as the cost and $65,000 as the cost of furnishing it) to purchase and furnish the New York condo. Aramony, chairman of the four-member Board, excused himself from the decision by the Board of Partnership Umbrella. Although the apartment was used by Aramony and perhaps other members of the small Partnership Umbrella staff, no information was provided that indicated that it was also available to United Way of America staff and the staffs of the other spinoffs.

The February 24 article concludes that Partnership Umbrella assumed the debts of PTS amounting to $215,000 ($140,000 due to United Way of America and $75,000 due on a Florida bank loan) in return for taking over its business. After various confusing explanations, Partnership Umbrella had evidently repaid the PTS loan of $140,000 to United Way of America in February 1988 by taking out a loan of its own, which was said to have been repaid by the summer of 1988—from the money provided Partnership Umbrella from the AT&T incentive program! Audited financial statements of United Way of America do not show that this loan was repaid by Partnership Umbrella, nor do the Board minutes of United Way of America show that Partnership Umbrella could have used some of the incentive money to repay the loan.

A companion article in *The Post* discusses the purchase of a Florida condo from the interest on a $1 million endowment given in Aramony's honor by Mutual of America, its pension insurer, known as the "William Aramony Initiatives in Voluntarism Fund." In 1990, Voluntary Initiatives America was incorporated in Florida to distribute the funds. Aramony was unpaid chairman, while his son, Robert, was the unpaid president. Of its $200,000 income in 1990, $125,526 was used to buy a condominium in Florida a mere three days after the organization was incorporated, reported *The Post*. In 1991, a year after its purchase, the condo was sold to Partnership Umbrella for $135,000 for the purpose of using it to support a nonprofit personnel service to be managed by Anita Terranova, a jointly paid United Way of America/United Way International employee living in Florida.[11]

The Post articles were followed up by extensive coverage by *The Chronicle of Philanthropy*. This publication printed numerous quotations from United Way volunteers, staff, and interested parties expressing their comments and profound concern regarding the allegations. An article dated February 25 also reported that Charities Funds Transfer, a nonprofit spinoff, provided financial statements containing notes from accountants indicating that the returns were incomplete. The paper also reported that the Board was undertaking a thorough investigation of United Way of America and the spinoffs and that the results would be released on April 2.[12]

LOCAL UNITED WAYS AND THE PRESS REACT

A few days later, Walter Annenberg, a million-dollar supporter of United Way's Alexis de Tocqueville Society, called for Aramony's removal to prevent "destructive fallout" that could "be fatal to the local United Way" groups. He said that if the reports were true, "This is indecent and disgusting and an immediate decision must be made regarding Mr. Aramony." I was told by someone who had spoken to one of his close associates that Annenberg was devastated by the revelations.

United Way members in San Francisco, Las Vegas, St. Cloud, Minnesota, Seattle, and Philadelphia took steps to withhold their dues.[13] In the next few days, 28 more United Way members agreed to do the same.[14] Efforts were extended to separate the local organizations from the national association. This was especially important to the United Way of the National Capital Area (located in Washington, D.C.) which shares the same name and is in the same geographical area. "It is particularly profane to have someone in the good work that the United Way has done all across the country be sullied, by finding out the kind of perks and personal leadership that has been revealed," said John Hechinger, a major donor in the area.[15]

The second article by Shepard in *The Washington Post* provoked extensive nighttime TV news coverage during the entire week of February 24. On February 25, "NBC Nightly News with Tom Brokaw" highlighted the salary and benefits, referred to chauffeured "limousines" (Shepard never referred to "limousines" in either of his articles), the Concorde flights, and the "high-paying" job for his son, Robert.[16]

The next night, February 26, "ABC World News Tonight with Peter Jennings" reported the same information. Jack Prater, the chief professional officer of United Way of Metropolitan Chicago, said that it was a very serious situation and that now it would be more difficult for the United Way to achieve the things it wanted to achieve.[17]

The same night, the local CBS affiliate in Washington, D.C. provided a very poignant interview with Jim Jenkins, a board member of the United Way of the National Capital Area in Washington, D.C., regarding *The Post* articles. He was among the first to call for Aramony's resignation.

> It presents to me the fact that you're uncaring, that you're not sensitive, that you don't know what's happened in America. You've lost touch. And that's what I think the people believe at this time.[18]

This United Way affiliate believed it had the most to lose because it shared a close geographical location with United Way of America. Too close for comfort!

DROPPING THE BOMB—THE FIRST TELECONFERENCE

On February 27, 1992, Susan Corrigan, the president of Gifts in Kind America called me at United Way International to see if I would be able to join her at a scheduled teleconference. She knew it would be a difficult and awkward situation and was looking for some moral support. She was right. One by one and in small groups, the staff of United Way of America filed into the well-appointed board room on the second floor of the national office. Many were in a state of profound disbelief, anticipating what might happen. A large projection screen was set up to carry the teleconference which was to take place in a production studio one floor below. Just prior to the teleconference, Tom Nunan, the prematurely gray general manager, walked in, obviously very shaken. His face projected his generally serious nature, only this time, even more than usual. He asked for quiet.

"I have something to say. Bill Aramony wanted the staff to know before it was announced during the teleconference." With his normally articulate voice beginning to crack, he said, "Bill wanted you to know that he will be announcing his retirement." We were all stunned, too shocked to consider the immense impact of Nunan's statement.

In the nationwide, closed-circuit teleconference carried by 93 affiliates, Aramony agreed to retire when a successor could be found. Dr. LaSalle D. Leffall, Jr., chairman of the Executive Committee, described the nature of the investigation regarding allegations of misconduct that had surfaced late in 1991. He said the investigation included a review of organizational documents and Aramony's business and personal records.

Some of the items that were examined were financial audit reports, materials related to the spinoffs, IRS Forms 990, financial records, and expense records. They also looked at Aramony's expense reports, travel calendars, individual tax returns, checking accounts, personal real estate transactions, his marital separation agreement, and other personal legal records. Leffall stated that the investigation had covered interviews with many individuals and collected other data independently.

This report, according to Leffall, was reviewed by United Way of America's Executive Committee. He indicated that recommendations would be forthcoming on policy and procedural issues that had surfaced during the investigation and that an investigation into the background of Mr. Merlo, the chief financial officer, had resulted in his being placed on administrative leave. He said that Aramony's compensation had been set in closed session by the Executive Committee based on comparative and competitive data supplied by Towers Perrin, an independent company that specializes in matters relating to compensation. He concluded that "Nothing new has surfaced" in regard to these investigations.

Then Berl Bernhard, partner in Verner, Liipfert, Bernhard, McPherson and Hand, who was assigned to oversee the investigation, made the following statement:

> The investigation conducted by the firm to which he [Leffall] referred is now over. And it involved a broad range of areas. What is important for everyone to understand is that there was no misappropriation found, no embezzlement found, no fraud, no malfeasance in office. There was no finding of diversion for personal enrichment by Mr. Aramony. Period.

He also had this comment concerning subsequent information about possible money owed by Aramony:

> For example, when we were looking at the reports and then we looked at additional materials, we found, for example, when you reconciled accounts you found that Mr. Aramony, instead of owing United Way anything, was owed about $1,200 on his personal expenditures from United Way of America.

He said that the investigators had found a number of specific areas that needed improvement, such as sloppy record keeping, inattention to certain detail and documentation, and certain issues raised about slowness in accounting and expenditures.

Areas that would be studied further, according to Bernhard, were United Way of America's relationship to the spinoffs. A whole series of recommendations were being made regarding United Way of America's governance, personnel systems, and bookkeeping systems, he reported, and many of the recommendations of the investigating firm would be implemented to restore public confidence.

He then reviewed the history of the five major spinoffs: United Way International, Gifts in Kind America, Partnership Umbrella, Charities Funds Transfer, and Sales Service/America. He indicated that Partnership Umbrella had saved 60,000 voluntary organizations $7 million, and that Sales Service/America had actually saved the United Way members over $60,000 on certain popular items, and had not raised their prices in two years. All spinoffs were discussed in a highly positive manner. He said that the validity and value of the spinoffs had saved United Way over $200 million!

Bernhard indicated that some changes had already taken place. The new policy stated that all staff must use the most economical air travel (no first-class airline seat or supersonic jet travel) and the most economical ground travel (no limousines).

Rich Adams, the narrator and Washington, D.C. TV personality, then asked Aramony to speak.

"I've devoted my entire life as a social worker in the United Way," he said in his opening remarks, much to the surprise of those most closely associated with him. Anyone who knew him well knew that Aramony never publicly referred to himself as a social worker, even though he has a master's degree in social work. His resume refers to a degree in "community organization." He preferred to be identified with business, regularly referring to his undergraduate degree in business administration, not his master's degree.

Aramony continued, "I would never do anything at all that would hurt local United Ways, the mission, or the people we serve." When asked by the narrator of the teleconference whether or not he would have done anything differently, Aramony replied,

> Well, you bet. I didn't pay enough attention to detail, or to the way some of my actions could have been perceived or my personal style could have been perceived by people. I'm a mover and I get things done, but the price I paid for that was not enough attention to that detail.

He discussed his first-class travel as necessary when he had back-to-back appointments, although he indicated he had not used first class since the year before and that it was probably a mistake in the first place. He said he flew the Concorde two or three times, once when he was sick and another time when he had to get to a meeting in Indianapolis on the Mobilization for America's Children program. (It would later be determined that he took at least nine flights on the Concorde.)

Actually, Aramony frequently went out of his way to fly the Concorde. During a meeting in Moscow, Mary Yntema, United Way International's local staff member, spent three days changing his ticket so he could return to the United States via the Concorde. He told me that flying the Concorde would allow him to arrive a few hours earlier, thereby giving him a chance to rest before an evening event in New York. This particularly difficult situation demonstrates how Aramony often operated without considering personal or financial consequences. I had asked him repeatedly not to change his ticket because of the difficulty of doing so from Moscow and the difficulty of receiving money back from Aeroflot, the Russian airline that handled all airline transactions. I instructed the staff to wait until the last minute, hoping we could arrange a ticket exchange rather than buy an entirely new ticket and hope for a rebate—a possible loss of $8,000 if we could not work it out.

At the last minute, a ticket exchange was not possible, and credit on Mary Yntema's American Express corporate card was denied because United Way of America's accounting department, headed by Tom Merlo, had not paid overdue bills. Aramony was furious that he did not receive his ticket, which he had expected several days earlier. I was upset because Mary would be in Moscow without the safety of a charge card. My chairman, who was present at the time, told me that I should have done what Aramony requested and gotten the ticket right away.

Another time, Aramony and I were returning from a trip on the Concorde. He struck up a conversation with a businesswoman as they both waited for luggage. When she discovered that he worked for the United Way and had just flown the Concorde, she walked away in disgust.

The second half of the teleconference shifted gears. Armony justified setting up the for-profit spinoffs, saying that the unrelated business expenses involved in Partnership Umbrella and Sales Service/America could have jeopardized United Way of America's tax-exempt status and that such subsidiaries were looked on with favor by the IRS. He alluded to a report that would be issued on April 2.

Leffall then dropped the bombshell. Aramony had submitted a letter offering to *retire* immediately. He said this decision was accepted by the Board, but that they had asked Aramony to stay on until a successor had been selected in order to provide for an orderly transfer of power. Chairman John Akers, who was not present, spoke on videotape, thanking Aramony for his contributions. Akers said United Ways would be involved in selecting a successor and asked everyone to keep focused on the organization's primary mission of helping people.

In response to a question by the narrator regarding full disclosure of the spinoffs, Bernhard said that he had not recommended full disclosure of the financial records of the two for-profit spinoffs (Partnership Umbrella and Sales Service/America) because such disclosure could put them at a competitive disadvantage. However, he said that one of the major accounting firms would be retained to see if information could be made available which would not jeopardize the operations.

Leffall mentioned that *USA Today* had taken a poll and four out of five people, or 80 percent, had thought his salary reasonable. In the question-and-answer call-in period following the teleconference, Charles Tower, a volunteer from Jacksonville, Florida, wondered why no consideration was given to the difference between being head of a charitable organization and being head of a for-profit corporation. He asked about the possible salary range for Aramony's successor. This was answered by Bernhard, who replied that compensation should be based on the *types of tasks and problems* faced by executives and not merely on the size of the company.

Among the most memorable comments made was one by Johnny Danos, chairman of the United Way in Des Moines:

> I'd like to make you aware that your message is not selling well here
> . . . Some of your independent investigators sound more like P.R. people and I would like you to clarify just who they are . . . We need full disclosure or we are going to be severely hurt in our marketplaces.

But the most poignant question, in my opinion, was asked by Jay Smith, Chairman of the Board of United Way of Metro Atlanta and publisher of the *Atlanta Journal* and *Constitution*:

> What I've not heard, quite honestly, is an apology. Do you think, Mr. Aramony, that we're owed one?

To which Aramony replied:

> Well, Jay, you absolutely are. I do apologize for any problems that my lack of sensitivity to perceptions has caused this movement. Absolutely. I do it happily and gladly to you and everybody else.[19]

Susan Corrigan and I were allowed downstairs in the teleconference area as it ended. Already there were his son, Robert, his former administrative assistant, Rina Duncan, and Linda Boyd, the AT&T consultant. Aramony, with tears in his normally happy eyes, obviously deeply shaken and saying but a few words, warmly greeted each one of us. He then immediately went to a private room to remove his makeup.

The universal reaction from the field was one of disappointment that Aramony's departure was not to take place immediately. Larry Walton, president of United Way Services of Richmond, Virginia, spoke for many when he said, "The national board has misread the anger that exists among our volunteers, our staff, the agencies we fund, and, most importantly, the donors."[20] There was a very strong feeling that the Board of United Way of America had not acted fast enough in recognizing the gravity of the situation.

Jack Costello, president of United Way Services in Cleveland, Ohio, said it all when he observed, "Now we begin a healing process. The United Way has been around for 105 years. The United Way is not going to go away."[21]

THE MEDIA BLITZ CONTINUES

Shepard, of *The Washington Post*, reported that on the morning of the teleconference, five large locals had withheld dues until the issues were resolved. They included Washington, New York, San Francisco, Minneapolis, and Seattle. He also reported that on the previous Monday, in a conference call with two United Ways representing the "big ten" of the largest United Ways, Aramony had rejected their request that he resign. He claimed that he had done nothing wrong. However, one of Aramony's top aides told me that Aramony soon realized that he had no choice but to step down.[22]

On the evening of the teleconference, "Nightline with Ted Koppel" devoted its whole show, entitled "United Way Under Fire," to many of the issues brought to the surface by the *Post*, other media, and the teleconference. In his introductory remarks, Koppel said that the United Way was the favorite of CEOs and that these events had given the United Way a "black eye." He reviewed the allegations briefly, but said that an investigation of the *USA Today* poll which had been cited as demonstrating that Aramony's salary had an approval rating of 80 percent was based on a "man in the street" interview of only five people, four of whom said it was okay!

Most of the public probably had sentiments similar to those of the young man interviewed by the "Nightline" staff on the street:

> I mean, as much money as this guy is making, half of that could go to his charity. This guy, I don't see how he needs $475,000, ya know, per year [sic] to survive.

Koppel also stated that United Way of America did not respond to the program's requests for an appearance by a national UW spokesperson. This proved to be a sore point with many local United Ways, who felt that Akers should have instructed the national association to appoint a spokesperson who would be available to the media. Jeff

Greenfield, a reporter for the show, concluded the first part of the segment with the following:

> In these hard times, anything that persuades hard pressed individuals to keep their hands in their pockets will wind up meaning less food for the hungry and less care for the sick, less comfort for the afflicted.

Koppel's guests included Charles Shepard, *The Washington Post* reporter, Kenneth Albrecht, president of the National Charities Information Bureau, and Jack Costello, the chief professional officer of the United Way in Cleveland (as no national representative was supplied by United Way of America). Albrecht said that although the creation of spinoffs was becoming more common due to the need for charities to raise funds in hard times, information on all charities and their related activities should be made available to the public. Costello indicated that his community, along with many others, was withholding dues and that his United Way was "not very happy."

Shepard, when asked about the problem with the spinoffs, which were said to have saved money for the United Way and other charities, replied that United Way of America staff had told him that the spinoffs were established to supply jobs for Aramony's friends and family. He said that they were suspicious about how the money was spent within these organizations and that the spinoffs were outside the system of accountability of United Way of America. Shepard also provided the audience with a clear articulation of the relationship between United Way of America, in essence a trade association, and its independent, autonomous affiliates.

The segment concluded with a discussion with Danny Bakewell, chairman and co-founder of the National Black United Fund, and Rees Lloyd, who had successfully sued the United Way over coercion of employees at the workplace. But Robert Bothwell, president of the Committee for Responsive Philanthropy and a long-time United Way critic, had the last word that night:

> Well, I think it's high time that United Way's 'motherhood and apple pie' image is shown for the unreality that it has always been. United Way's been a dinosaur. The pattern that's been established by Bill Aramony in twenty years of the United Way trying to be the most important charity on the earth, is simply one that has got to go.
> "We've had a major revolution in the nonprofit sector. There are more charities serving very many different kinds of constituencies now than twenty years ago. It's time for a change.[23]

In a response to a negative editorial in *USA Today* on February 28,[24] Dr. LaSalle Leffall defended Aramony and pointed out that he had declined to accept a raise in 1992. But Aramony told me privately that he had had no practical choice but to reject the raise because it had been widely reported in the news media that John Akers, then current chairman, and W. R. Howell, the next chairman, declined raises in their own companies.

In the February 28 follow-up article to the teleconference, Felicity Barringer of *The New York Times* published a complete list of United Way of America's Board of Governors, including their corporate affiliations.[25] On February 29, Charles Shepard and Wendy Melillo of *The Washington Post* reported that Aramony had retired the day before, effective immediately, and that Al Cooper had been appointed acting president. Sunshine Overcamp, United Way of America senior vice president for Corporate Communications, confirmed this in a memo to United Way of America staff later in the day.[26]

On March 2, Kathleen (Kitty) Telsch, a well-known *New York Times* reporter who covers the charitable beat for the paper, described the opportunities the United Way events presented for competing charitable federations, led by Robert Bothwell to "break" United Way's monopoly on campaigns at the workplace. Since the 1960s, these groups, which represent women and minorities and many other "causes," had put pressure on the United Way to open up its system. A major breakthrough came in 1981 when the federal government opened up the Combined Federal Campaign to include 20 additional charities. It reported that the United Way of the Bay Area in San Francisco has listed six competing federations on their pledge cards furnished to donors.[27]

The Second Teleconference

On March 5, Charles Shepard reported in *The Washington Post* that five file drawers of financial material had been discarded at United Way International, an organization I headed for eighteen years.[28] The same day, at a second closed-circuit teleconference beamed to United Ways throughout the country, John Akers, chairman of the Board, announced that he had appointed lawyer Kenneth W. Dam, a vice president at IBM, as interim successor until a permanent replacement for Aramony could be found. Dam, a former deputy U.S. Secretary of State and provost of the University of Chicago, was rustled out of bed by Akers at 12:30 in the morning while on business in Australia—Akers asked him to take the job. It was made clear that Dam would continue on the IBM payroll until his own retirement from the company in September 1992. Dam said that he saw his role as one of establishing credibility by overseeing the completion of the continuing investigation of United Way of America's governance policies and personnel practices, restoring public confidence, and addressing the concerns of volunteers, professionals, and staffs in local communities.

One of the best pieces of news for United Way was the announcement by Dan Rooney, owner of the Pittsburgh Steelers, that he had spoken with Paul Tagliabue, NFL Commissioner, who asked him to assure the United Way that the football spots would continue to be aired during NFL games.

Akers requested that suggestions regarding the appointment of a new president for United Way of America be sent to the Search Committee. Board member Dr. Thomas F. Frist, Jr., chairman of the Hospital Corporation of America, was appointed chairman of the Search Committee. It was also revealed at the teleconference that the company which Aramony had originally retained to look into the earlier allegations was the Investigative Group, Inc. (IGI) headed by Lenzner.

Berl Bernhard, also participating in the teleconference, reviewed the purposes of the original investigation, that is, the misuse of personnel and resources, the relationship of Aramony and his associates to the spinoffs, and the hiring of a chief financial officer without an adequate investigation. He emphasized that the original investigation focused only on the allegations and did not extend to other employees and that there had been no financial audit. Lenzner's group, he said, did review expense and travel records, corporate credit card records, telephone logs, and other material related to the United Way of America's relationship to the spinoffs. As a result of this limited investigation, it did find procedural omissions in the office of the president and the chief financial officer, as well as interlocking board memberships with the spinoffs, acquisition of certain real estate in Florida and New York, and allegations of nepotism and benefits to Aramony. The investigators, he also pointed out, found no evidence of misappropriation of corporate assets by Aramony. However, United Way of America in certain instances may not have been reimbursed for personal expenditures.

Bernhard reported that he had asked Larry Horner, the chairman of United Way of America's Audit Committee (the Board's only "internal control" committee), to "superintend the mission for the board." He indicated the final recommendations would be made to the board at its meeting on April 2.

These recommendations, which resulted from the work of the IGI, would include the relationship of management to the board, financial controls, personnel systems, compensation and benefits, relationship of spinoffs to United Way of America, procedures for screening job applicants, etc.[29] It is unclear why Verner, Liipfert, as represented by Bernhard, was qualified to make recommendations on these particular subjects.

THE PUBLIC RESPONSE

Akers and the others responded to additional calls phoned in following the formal presentations that took place at the teleconference. There was considerable concern expressed that Aramony was still collecting his salary.

In response to a question regarding the relationship between local United Ways and the national organizations, Akers indicated that there was too much "we/they." He hoped that a better working relationship could be developed. Another questioner expressed concern that the Board was not responding to requests from the media, mentioned on the "Nightline" show on February 27. A question was also raised regarding the cost of the investigation.

Some of the questions raised had to do with the discarding of files at United Way International, which had been reported by the press. In responding to a question in that regard, Bernhard said the following:

> Let me point out on that the records involved were records of United Way International. They were not United Way of America records. It appears that there was destruction of certain records. What is not clear to us yet, and this is an ongoing investigation, is whether these records were duplicative records, whether they were done prior to, or after an audit. None of that is yet clear. We don't know why these records were destroyed.[30]

I will discuss this issue in greater detail later in Chapter 7.

During a press conference following the teleconference, some questioned the propriety of hiring the law firm of Verner, Liipfert, et al., which had previously done work for United Way of America and the defunct Professional Travel Systems and was also the former employer of the United Way of America's legal counsel, Dr. Lisle C. Carter, Jr. (Although he was only on staff for four years, Sales Service/America, Voluntary Initiatives America, and Mobilization for America's Children were incorporated on his watch.) *The Chronicle of Philanthropy* quotes Walter Annenberg, a major United Way benefactor, charging that for Verner, Liipfert to investigate allegations of wrongdoing was "like asking a cashier to audit his own books."[31] Since this whole affair has more to do with propriety than illegality, these points are important in determining whether or not justice and fairness were well served.

The New York Times reported that there were two reactions to the teleconference: one, considerable relief expressed at the appointment of Kenneth Dam, and two, a desire for any actions which would stem the unfavorable publicity.[32]

On March 17, Ken Dam announced that Aramony would receive no severance pay and that his pension benefits had not yet been decided pending the resolution of certain legal issues. Merlo's employment was also terminated without severance pay, and he was not eligible for any pension.[33]

"LISTENING" AT THE VOLUNTEER LEADERS CONFERENCE

"I want to tell you how sorry I am and my fellow board members are for the situation that exists in Alexandria," said John Akers, addressing over 1,400 local United Way volunteers and professionals at the annual Volunteer Leaders Conference in Indianapolis on March 22. Board member Tom Frist added, "I was not perceptive enough; I was not sensitive enough." Frist provoked laughter when he said that he found the dog whose droppings he had stepped in outside the convention hall. He had expected the dog to bite him, but it licked him instead. "I looked at this as an opportunity," he said. The analogy was not lost on those present. Dam reported to the group that United Way of America was using a line of credit to pay bills and was considering borrowing against the Alexandria office building. He reported that the budget had been cut 10 percent, and that a hiring freeze had been imposed. W.R. Howell, chairman of J.C. Penney Company and chairman-elect of the board, led everyone in a somewhat strained "group hug."

The conference was unique. It set up "listening forums" headed by board members who handled a barrage of questions about what went wrong, and heard suggestions about what needed to be done to reestablish credibility. It became very apparent from this meeting that everyone was waiting for April 2 when the results of the investigation would be reported to the country.[34]

THE APRIL 2 REPORT—A STORY OF EXCESS AND LOST VALUES

The Investigative Report (called the "Report to the Board of Governors of United Way of America") hit the front page of *The Washington Post* and *The New York Times* on April 4. *The Times* published another list of the current board members of United Way of America. The following comments are samples which appeared in the press during this period. They speak for themselves:

Kenneth W. Dam: "These conclusions are disturbing and will certainly outrage people who have given their hard-earned money week by week to help the United Way help those in need. They will, and should, feel betrayed."

Kenneth L. Albrecht, president of the National Charities Information Bureau: "I'm astounded. This kind of stuff leaves you grief-stricken. It doesn't just affect United Way of America, it affects local United Ways, it could affect local senior citizen centers and day care centers. It affects every single one of us who are involved in the charitable field in this country. We are all diminished and the public trust has been diminished."

Amanda Bowman, senior vice president, United Way of New York City: "We were shocked, especially the amount of money that was involved and actions that seem more severe than just errors in judgment."[35]

Larry Horner, chairman of United Way of America's Audit Committee: "[. . . the Board might have been] a little more quizzical."

Regan A. Henry, partner, Wolf, Block, Schorr & Solis-Cohen, and a member of the Board of United Way of America: "You have a board at United Way of America that has been taught a lesson or learned a lesson. Certainly I have learned a lesson: I'm not going to take things at face value. When you deal with a trusted executive who's been around a long time, there is a tendency to take a lot of things that he says at face value, and not delve into it and look around a lot. If he's not conveying the reality, you're not going to know what the reality is.[36]

David A. Paradine, president, United Way of the Columbia-Willamette Valley (Portland, Oregon): "Overall the system will survive. But it's what happens in the short term that everyone is worried about."[37]

Bill Aramony: "I reject categorically any suggestion of misappropriation or breach of trust during my tenure at United Way of America."[38]

The charges and allegations in the Investigative Report (many of which have already been aired in the press) will not be discussed at this stage. Instead, I have woven its content throughout the narrative in order to make it more relevant to the particular issues under discussion.

ARAMONY APPEARS ON "NIGHTLINE" ON APRIL 3

In the days of the Old Testament, the Levites, the priests of ancient Israel, would take a goat on the Day of Atonement symbolically loaded down with the sins of the community and drive that goat into the desert. Good for the community, tough for the goat. That, in fact, is where we got the term *scapegoat*.

Thus did Ted Koppel set the stage for this interview with Bill Aramony. It was a unique interview for Koppel. Normally, he interviews via a TV monitor or across a table. In this scenario, Aramony was tight up against him. This is the kind of situation that is most comfortable for Aramony—the "one on one," the *mano a mano* that has characterized his success.

Koppel began by referring to Aramony's "limited apology" and to his "questionable" reasons for the spinoffs. He listed them all, including the dollar amounts along with the alleged abuses (i.e., the limousines, the Concorde flights, and the Las Vegas and Florida trips).

ABC commentator David Marash said that the investigation had focused all of the blame on William Aramony. He said that sources inside the organization reported that the board had ignored several whistle-blowers' reports about Aramony's activities. Also, Arthur Andersen & Co., the firm which had audited United Way of America's financial records, still hadn't explained how it witnessed Aramony's expensive lifestyle and the creation of "several incestuous spinoff companies" yet had failed to inquire into the "appropriateness" of such activities.

In hard questioning regarding the alleged abuses, Aramony stated again that with back-to-back meetings, he couldn't have been expected to stand on street corners and hail taxis. He replied that he reimbursed the company for personal flights to Gainesville, Florida and no company funds were used to pay for his companion on a business trip to Egypt. (Aramony did engage in business on that trip and charged United Way International only for his airfare and two nights lodging, even though he stayed there for a longer period of time. The issue is whether or not $6,100, the cost of the flight, was justified for a day's meeting. He eventually reimbursed United Way International for the flight expenses.) He also said that the Florida condo was used as an office to handle United Way International's Latin American program.

Aramony claimed that the Board of Governors had been sent extensive information on the purposes of the spinoffs prior to their establishment and had been informed of all of the transactions. Koppel concluded the interview by expressing a sentiment which appeared to reflect the prevailing opinion of the public at the time:

> ... there is a flat-out assertion that what Bill Aramony did was arrogant, self-serving, self-benefiting, self-profiting, and that he ran this kind of organization in a high-handed way. That doesn't *look* right. That's the gentlest, kindest, most charitable way it can be said.

Aramony claimed that such a characterization was grossly unfair and that he had been denied the right of "due process" by not having a chance to see and respond to the April 2 report prior to its publication.[39]

A CONTINUING BARRAGE

Articles on United Way issues continued to receive heavy play throughout the summer of 1992. *The Chronicle of Philanthropy* featured an article on the pay and perquisites of United Way executives in its May 5 issue. It indicated that the top ten United Way chief professional officers are provided with either a car or a car allowance and sometimes business club memberships.[40] In an article published on May 19, it was reported that of approximately 1,400 dues-paying United Ways, 29 percent (or 411) had paid at least part of their dues and that 32 of the 67 largest United Ways (those raising $9 million or more) were still paying dues. It also reported that a three-member committee composed of counsel from companies of two former United Way board member chairmen and a counsel representing local United Ways was formed to resolve the various disputes between United Way of America and Aramony. These disputes included restitution of any undocumented expenses by him, payments made under consulting agreements to friends and former associates, and for payments to the spinoff organizations.[41] The same edition published a letter from Aramony to Akers responding to selected items in the Investigative Report, particularly on the background for the recommendations on his compensation and inaccuracies concerning work performed by consultants, especially that of Frederick J. Ryan, Jr., once a top aide to former President Reagan.[42]

The Washington Post reported on the results of United Way's Rochester, New York campaign, the only one in the country conducted in the spring. It was watched very closely to determine what the effects of the crisis would have on donations. Although the campaign was $2 million down from last year's results, the decrease was attributed to the local economy and a dispute concerning Planned Parenthood, not to the crisis.[43]

On May 28, both *The Washington Post* and *The New York Times* reported that the Justice Department issued subpoenas to a number of organizations, including United Way of America and numerous individuals associated with the spinoffs.[44] *The Post* also reported on June 3 that United Way of America, in an effort to downsize, offered staff an additional two months' severance pay (up to five months) for anyone who resigned by June 19.[45]

THE POWER OF THE MEDIA

It is certainly clear that the press played a major role in informing the public about the extent of the crisis, and subsequent articles compounded public awareness in a negative way. Although Aramony's salary figures were readily available to the public and were frequently published over the years, it was this lethal combination of high salary and perks that created the impression of excess and abuse. Among the most often repeated abuses were the car and driver (which at some point in the public disclosure arena turned into a chauffeured limousine) and the flights on the Concorde. Other areas of public outrage included the purchase of an apartment in New York and a condominium in Florida with charitable dollars.

Compounding the press exposures were Aramony's attempts to justify his behavior in ways that provoked even more outrage. For example, Aramony was quoted as saying, "I can't afford to be waiting for taxicabs" (too arrogant), that he didn't know about Merlo's legal problems despite a close relationship that spanned 30 years (unlikely), and that he had no influence in the hiring of his son to run a major subsidiary (not believable).

Bill Aramony's style of management and penchant for high living were well known at United Way of America and among local United

Way members. Even though some may have cautioned him to be more careful, it is not certain he would have listened to any of them, with the possible exception of his Board chairman. If he were to be called on any of these matters, he reasoned that the Board, who understood this lifestyle as being necessary for the chief executive officer of a large organization, would protect him. The press had merely collected everything that was already available from public and private sources, followed leads, and published the results in two major segments in one of the most prestigious papers in the nation. The public, which had not been conditioned to these kind of activities regarding charitable organizations, was understandably outraged.

REFERENCES

1. Closed-circuit teleconference, United Way of America (March 5, 1992).
2. Conversation with William Aramony and Robert Aramony on February 28, 1992. The four papers were *USA Today* (February 28–March 1), *The New York Times* (February 28), *The Washington Post* (February 28), and *The Wall Street Journal* (February 28).
3. Jack Anderson and Michael Binstein, "Charity Begins at Home For United Way," *Edmond Evening Sun*, Edmond, Oklahoma (February 12, 1992).
4. Letter from LaSalle D. Leffall, Jr., M.D., to Andy BeDell, Senior Editor (February 11, 1992), United Features Syndicate.
5. Verner, Liipfert, Bernhard, McPherson and Hand. *Report to the Board of Governors United Way of America* (April 2, 1992), p. 1.
6. *Ibid.*
7. "Perks, Privileges, and Power in a Nonprofit World," *The Washington Post* (February 16, 1992).
8. Mundy, Alicia, "It Works for All of Them," *Regardies* (February/March 1992), pp. 20–26.
9. "A Charitable Story," *The Washington Post* (February 20, 1992).
10. "United Way Under Fire," *The Chronicle of Philanthropy* (February 25, 1992).
11. *The Washington Post* (February 24, 1992).
12. *The Chronicle.*
13. "National United Way Under Fire," *USA Today* (February 27, 1992).
14. "United Way Chief Bows Out," *USA Today* (February 28–March 1, 1992).
15. "Charity Leaders Success Was Also Undoing," *The New York Times* (February 28, 1992).
16. "NBC Nightly News" (February 25, 1992).
17. "ABC World News Tonight" (February 26, 1992).
18. WUSA (CBS News).
19. Teleconference, United Way of America (February 27, 1992).
20. "For United Way, the 'Slate's Not Clean,' " *USA Today* (February 28–March 1, 1992).
21. *USA Today* (February 28–March 1, 1992).
22. "United Way President Is Urged to Resign," *The Washington Post* (February 27, 1992).
23. "Nightline—United Way Under Fire," ABC (February 27, 1992).
24. Editorial, "New United Way Leaders Must Clean Up Problems" *USA Today* (February 28, 1992).

25. "United Way Head Is Forced Out In a Furor Over His Lavish Style," *The New York Times* (February 28, 1992).
26. "United Way Chief Exists Abruptly," *The Washington Post* (February 29, 1992).
27. "Charities See Opportunity in Troubles at United Way," *The New York Times* (March 2, 1992).
28. "United Way Unit's Files Discarded," *The Washington Post* (March 5, 1992).
29. Teleconference, United Way of America (March 5, 1992).
30. *Ibid.*
31. "United Way: The Fallout after the Fall," *The Chronicle of Philanthropy* (March 10, 1992).
32. "United Way Head Tries to Restore Trust," *New York Times* (March 7, 1992).
33. "United Way Committee Votes to Stop Aramony's Salary," *The Washington Post* (March 18, 1992).
34. "United Way Volunteers Hear Apologies From Board," *The Washington Post* (March 23, 1992).
35. "United Way Finds Pattern of Abuse By Former Chief," *The New York Times* (April 4, 1992).
36. "Charity Board Learns to be Skeptical," *The New York Times* (April 19, 1992).
37. "Affiliates Fear Bitter Fight by Ex-head of United Way," *The New York Times* (April 5, 1992).
38. *The New York Times* (April 4, 1992).
39. Nightline—"United Way Under Fire," ABC (March 3, 1992).
40. "A Closer Look at Pay and Perks," *The Chronicle of Philanthropy* (May 5, 1992).
41. "Local Dues to United Way of America Rise, Easing Fiscal Crisis," *The Chronicle of Philanthropy* (May 19, 1992).
42. *Ibid,* "Text of Letter in Which Former United Way Chief Replies to Some Charges."
43. "Rochester United Way Finds Recession is Biggest Threat," *The Washington Post* (May 22, 1992).
44. "U.S. Probing Operation of United Way Under Aramony," *The Washington Post* (May 28, 1992) and "Justice Department Seeks Records of United Way and its Companies," *The New York Times* (May 28, 1992).
45. "United Way Urges Staff to Quit or Take Leave Without Pay," *The Washington Post* (June 3, 1992).

CHAPTER 2

Freedom, Charity, and the United Way

"Then thou shalt strengthen him: Yea, though he be a stranger and a sojourner; that he may live with thee."
Leviticus 25:35

"So there abide faith, hope and charity, these three; but the greatest of these is charity."
1 Corinthians 13:13

In order to understand "what went wrong and why" with the United Way movement, a clear understanding of its roots in charitable giving and activities is essential. Rising from Judeo-Christian ethics and democratic traditions, giving, caring, and serving became deeply ingrained in the American psyche. Gordon Manser and Rosemary Higgins Cass, who for many years led the National Assembly for Social Policy and Development, a group of charities involved in social welfare planning, said it best when discussing the historic circumstances which promoted the common good in the nation: "The impulse for these acts is to be found in the Judeo-Christian ethos of love, justice, and mercy. The millions of volunteers of every type in our society today can trace their lineage and inspiration to these devoted efforts."[1] Over time, this ethos created a clear perception among great numbers of American people of what they understood charitable activity to be. The United Way, the premier charitable organization in America, had become antithetical to that understanding and betrayed those traditions. It had forsaken its humble origins. It had betrayed American society, itself.

In this chapter, we will trace the roots of the voluntary sector in America in order to show that the past cannot be separated from the present. The voluntary spirit and the charity it engenders are not especially unique to America, although they may have reached their zenith in this country. As a result of having spent many years in the international arena, I have been made very much aware of the fact that charitable activities are present in every society. They may be known by different names, and they may often be taken for granted, but they are *always* present—people reaching out to help others in need is a trait common to all people and quite possibly a common human need as well.

AMERICAN SOCIETY AND THE VOLUNTARY SECTOR

American society is commonly viewed as having three sectors. They are *Government, Business*, and the *Voluntary Sector*, sometimes called the Third, or Independent Sector. (I will refer to it as the voluntary sector). In carrying out their separate purposes, each of the sectors benefits society in its own special way. The elements of the first two sectors, government and business, are obvious to most people. The elements of the voluntary sector may not be as clear. Simply put, the voluntary sector represents the vast array of institutions, organizations, and acts of giving, caring, and serving which increase the quality of life in America. It is called "voluntary" because its support and activities are derived from the efforts of millions of citizens who donate their time and money to solve others' problems or enhance another's quality of life in ways that are not provided by the other sectors. Its creations range from colleges and universities, hospitals, museums, family service associations, Boy Scouts, girls' clubs, and arts and cultural centers to veterans and citizen's associations, the Elks, churches, and synagogues.

In 1991, *Giving USA*, probably the nation's most definitive source in such matters, reported that total private giving in the United States was $124.77 billion, a 1.4 percent increase over the previous year.[2] The same year United Way organizations raised $3.17 billion, slightly over 2.5 percent of the total. Yet United Way's influence on philanthropy in the country belies these statistics. Because of its centrist position in communities involving millions of citizens across the country in giving and receiving, its influence is far greater than these figures indicate.

Brian O'Connell, president of the Independent Sector, Inc., once wrote in describing the impact of the sector on American life:

> This sector provides an enormously important extra dimension in our pursuit of happiness and inalienable rights. Its impact is clear in just about every field of endeavor including fields as different as architecture, health, human rights, historic preservation, international under-

standing, arts, neighborhoods, empowerment, patriotism, agriculture, rocketry, physics, the homeless, and astronomy.[3]

Waldemar Neilsen's impassioned defense of the voluntary sector (he refers to it as the "third sector") calls for its revitalization and recognition by the government as being a critical and essential part of American life. Although he recognizes that the sector is not a substitute for the humanitarian programs of a modern welfare state, he believes that the voluntary sector can lessen the fiscal, psychological, and political side effects of excessive bureaucracy and the centralization and depersonalization of government-style programs.[4]

There are over 900,000 tax-exempt organizations in the United States. Contributions to approximately 500,000 of these organizations are tax-deductible under Internal Revenue Code section 501(c)(3).[5] The United Way was founded in response to the need for health and welfare funding and for the purpose of distributing those funds effectively. The United Way, because of its neutral position in most communities, frequently can gather members from local businesses and governments around a *community table*. In this role, United Way can also serve as a meeting ground to discuss ways in which the three sectors can work together for the benefit of the whole community.

INTERNATIONAL VOLUNTARISM

I have always taken strong exception to those who, in speeches and in articles, state that voluntarism (if not charity) is a special American creation as if to intimate that we have cornered the market on good deeds and good works. A closer look at charities in other countries will show they also have organizations through which people can express their concern for others. James Joseph, in the opening chapter of his book, *The Charitable Impulse*, which describes the motivations and activities of philanthropists in a variety of countries and cultures, says that "tales of altruism, charity, and philanthropy can be found in every culture and every community among those with abundant wealth as well as among those who live on the margins of the economy."[6]

In the former Soviet Union, for example, secret volunteer-like institutions arose even in a Communist state to assist victims of that state by feeding, protecting, and sheltering them. The individuals who participated in these organizations, often at great personal risk, never referred to themselves as "volunteers." They only did what they thought was necessary or right. Mary Yntema, the first director of United Way International's Moscow Liaison Office, tells the story of a woman who would help out a neighbor by delivering food and running errands. She had never realized that she, too, was a volunteer. She was only doing what she thought was right. When people are hurting or in need of nurturing, there will always be those who will respond with both heart and soul, oblivious to any possible personal danger.

WHAT MAKES AMERICAN CHARITIES SPECIAL?

If we believe that volunteering, giving, caring, and serving are not unique to America, then what makes us special in this regard? Is it the fact that we, as a nation, have not developed the governmental and socialistic models of our European forbears? Or is it that we do not possess the cultural, religious, and extended family loyalties of the Asian, Hispanic, Native-American, and African-Americans? Is it that American efficiency has created an "organized" voluntary sector and, therefore, institutionalized it?

Although American society could never be described as culturally homogenous, the overall ethos of our nation cannot be separated from our British heritage. The efforts of the "mother country" to deal with human misery over the centuries have had a lasting and profound impact on the social fabric of our nation. In addition, the challenges faced in the New World where people had to depend upon themselves and their neighbors in the absence of effective, or, in some cases, any government, added to the special character of American voluntarism. Eventually, England would pursue its own path toward socialism based largely on the philosophy of the great nineteenth-century reformer Robert Owen, whose utopian socialism had failed to take root in this country.

One of my many jobs when I first came to United Way of America was writing speeches for Aramony. In researching a particular speech, I came across an address by Richard Lyman, then president of Stanford University, in which he drew upon the observations of Edmund Burke, the great British (actually he was Irish) statesman and orator, who referred in one of his writings to society's "little platoons." He was referring to those intermediate institutions between the individual and the state which mediated the power of the government to protect and serve the needs of the individual. Today these "little platoons" would

be referred to as voluntary organizations. He bemoaned the fact that
the French Revolution, through the zeal of its leaders to purify society,
aggressively sought to destroy these very special social structures. You
could say that society, in order to maintain its stability, requires the
existence of certain institutions which are responsive to those needs of
certain groups and individuals whose deeply personal concerns the
state, throughout history, has always been unable to meet.[7]

My friend and colleague Richard C. Cornuelle, a well-respected
student of American voluntarism, wrote:

> What may be most original in the American experience is not that our
> commercial sector is organized more or less along free enterprise lines,
> or even that our political institutions permit very nearly universal
> participation, but that Americans for nearly a quarter of a millennium
> have found better and better ways to act *directly* on their common
> problems by forming literally millions of voluntary organizations of
> every imaginable shape and size.[8]

THE CONCEPT OF COMMUNITY

Voluntary activity represents the best instincts of the American people.
Voluntary associations began to form as soon as the first Europeans
rowed ashore. Their Judeo-Christian values were expressed through
the Protestant Ethic which they carried with them. The class structures
inherent in British and other European societies were ill-suited to the
strenuous frontier life of the colonies. Birth rights and special treatment
did not serve people well in this newest, yet harshest of new lands.
What developed was a concept of *community*—the basic social institution upon which the United Way largely rests. The community eventually transcended both religion and class.

Starvation, danger, illness, and natural disasters made no distinction among the rich and the poor in the early days of our country.
Against the elements, all people were equal. Self-help and cooperation
were the only options available. Basic survival depended upon it. Mutual dependency became a way of life. This environmentally imposed
equality superseded class differences and created the democratic environment which allowed our emerging republic not only to survive
the early years of desperation, but to prosper into a great society soon
to be envied throughout much of the world.

PHILANTHROPY BECAME THE ENGINE

If voluntary cooperation characterized these early communities, *philanthropy* became the engine—the driving force. Philanthropic activity nurtured voluntary organizations and enabled them to meet the needs of people more effectively. Together, philanthropy and voluntary service brought out the best instincts of the American people. It was from these seedlings that the United Way movement grew, was nurtured, and developed into the hugely successful charity it eventually became.

THE UNITED WAY: AN OUTGROWTH OF AMERICAN INGENUITY

Organizations, like people, are products of their past. Over time, they evolve and form their own special qualities which separate them from others of their kind. Sigmund Freud observed that "the child is the father of the man." The United Way of today is the product of multiple historic influences simply because it has touched virtually every aspect of American life in one way or another. Simple acts of charity, of people helping people, became the basis for the first United Way and others which were to follow. Organizing this charitable activity in order to make it more effective in meeting human needs was a logical outgrowth of American ingenuity. Call it a better mousetrap. The United Way has had its fits and starts over the years, but because it made sense, because it was steeped in American tradition, because it was community based and, therefore, reflected community needs, it worked. Maybe it didn't work "for all of us," as some critics say, but it has worked reasonably well for many, many years.

When Bill Aramony took the reins at United Way in May of 1970, he inherited an entire history which extended back centuries in time. Because America is based on a political democracy with a free market economy, America's society and culture are determined by events over which it has only limited control. A centrally planned economy with an autocratic leader can control, at least for a time, the economic and social resources which inevitably cause change if left unregulated. Fortunately, we in America have a different tradition. The best leaders of our great institutions are able to adapt to change while at the same time adhering to certain values which are unchanging. This challenge is difficult at best, even for the most able of leaders. What went wrong with the United Way may possibly be found in the inability of its volunteer and professional leaders to understand the balance between social change and the American ethical imperatives which never change.

The United Way owes its success to two enduring institutions of American life: corporations and organized labor. These two institutions have thrived in our capitalistic and pluralistic society. Although each has pursued different directions since the Industrial Revolution, one of the forums in which they have always found a common cause has been with United Way.

Business and the United Way

When the United Way began in Denver in 1887, corporations, particularly those run by northern industrialists, had begun to prosper with the opening of western markets and the rebuilding of the South. Eastern banks extended considerable credit, which led to the accumulation of large sums of capital by a few companies. In this environment, free market competition declined and wealth became concentrated. Between 1879 and 1899, capital investment had quadrupled. The number of factories had grown from 140,000 in 1860, with a million workers, to 208,000 in 1900, with 4.7 million workers. Between 1860 and 1900, the gross national product had tripled.[9]

Despite antitrust laws and laws regulating monopolistic practices, today only a few corporations account for the great majority of business activity in America. Of three million businesses, just 2 percent have assets of more than $10,000,000. The largest 200 companies employ 80 percent of all the people who work for companies. Of all the industrial organizations, the largest 100 corporations controlled half of all industrial assets, such as land, buildings, and equipment by 1983.[10]

These facts are very important to the United Way. Aramony would become more successful than his predecessors because he understood how to "work" these forces to serve the public good. Once this support was assured, so, too, would be the success of the United Way. A generation ago, C. Wright Mills wrote in *The Power Elite*:

> The power elite is composed of men whose positions enable them to transcend the ordinary environments of ordinary men and women; they are in positions to make decisions of major consequences . . . for they are in command of the major hierarchies and organizations of modern society. They rule the big corporations. They run the machinery of the state and claim the prerogatives . . . they occupy the strategic command posts of the social structure . . . in which are now centered the effective means of the power and the wealth and the celebrity which they enjoy.[11]

Aramony understood the absolute necessity of recruiting top corporate leaders to "the cause" in order to secure a lock on corporate and employee charitable dollars for United Way distribution. Most importantly, corporate involvement in the United Way created an opportunity to expose these elite to social problems. Their involvement took them, albeit for short periods of time, out of their boardrooms and private clubs and acquainted them with their community's social problems, thus giving them an opportunity to exercise their corporate social responsibility.

Some corporations began to realize that enlightened self-interest expressed in responsible corporate activity was not only good for business, but good for society as well. This attitude was very important to the involvement of corporations in charitable activity.

On March 26, 1981, The Business Roundtable issued "The Business Roundtable Position on Corporate Philanthropy," a landmark statement endorsed by the U.S. Chamber of Commerce and the National Association of Manufacturers. It reads in part:

> The Business Roundtable believes that corporate philanthropy, primarily through contributions, is an integral part of corporate social responsibility. All business entities should recognize philanthropy as good business and as an obligation if they are to be considered responsible corporate citizens of the national and local communities in which they operate.[12]

Business leaders have been instrumental in the development of United Way organizations since the turn of this century when the Cleveland Chamber of Commerce conducted a series of studies which led to the first modern Community Chest (a name which subsequently became widely used by many other communities). It was obvious that business was a significant donor force in virtually every urban or semi-urban community. If contributions were to be requested from business for charitable purposes, it was essential that the funds be raised and distributed efficiently. In other words, charities had to maintain the same "business" standards as business itself.

The Community Chest movement continued to accelerate its drive to involve businesspeople in its operations. By 1936, most companies in most communities stood behind the concept of federated or combined, community-wide fund-raising. At that time, one-fourth of the money contributed to the chests came from corporations. At the beginning of World War II, giving by corporations to the War Chests nearly doubled in a space of just five years. Today, direct corporate contributions to the United Way account for almost a fourth of total contributions.

In 1940, Congress passed a law which allowed banks to contribute to community funds. This was followed by similar actions in the mutual life insurance area. By 1952, the standards of how much to give were becoming more sophisticated and included consideration of the community's pattern of giving, net profits, the economy, etc. Today, most communities consider a wide range of indices in determining how much money can be realistically raised in any particular campaign. Yet, the most significant step to involve corporations in the United Way did not occur until the formation of the National Corporate Development Program (NCD) in 1975, now known as the National Corporate Leadership Program (NCL).

Organized Labor and the United Way

Following the growth of big business came big labor. In the late nineteenth century when immigrants began to flood the workforce, real wages began to drop. The labor force at the time consisted mainly of women, immigrants, African-Americans, widows, and children. They worked 12- to 14-hour days, six days a week. At the turn of the century, 50 to 66 percent of working families were poor, and 33 percent lived in abject poverty. This situation provided grist for the mill of organized labor.[13] It was not, however, until the 1930s that unions were given the right to organize and bargain collectively.

One of the great successes of the United Way system is its capacity to unify communities. Both management and labor recognize that the United Way provides the only significant forum where they can sit at the same table in a neutral setting to work together to meet the needs of the community. One of the most dramatic sights I ever witnessed was John D. de Butts, president of AT&T, embracing Glen Watts, president of the Communications Workers of America (AFL-CIO), after they had just left a meeting where they had worked closely together in order to resolve an issue concerning what was then called the National Corporate Development program.

In 1974 in Detroit, Douglas A. Fraser, vice president of the United Auto Workers, became the first labor leader to head a major United Way campaign. Throughout the last 25 years, top labor leaders have been deeply involved in the United Way system at all levels. These have included William Green, AFL President; Philip Murray, CIO president; George Meany, who served as the national campaign chairman; and the beloved Joseph A. Beirne, who was the chairman of the Board of the national association from 1966 to 1967. Leo Perlis, the first head of the AFL-CIO Department of Community Services, served on United Way of America's Board of Governors for many years. Until recently, this position at the AFL-CIO was held by Joe Velasquez, considered the most creative and dynamic leader since its inception.

"A Cooperative Memorandum of Understanding Between The United Way of America and the AFL-CIO" calls for labor participation in United Way activities, representation by labor in the area of policy-making, and the appointment of a Director of Labor Participation at United Way of America. This position is currently held by Jordan "Bud" Biscardo, a former streetcar operator from Pittsburgh, considered an extraordinarily bright and capable leader who easily bridges management and labor issues with great ability and finesse. One of the most important activities of this office is securing campaign endorsements from AFL-CIO affiliated unions for the annual United Way campaign.

The labor movement is the foundation upon which the United Way movement rests. It is the factory workers and employees of large business corporations who provide, through payroll deductions, over 60 percent of United Way funds. A visit to any factory setting during the annual fund-raising campaign will demonstrate the enormous enthusiasm workers have for the United Way. The creative and indefatigable chief professional officer of Kansas City, Missouri, John Greenwood, carried the relationship between United Way and employees to new heights when he focused his organizational efforts on training factory workers to provide information and referral services to their fellow employees, and in other ways help them with virtually any problems they might have. The principles and practices of these "workplace presence programs," first pioneered by Greenwood among auto workers in Flint, Michigan were carried on in concert with the representatives of organized labor. I visited this program in Flint at Aramony's suggestion. It was the single most powerful program for generating community spirit for the United Way I had ever seen before or since. It was widely promoted by United Way of America and has had an important impact on the movement. In 1992, Greenwood received a special award from the local AFL-CIO in recognition of his contributions to helping working people through the United Way.

The AFL-CIO Union Counselor Program trains rank-and-file union members to assist their "brothers and sisters" throughout the country in cooperation with United Ways. These counselors help coordinate participation in United Way campaigns, conduct institutes on health and welfare issues, and provide information and referral regarding community services.

Leo Perlis was the director of the Community Services Department when Aramony became the National Executive. Both were very strong leaders who constantly disagreed on several key issues. Perlis wanted to establish United Way funded labor agencies, which would focus attention on providing direct services to union members. Aramony flatly rejected this alternative. He thought it would be divisive to community cohesiveness. He believed that it was the responsibility of the United Way to provide services to everyone who needed them. Aramony was highly trusted by the labor movement, and his word, based on a simple handshake, was considered sufficient to implement major program initiatives. Labor union leaders remain among his most ardent supporters. Aramony's careful cultivation of labor is a significant factor in its support of the United Way movement. In 1990, he received the AFL-CIO's Murray-Green-Meany Award, the labor federation's most prestigious community services honor. It was reported to me that most labor leaders associated with the United Way understood that Aramony had to leave but resented how it was handled by the leadership of the board.

The United Way provided unique opportunities for both management and labor. Each group came from radically different perspectives, a reality which created a continuing adversarial relationship. Over time, with the help of United Way, both eventually recognized that the well-being of American society depended on the well-being of its communities. This made only good sense, and United Way was ready to help. Through the United Way, they could both together direct their energies and considerable resources toward something every prudent citizen desired—a stable community in which to live and raise children. Stated another way, happy workers make happy customers. Social disorder—crime, broken families, drug and alcohol abuse—undermine the harmony of communities.

Big business and big labor found common purpose in the United Way. It met not only their own divergent needs, but the needs of the United Way as well. By lending its support, these pillars of American society gave the United Way a power and influence which separated it from other health and human service organizations and made it the preeminent and distinctive charity in the nation. It seemed that with the support of these major American institutions, everything was possible and nothing could go wrong.

A NEW UNITED WAY ERA BEGINS

Bill Aramony became the National Executive of what was to become the United Way of America on May 18, 1970, 83 years after the first United Way began in Denver in 1887. At the time of his selection, the press releases indicated that, at 42, he was the youngest individual ever to occupy the post since the national office came into being in 1918. In fact, he was the fourth such person to serve in that position. He had told several friends and colleagues that he would stay just ten years. He stayed almost 22, and, had the events of 1992 not taken place, he would have been at the helm for at least another two years, before retiring at age 66. It was important to Aramony, as he articulated many times, that he break the expected "mandatory" retirement age of 65 in order to show that his departure from the movement was undertaken at his own initiative and in his own time.

HOW ARAMONY CAME TO POWER

There are many stories regarding how and why Aramony was selected which are not well known to the public. In the late 1960s, the United Community Funds and Councils of America (then the name of the national association representing community-wide fund-raising organizations in local communities) had stalled, not knowing quite what direction to take as a result of the tumult of the 1960s and the tremendous amount of public funding of services during that period which had previously been supported by the private sector. With so much public funding of health and social services, was organized voluntary giving that necessary? Is there a significant role a national organization can play in helping to solve community problems? How do voluntary organizations accept public money and still maintain their independence? How can money be raised for voluntary services if the public perceives needs being met by the public sector? These were just a few of the questions asked by the national officials.

The national association retained a management and accounting firm, then called Peat, Marwick, Mitchell and Company (PMM), to undertake a comprehensive study of the national organization in order to help it define its role, its pattern of services, its administration, and its financial structure. Bayard Ewing, chairman of United Community Funds and Councils of America and a prominent attorney from Providence, Rhode Island, presided over the transition to the new organization.

The impact of the report was profound and far-reaching. Twenty years later, the field is still benefiting from the impact these farsighted recommendations have had on the United Way movement and, to a lesser extent, American society. It was this study that served as the platform upon which Bill Aramony launched his career as a national leader of what was to become one of the most successful charitable organizations in America.

The Selection Committee, headed by the late Board member Harry T. Sealy from Cleveland, considered many options for the type of individual they wanted to lead the national association in order to bring it into a new era of progress. Among the debates that ensued within the committee was whether to recruit a figurehead with credibility (it was said that General Westmoreland was under consideration) *or* to find someone among the local United Way chief professional officers.

At the time, Aramony was well known among his peers across the country as an innovative, creative thinker. He had led the United Way of Dade County in Miami, Florida to record fund-raising results. It had been more or less assumed that the new chief professional officer would come from one of the larger cities. Miami was not included on that list. However, most of the leaders of the larger communities had just been placed in good positions or preferred to stay where they were.

When Aramony heard that the Selection Committee might choose someone from outside the field, he told me that he rallied his friends from around the country and presented Sealy with an ultimatum. Either choose someone from the field or he, Aramony, would lead a boycott of the movement. "The leadership of the national association belongs to the pros in the field," he said. He believed that it was totally unacceptable to follow the pattern of the American Red Cross, which had always selected an outsider to head its national office. He considered this an insult to the professional Red Cross worker.

The final choice came down to Dan MacDonald, currently the chief professional officer in Indianapolis, and Aramony. Aramony related to me, although I have not been able to verify it from any other contemporary sources, that the Selection Committee hired private detectives to report on any aspects of the personal lives of the finalists which could be embarrassing to the national association if uncovered. Aramony was informed of the investigation by inside sources and chose not to change his lifestyle. "My private life is my own business," he would say. "If I have to sell my soul to get the job, it's not worth it." When confronted with compromising information by Bayard Ewing, then chairman of the Board, he successfully used this reasoning to mitigate the issue. Aramony later indicated that he provided assurances to Ewing on these matters which had apparently satisfied both him and the Selection Committee. Twenty-three years later, this attitude towards his personal lifestyle would help contribute to his downfall. It was also an attitude that one could say was "pure Aramony."

Aramony reportedly used all the political means he could to obtain intelligence on the deliberations of the committee and to further his chances for the top job. These methods included lobbying both his friends (whose volunteers sat on the Steering Committee) and well-placed staff people in the national association.

Another recommendation was said to have come from John Gardner, who received good reports about Aramony from Frank Sullivan, chairman of Mutual Benefit Life of South Bend, Indiana, where Aramony had served as the chief professional officer. Sullivan had been chairman of the local operation of the Urban Coalition, which was founded by Gardner.

One of the main issues for the Board was whether or not the new leader would accept the recommendations of the PMM study in which the board had invested so much effort. Aramony indicated that he agreed with most of the recommendations. But he said that he would *not* accept the recommendation which called for two major staff positions—one which would handle internal United Way system (membership) matters and one that would handle external (voluntary services) relations. Aramony said that he would assume both functions. So, with his selection began the most far-reaching and dramatic changes in the United Way since its founding nearly a century before.

Bayard Ewing, at the annual meeting of the trustees on December 3, 1970, in Dallas, Texas, said:

> A dynamic new jet force was introduced into all of our preceedings with the appointment of Mr. Aramony. I can't tell you what a breath of fresh air this man has been. There is nothing soggy about his thinking. There is no slavish dedication to the way things have been done in the past, unless that past has wisdom that is demonstrably useful to us today.[14]

Ewing would later remark to me many times how proud he was to have been responsible for taking a major risk by hiring a "maverick" like Bill Aramony. This gracious patrician passed away in late 1991 and was thereby spared having to bear witness to the events which transpired a few months later.

THE "MAVERICK" TAKES OVER

One of Aramony's first priorities was to develop a new national staff
and unload most of the present staff while staying within budget. He
knew that he would have to pay more to get the staff he wanted, but
he believed that a few good, well-paid people could do the work of
several lower-level employees. He is justly proud of the fact that no
one was let go without first having been provided a generous measure
of personal security. Pensions were bought up, large severances were
granted, consulting contracts were arranged until retirement benefits
could be collected and new jobs found.

Aramony personally told me a story about one of the staff in the
personnel department who was considered to be a bigot. This individual supposedly denied openings in the United Way to ethnic minorities, Jews, and others. Aramony told me that on his first day on the job,
even before taking off his coat and hat, he marched into the individual's
office and announced, "You're fired!" Even so, arrangements were
made to ease that person into retirement. This was another example of
"pure Aramony." I was unable to verify this story from contemporary
sources.

Launching the New United Way: The First 200 Days

With the selection of Bill Aramony as National Executive, volunteers
and professionals associated with the United Way had great hopes that
the movement under his leadership could be revived and once again
become a relevant and major force in American life. During the 1960s,
as difficulties in coping with radical change increased and government
financing of social services expanded, the United Way had begun to
lose its confidence. Aramony changed all that. His "honeymoon period" produced the most impressive and far-reaching changes in the
United Way since its inception.

Shortly after his appointment in 1970, he addressed an enthusiastic
staff gathered from across the country in Hollywood Beach, Florida.
He promised that the new United Way would be more inclusive and
committed to service delivery systems which met the needs of people,
not the needs of charities. He graciously recognized the contributions
of his predecessor, Lyman S. Ford, and his service to the movement.
He encouraged local United Ways to recruit strong business leaders to
their boards (as he had done) and to adopt sound administrative and
management procedures;[15] in effect, to become more like business.

At the annual meeting of the Board of Trustees in Dallas, Texas, later that year, five major actions were taken:

1. Approval of the revised charter and by-laws for United Way of America.
   Note: These changes involved, among other matters, changing the name and redefining the mission.

2. Reduction of the size of the Board of Directors from 62 to 32 members and an election of new Board members.
   Note: The previous Board consisted of both United Way professionals and agency executives. Aramony and Ewing had asked the Board to resign so that a top-level group of ethnically diverse business and labor leaders could be selected.

3. Change of the title of the volunteer head of United Way of America from "President" to "Chairman of the Board," the title of the chief salaried executive officer from "Executive Vice President" to "National Executive," and the name of the "Annual Trustees Meeting" to the "National Congress."
   Note: These changes were made in order to bring the United Way terminology and organization closer to that of the business community. At the time, Aramony had said that the field was not yet ready to refer to him as "President."

4. Change in the method of member organization voting from one vote for each United Way of America member organization to one vote for each, plus one vote for each $5,000 of dues paid to United Way of America, and one additional vote for each 5,000 population figure within the member's solicitation and/or planning area.
   Note: These measures were taken to encourage the increase in dues and to give greater influence to the larger communities. They were largely cosmetic as the annual congress was essentially a rubber stamp for actions already taken by the Board.

5. Agreement to increase the annual membership dues from $3/10$ of 1 percent (approximately) to $5/10$ of 1 percent of the amount raised in the previous year's campaign to implement the program plans for 1971 and 1972.
   Note: This point was a key element in Aramony's ability to implement his program goals after reducing the budget from what it had been the year before. It would allow him to hire fewer staff and pay them more, generally increasing the qual-

ity of services and products produced by the national association.[16]

The 13-Point Program—Rebirth and Renewal

Aramony developed support for his program by meeting with hundreds of local United Way executives from across the country during the second half of 1970. From these face-to-face meetings, he developed a *13-point program* which set the stage for all that was to follow in the coming years. The 13-point program included:

1. **United Way Systems Institute.** To increase the ability of United Way organizations to handle the ever-increasing flow of data and basic management information. To expedite the implementation of systems management resources in local communities through training, consultation, and EDP services to local communities.

2. **United Way Census Project.** A special effort will be made to plan programs to optimize utilization of the 1970 census data. Local community needs for census data in the planning, programming, and budgeting areas will be reviewed and relevant tables and other tools will be prepared to enable local United Way organizations to utilize data.

3. **United Way Foundation Grantsmanship.** To develop an effective ability of United Way organizations to secure foundation grants to augment local efforts to plan and provide innovative and relevant health and welfare services.

4. **Government Grants and Relations.** To develop a strong voluntary participation in government programs that relate to problems with health and welfare import. Activities would include:
    —establishment of linkages with regional offices of governmental agencies.
    —active efforts to assure that the voluntary intent is reflected in health and welfare legislation and policies.
    —a systematic program of obtaining federal grants to augment local resources for health and welfare services.

5. **Allocating Systems.** To build a strong workable process—at the local level—for judicious and relevant use of federated voluntary dollars to meet voluntarism's fair share of health and welfare costs locally, regionally and nationally.

6. **Information/Referral Services and Volunteer Bureaus.** Un-

dertake a thorough review of volunteer bureaus and information and referral service programs for the purpose of clarifying and defining future activities in these areas.

7. **Representation of Local Interest with National Voluntary
Agencies.** This new program thrust was aimed at a definitive
effort to assure that local interest is brought to the attention of
all national voluntary agencies. Specific efforts will be made
to secure better use of the old United Way dollars spent by
national agencies. This would include continuous consideration of the acquisition of new dollars from other sources.

8. **Planning and Delivery Systems.** The objectives of this program are to:
    a. Define what community-wide social planning is.
    b. Decide what United Way's role in social planning should
       be.
    c. Settle the question of who's going to do it under the United
       Way banner.
    d. Build the kind of mechanism that will deliver the necessary
       punch.

9. **National Corporation Cultivation.** Objectives include:
    a. Upgrade corporate giving.
    b. Promote new corporate ability to give standards.
    c. Secure payroll deduction wherever not available or avail-
       able for only limited time.
    d. Promote more effective employee and executive cam-
       paigns through all-out promotional efforts by the corpo-
       ration in all of its operations. These will include:
       ■ promotion of local United Fund fair-share standards.
       ■ payroll deduction availability and promotion.
       ■ separate solicitation and reporting of employees versus
         executives and/or management personnel.
    e. Identify and cultivate national corporate leaders who are
       active locally in the United Way and are potentials for na-
       tional United Way leadership.
    f. Identify and cultivate other national corporate leaders in-
       cluding those active with United Way member agencies
       and non–United Way agencies.

10. **Voluntary Accreditation of Funds and Councils.** On recommendation of a professional advisory committee, the Board of
Directors of the United Way of America, at its meeting on January 30, 1970 voted: 1) to establish a commission on voluntary

standards and accreditation and 2) that the following be a major objective of the national association.

   a. Assist communities to achieve their maximum capacity and maximum results by developing acceptable procedures.

   b. Helping communities help themselves through local community initiatives.

11. **United Way Projects for Youth, Minorities and other Groups.** This program reflects the special effort of the United Way to expedite the participation of youth, minorities and other groups in the United Way movement.

Objectives include:

   a. To document existing data on minority and youth groups, their leadership, concerns and programs.

   b. To develop a program for recruiting and developing qualified people for professional positions in our field.

   c. To provide crisis counseling to local United Way members.

   d. To assist youth and minority groups to get involved in policy, program, and service aspects of the health and welfare system.

   e. To improve the sensitivity of United Way organizations to social issues so they can anticipate and avoid disruptions and confrontations.

12. **Measuring Public Opinion.**

   a. To increase public relations effectiveness of local Funds by providing research findings that can be used locally.

   b. To make United Way organizations sensitive to public attitudes so that they may adjust programs to meet needs and counteract false opinions.

   c. To uncover public attitudes on community problems of funds, councils, and member agencies and assist in charting changes in these attitudes where needed.

13. **National Academy for Voluntarism.** The aim of the National Academy will be to increase the ability of the thousands of volunteers in the United Way movement to meet their responsibilities for the policies and programs of the voluntary agencies with which they are affiliated at the local level. It will also provide for the continuing education needs of the professional staff in the United Way affiliates across the country.[17]

In the first year of his tenure, Aramony sought to bring unity to what were essentially many disparate and separate United Way organizations with different names and no national identity as a movement. The PMM report stated that most respondents who commented on suggested names liked the name "United Way" best. Most believed that the name "United Way" would position the movement as an iportant unifying force in the community and not simply as a mechanism to raise funds, as the previous names had implied. This recommendation was not only wholeheartedly endorsed by Aramony, but aggressively promoted by him. Saul Bass, the world-renowned graphic artist, designed the current "helping hand" logo as the unifying symbol of the United Way movement. Although initially considered to be somewhat complicated because of its many-colored rainbow, it eventually gained widespread acceptance.

Setting Up the New Headquarters

Aramony had obtained approval to move the organization out of New York City to the Washington, D.C. area where a site had been selected on an underused piece of property in Alexandria, Virginia on the Potomac River. Immediately to the east was a fat-rendering plant and to the south, a lot on which sat huge, unused stationary gas tanks owned by Texaco. However, the location choice proved to be a wise decision from practical, financial, and symbolic standpoints. It was also important that the office leave its quarters in a flat across from the United Nations on the East River in New York and relocate to the Washington, D.C. area where it would be closer to the central government.

A significant part of future programming involved the development of broad-based public/private partnerships with government for social welfare programs, as well as the hope of supplementing program activities of the United Way with government funds. United Way of America's new top-level board of corporate and labor volunteer leaders would then be able to impact their peers in government on behalf of the United Way as well. Aramony firmly believed that the voluntary sector needed a highly visible symbol to express its importance to society and the country. He rejected less expensive office space in Washington in favor of a separate facility which would be a monument for the United Way and a demonstration of the strength and vitality of the voluntary sector in America.

The financing for the building was a major problem initially. However, with the help of his board members and others, he was able to establish lines of credit and convince the banks that he would be able to pay back the loan. It worked. Ground was broken on April 2, 1971, almost a year after Aramony had become the National Executive (and 21 years to the day before publication of the investigators' report on United Way of America, Aramony, and the spinoffs). The building was designed by a United Way of Dade County volunteer and Miami architect, the late Edward G. Grafton. It was constructed according to what was then called the "fast track" construction method, which is less expensive and much faster than more conventional methods. It was completed in less than nine months *"to bring the presence of the voluntary sector to the doorsteps of our nation's capitol. . . . A shining example of our commitment to the cause of voluntarism."*[18]

Although there was some grousing about its apparent opulence by conventional standards for voluntary organization facilities, these feelings soon dissipated. The idea of a symbol literally had become a concrete reality. City planners in Alexandria objected to the design, preferring it to be closer to the Old Town Alexandria federal style. However, the location was outside of the area where historic housing codes applied. The Alexandria branch of the local United Way, which covered the capital area, was embarrassed by it and sought to distance itself from the facility by clarifying that none of its cost was borne by local contributors. To avoid the designation as an office or building, it was euphemistically called the National Service and Training Center. Eventually, it was simply known as the "United Way Building." Some would call it the "Taj Mahal."

Aramony moved quickly to implement the 13-point program. Among the important achievements of this period (1970 to 1971) were:

1. The establishment of the *United Way Systems Institute,* whose purpose was to assist United Way members in developing sound management, financial, and data processing systems.

2. The development of *guidelines for assisting United Ways in making the best use of the 1970 census data.* The Department of Commerce cited its *Guidebook on Census for United Way* as the best private effort on census data use.

3. Accountability products called *the house of accountability* included guidelines for allocations systems, the publication of *UWASIS (United Way Service Identification System [1972]).* This system, developed by United Way scholar Russy Sumariwalla, succeeded in not only defining, but classifying virtually *all* human services under six major social goals. *UWASIS II,* revised in 1976, improved on the first *UWASIS.*

Aramony believed that a major problem in the human service area was the lack of precise and mutually exclusive definitions of program services. With agreed-upon definitions, it would be possible to measure and compare results. He felt that it was essential to demonstrate to the public that its contributions were producing measurable outcomes. *UWASIS* and its related accountability tools and its various revisions over the years not only defined human service programs, but provided suggested measurements for other programs as well. It has been used by thousands of government and voluntary organizations throughout the world.

The creation of *MACSI (Management and Community Studies Institute)*, run by the late Harold Edelston to assist communities (for a fee) in evaluating their management and programs, was the chief method that the national association used to serve local United Ways by installing its management tools in local communities.

4. The publication of *National Standards for Information and Referral Services* and the development of closer relations with volunteer bureaus was my particular responsibility. Aramony considered information and referral, a service which received requests from anyone needing help, usually by phone, and referring them to the most appropriate public or private agency, as very important to United Ways. It was, he reasoned, one of the few opportunities that the United Way itself had available to provide services directly to people. People are more inclined to give money when they can receive direct assistance. Through information and referral, the United Way, therefore, could help demonstrate that even the United Way itself can be relevant in helping people. He wanted to reach out to volunteer bureaus because he believed they exemplified the public expectations of volunteerism, that is, people helping people in direct and personal ways.[19]

An update on "Rebirth and Renewal" published a little over a year later outlined these additional accomplishments:

1. *Government Relations*—the establishment of high-level contacts with public officials to develop better voluntary sector relations, governmental relations, and public/private partnerships.

2. *Conferencing*—a new conferencing format was created by folding planning, budgeting, and fund raising into one annual Volunteer Leaders Conference.

3. *Metro structure*—a metro (city) structure was created to focus on urban problems. This structure ranked cities by fund-raising results. Emphasis was given to the larger communities which provided most of the dues support to United Way of America.[20]

THE TOP 17, THE BIG 10, AND OTHER CLIQUES

The leaders of the largest voluntary organizations in the country would begin to meet at least twice a year over the next two decades with Aramony personally. It became known as the *Top 17*. Also, over the years, several informal, affinity groups had developed among United Way professionals. They appear to have met various information sharing and social needs of the participants. The most influential of these "clubs" was the *Big 10*—a group of chief professional officers of the largest cities which had first begun meeting after World War II. Since 1961, the group along with its members' top staff had begun to convene for five days in New York City following the annual campaign. This group influenced the establishment of the National Professional Advisory Council (NPAC) as a way to put a check on Aramony by establishing formal procedures for advising him on his latest program initiatives. Over time, it grew and became very influential in advising on policy areas. "Ten Key Cities" first met in Orlando in 1962. Its members kept each other up to date on the latest fund-raising, planning, and marketing issues. "Select Cities" was a different clique. At one time, some members of this circle wanted to start a union of United Way professionals, but none of these groups had much influence on national policy, with the exception of NPAC, which had impact only in later years.

UNITED WAY AND THE SOCIAL PLANNING COUNCILS

Efforts were also made to clarify the relationships between United Way and its closely related social planning councils. Historically, these councils had grown up in communities as separate bodies charged with conducting studies to determine the most important needs requiring funding. Aramony had a history of defunding planning councils in the communities in which he had worked in order to bring the planning function directly under the United Way central fund-raising apparatus. He believed that planning was as much a political and public relations process as it was a rational one. Funding of services was a compromise between the "heart and the mind," he would say. He wanted the fund-raising portion of the United Way, not the planning portion, to determine the nature of that relationship.

Aramony liked to relate a story about a local director of a planning council who he asked to come to his office with all the studies his group had conducted over the past several years. The hapless soul appeared with an enormous stack of documents, which he proudly laid out on a large table.

"How many of these studies have resulted in funded programs?" Aramony asked.

"I don't believe any of them, sir."

"Then your organization is a waste of time and money!" he yelled as he reached over and swept all of the reports on the floor. The director resigned shortly thereafter, and the planning functions were brought under the direct control of the United Way.

THE NATIONAL ACADEMY FOR VOLUNTARISM: WELDING THE HEART AND MIND

The creation of the National Academy for Voluntarism under the capable leadership of Donald L. Plambeck was another way Aramony sought to weld the heart with the mind. Not only would the United Way be a chief funder of charities, but it would set the standards for the management of voluntary organizations, a factor long acknowledged by much of the public as a weakness of the sector. Plambeck, an inspiring teacher, developed the instructional program and initially taught many of the courses, particularly those in his forte (management).

Over the years this group has trained thousands of volunteers and professionals from across the country with hundreds of courses. A unique system of credits, an original suggestion by John "Jack" W. Hanley, past chairman of the Monsanto Company and past chairman of the board of United Way of America, allowed payment for courses to be charged against dues payments (providing the community had paid its "fair share"). These "credits" provided a major incentive for United Way members to send their staff to the courses since they had paid for them anyway as part of their dues contributions.

When United Way of America, some months after Aramony departed, attempted to make participation in these courses an extra cost beyond the regular payment of dues, Bobbi van der Voort, one of the United Way's most respected chief professional officers, as well as an accomplished teacher, strenuously objected. She believed that training was so important that it should be a basic service.

REGIONAL OFFICES WERE ESTABLISHED: REACHING THE HINTERLANDS

In addition, four regional offices were established (San Francisco, Atlanta, Chicago, and New York) by United Way of America in order to bring the national association closer to its constituency. Aramony was specifically advised by the past president, Lyman Ford, that such a move would eventually prove to be nonproductive and too costly. However, initially Aramony saw it not only as an opportunity to move his programs into the hinterlands, but as an outlet for professional staff who, for one reason or another, were not working out at headquarters yet weren't ready for retirement. Eventually, many excellent people actually served in these offices and provided valuable feedback to the national association on what was really happening "out there."

THE ESTABLISHMENT OF THE TOCQUEVILLE SOCIETY

Among the other initiatives completed in the next few years was the Alexis de Tocqueville Society Award, which honored outstanding volunteers. John W. Gardner, Vernon E. Jordan, Jr., and the Haas family of the Levi Strauss Company were among those honored by the program. Eventually adopted by local United Ways, it became a primary vehicle to raise money from individuals of "high net worth." With outstanding United Way of America staff leadership from Ruth Maldonado and volunteer leadership from board member Thomas F. Frist, Jr., chairman of the Hospital Corporation of America, the program grew from $3.6 million in 1984, shortly after it began, to $76 million by 1991. Twenty-four people had give a million dollars each to local United Ways by the end of 1992.

COMMUNICATIONS PROGRAMS

One of the major advances at this time was the development of a full-fledged communications program under the leadership of Mario Pellegrini, who had come with Aramony from Miami. He had been a producer of audio-visual materials for the American Cancer Society. Under his direction, sales of public relations materials increased by a third in just two years.[21] This program eventually became a major source of funds for the national association and ultimately was "spun off" as

Sales Service/America. By 1974, the program had received numerous trade awards. Loretta Lynn, Dean Jones, David Jansen, Cliff Robertson, and other stars were recruited to participate in these promotions for United Way.

By far the most significant event was to capture an agreement with the National Football League, headed by Commissioner Pete Rozelle, to air United Way–produced spots during every major league football game during the season. The NFL had previously provided free advertising for what was to become VOLUNTEER: The National Center for Citizen Involvement, which promoted the recruitment of direct service volunteers. Pondering what to do, Pellegrini called me into his office.

"Glaser," he said, "help me with this. You work with [direct service] volunteers. I need you to give me a reason why the NFL should give us public service time."

"Mario," I replied, "We represent thousands of agencies, including volunteer recruitment. That's the case to make. It's an ideal situation for the NFL and the United Way. More bang for the buck."

"Write something up for me. I'm going to New York tomorrow to talk to them."

It worked due more to Pellegrini's incredible salesmanship ability than anything else. Today, these public service announcements are worth $45 million in free advertising and are watched by an estimated 80 million people weekly. They are aired in every community that televises NFL games, reaching millions of United Way contributors on a weekly basis during the fall football season. It was a particularly powerful tool because it focused on United Way's primary constituencies.

THE STANDARDS OF EXCELLENCE AND THE PDP: TWO OF ARAMONY'S EARLY PET PROGRAMS

In my opinion, the *Standards of Excellence*, a publication completed by the end of 1971, was one of the most significant contributions during these years. Aramony had always believed in defining what he called the "ought" of the United Way, that is, the standards against which an effective United Way should be measured. The *Standards of Excellence* became that model. It was developed after extensive review by volunteers and professionals from across the country. It later added a code of ethics.

The development of the *Personnel Development Program* (PDP), ap-

proved by the Board of Governors in November 1973, was an effort
to recruit young interns to the United Way. One of the first interns
was Ed Allard, a young career military officer, whose fate was sealed
when he sat next to Aramony on an airplane and was convinced by
the time the plane landed to leave his chosen career and join the
United Way. Allard would say later that he made the decision because
someday, when his daughter would ask him what he did for a living,
he wanted to be able to tell her that he worked to save lives rather
than destroy them. In addition, the PDP program sought to enhance
training for professionals and conduct on-site organizational development to assist United Ways in functioning better as a team. A section of the program that provided funds for early retirement was rejected by the field, even though Aramony argued that it was
important to open up "the top" to make room at the bottom (I'm sure
the irony of this part of the program is not lost on the reader!). The
PDP program was very important because Aramony firmly believed
the United Way could survive only if there were top professionals
who would be able to recruit the best volunteers from major businesses to serve on their boards and help raise money. "Top volunteers," he would say, "would only be attracted by top professionals."
The program received start-up money from the Lilly Endowment and
other funding from the W.K. Kellogg Foundation.

THE LARGE UNITED WAY COMMUNITIES EXPAND

By the mid-seventies, the focus of the national organization and most
charities was on *tax reform*, and the clarification of allowable *lobbying
activities. Area-wide arrangements* were also being encouraged in order
to develop more efficient United Way organizations in the large metropolitan areas. A major problem for the United Way was moving
money from the wealthy suburbs of large communities into the inner
cities where the needs were greatest. These large regional United Ways
would centralize the fund-raising and coordinate media efforts, while
at the same time distributing funds within the region based on area
needs. These regional United Ways were often very complicated. The
largest and most comprehensive was the United Way of Tri-State,
launched in 1977. It covers New York City as well as portions of Connecticut, New York State, and New Jersey. For many years it was led
by Calvin E. Green, a career United Way professional who succeeded
in raising a lifetime sum of $2 billion, probably a world record by a

fund-raising manager. United Ways were also encouraged to help develop United Ways if none existed in nearby communities.

THE FOUNDING OF UNITED WAY INTERNATIONAL

Nineteen-seventy-four saw the beginning of United Way International. Since 1928, when the first United Way outside of Canada and the United States was formed by a Rotarian from Cincinnati in Cape Town, South Africa, the concept of United Way giving had proliferated around the world. There had never been a formal mechanism at United Way of America to respond to the continual requests for training and consultation from these overseas organizations. United Way International, the oldest of the spinoffs, was formed for the purpose of assisting current and emerging United Ways in an organized manner. Its goals were to conduct feasibility studies for communities in other countries that wished to begin United Way organizations, provide special training and technical assistance for their volunteers and professionals, and encourage giving by U.S. companies operating overseas and foreign corporations operating in the United States. Aramony probably correctly recognized that domestic priorities were the most important ones in the early days and that international concerns should only be addressed as an important, but not a principal activity of the national organization. From the beginning, I held this portfolio. It did not become a full-time job until over a dozen years later. An international organization without the name "America" was preferred in order to ensure credibility and sensitivity to the cultural and special needs of the United Way volunteers and professionals from other nations.

THE FORMATION OF THE NATIONAL CORPORATE DEVELOPMENT PROGRAM AND THE LONG-RANGE PLANNING COMMITTEE

In 1975, United Way campaigns across the country achieved a landmark billion-dollar mark for the first time in history. This was based on anticipated annual increases which were occurring with some predictability. That same year, *the National Corporate Development Program* was created. It was originally chaired by John D. deButts, then chairman of AT&T. Its goals were to develop a strategy, based on new fair share corporate giving guidelines, to reach national corporate leaders to support local United Ways. These guidelines were developed by AT&T and tested out on other companies. Although modified over time, they provided benchmarks by which adequate participation in United Way would be measured.

The Long-Range Planning Committee, formed in 1975, was first chaired by John W. "Jack" Hanley, chairman of the Monsanto Company. Its purpose was to determine the issues facing the United Way movement, and to decide how best to deal with them in the future. Eventually, its highly professional reports under the direction of the capable and erudite George Wilkinson provided important information to United Ways in predicting trends for the future. The entire country was contacted to determine what help they needed. The results were summarized into five main areas of concern:

1. The decline in real terms of corporate support.
2. The need for more national media support for local campaigns.
3. Public policy decisions by government affecting United Way services without their involvement.
4. The effective use of volunteers.
5. The need for expanded area-wide arrangements.[22]

THE PROGRAM FOR THE FUTURE WAS ESTABLISHED TO ANSWER THE CALL

These efforts resulted in the creation of the *Program for the Future*, approved at the December 1976 meeting of the Board of Governors. This program became a national priority, and most other national programs were subsumed under it. The overriding purpose of the program was to put forward the case for the voluntary sector and its place as an essential counterpoint to government. This positioning was considered critical in order to ensure the ongoing voluntary participation of people in American life and therefore help promote citizen participation and pluralism. The United Way would become the standard-bearer for a more defined and stronger voluntary sector. To achieve this role, United Way itself would have to become stronger as well. The program's specific elements included:

1. Testing the ability of the National Corporate Development Program's guidelines to triple fund-raising results.
2. Developing a stronger media relations program.

3. Establishing a strong federal legislative program to impact decision making at the highest levels of government.
4. Locating new sources of funding, such as deferred gifts, endowments, and donations from foreign countries increasing their investments in the United States.
5. Provide services to United Ways in small communities.[23]

In the first year of the program, major progress had been made. Over a thousand staff and 300 volunteers had attended regional meetings on the need, purpose, and process of long-range planning. It was the year that United Ways achieved a 9.1 percent increase in fundraising results, the highest percentage increase in 20 years. The National Corporate Development Program had recruited 106 corporations representing 3.2 million people.[24]

ARAMONY WINS OVER THE AMERICAN CANCER SOCIETY

Aramony's operating style, often very effective, is best exemplified by his success in bringing the American Cancer Society into the United Way family. The American Cancer Society had pulled out of the Community Chest movement in the 1950s due to irreconcilable differences, even though their local chapters had begun to lose money. Unlike United Way of America, which exercises no control over its independent and separately incorporated members, the American Cancer Society (as well as the American Red Cross and the American Heart Association, to name a few) is a unified system in which units or affiliates must comply with policy directions from their national office. In his book, *The United Way—The Next Hundred Years*, Aramony related that he began to meet with Lane Adams in the mid 1970s, even before he had become executive vice president of the American Cancer Society. Adams had arranged for Aramony to meet with a key American Cancer Society Committee involved with future relations with United Way.[25]

According to a staff member who was involved in this process of *rapprochement* with the American Cancer Society from the very beginning, success was due to Aramony's special ability to engage top leaders in developing a personal, trusting relationship with him in social situations before serious negotiations would begin. Thus, several meetings were held, followed by golf games and informal discussions.

At one critical meeting, Bob Beggan, a senior vice president of United Way of America, went quietly to the telephone in Lane Adams's office. He had left Aramony arguing with Adams and his deputy, Dick

McGrail. They had been discussing the incorporation of a fund-raising coalition of health agencies opposed to the United Way in an important Midwestern state.

Beggan was talking on the telephone to the chief professional officer of a United Way located in a major city in that state. "You're going to have a big problem soon," said Beggan. "We'll meet them with guns blazing," the executive said to Beggan. Beggan responded, "There's a better way. Can you get here tomorrow?"

The local United Way executive flew to New York the next day and immediately began to negotiate for a possible joint effort in his community with Adams, McGrail, and the executive vice president of the state division of the American Cancer Society. If the joint effort worked, it would be among the first United Way–Cancer Society contracts in the nation. It would prevent a competitive situation from developing, and both organizations could team up to save lives and reduce suffering.

As negotiations continued, the United Way executive slowly began giving away the store! In a nonverbal but clear way, McGrail looked over at Beggan and indicated, "We've got you, but we're not going to take advantage."

"Bob, it's okay. We'll call it a night and continue tomorrow when we're all more refreshed," McGrail announced. This timely comment kept Beggan from having to dispute his own colleague who had not had the opportunity to know McGrail in a personal and trusting way.

When negotiations began again the next day, one of the most successful contracts had been established. It eventually set the pattern for those that followed. Aramony's ability to gain trust and faith had been achieved as a result of many previous, mostly informal meetings between the negotiators. No one had taken advantage. The result is that today, over a decade later, there are currently about 145 local arrangements with local units of the American Cancer Society, and it all began among friends. Similar arrangements were worked out with about 140 local affiliates of the American Heart Association. Aramony's style at its best.

NEW PROGRAMS PROLIFERATE

Over the next couple of years, United Way of America expanded many other existing programs and initiated many new ones. The year 1977 also saw the development of a special office to serve smaller communities. United Way staff from many different cities and I produced a self-study guide for information and referral. A joint effort with the AFL-CIO produced a booklet to help assist communities experiencing sudden economic disruption caused by plant closings.

A program with the Department of the Navy was launched to develop joint family service centers as well. This program was based in Norfolk and was successful due to the pioneering work of Gene Berres, chief professional officer, and his staff at the United Way of Norfolk and Hampton Roads.

By 1980, an Hispanic Development Program had been established to recruit more Hispanic volunteers and professionals to the United Way. The growing economic purchasing power of the Hispanic community became increasingly recognized by local United Ways. Hispanic involvement in local United Ways had become imperative.

Two major reports were issued by the long-range planning process, one dealing with the expected impact of the 1980s on the United Way, and the other dealing with the world of work. Based on an effective management assistance program begun by the late Joseph Weber, chief executive of the Greater New York Fund, the Community Outreach Division which I led began to promote the concept nationwide. With this program, United Ways recruit mid-level corporate executives to provide *pro bono* services to United Way and its affiliated agencies and conduct management training programs.[26]

In 1982, a new National Service and Training Center opened its doors, just over a decade after the first building had been constructed. This entire process was representative of Aramony's legendary ability to wheel and deal to get the best of all possible results. The new building was located on the lot owned by Texaco just south of the previous building. Through the efforts of Jack Hanley and others, the property was conveyed to United Way of America through a "bargain sale." (A bargain sale takes place when the property is sold to a charity for less than its value; the difference becomes a charitable deduction.) By the time the old facility had been sold and an additional $6 million raised by a committee headed by John Opel, former chairman and chief executive officer of IBM, the mortgage on the old building had been retired, without the new building carrying any mortgage whatsoever. Thus, Aramony was able to build an office twice the size and carrying no debt!

The Emergency Food and Shelter National Board Program, etc.

"I don't want one cent from this program to go to the United Way. All of it is to go to those who need help," said Aramony in 1982 in announcing a program which continues to have a tremendous impact on the country a decade later. He was referring to the Emergency Food and Shelter National Board Program, which was given an initial grant of $50 million by the government to distribute to the increasing number of hungry and homeless as a result of a recession that had peaked in 1982. Congress deemed that the United Way could distribute the money far more effectively than the states (although in the first year, the states were given $50 million as well).

Investment of the funds resulted in an additional $250,000. Aramony insisted that United Way of America not take any administrative cost for the program and that it was to act only as the fiscal agent for the participating agencies. Those agencies are the Catholic Charities, the Salvation Army, the American Red Cross, the National Council of Churches, and the Council of Jewish Federations. The Board was to be chaired by a representative from the Federal Emergency Assistance Program. The current staff director is the extremely capable former minister, Wiley B. Cooper. Its staff is employed by United Way of America, which is under government contract to execute the program (therefore it is not a spinoff). Since its inception 10 years ago, the program has received over $1 billion from the federal government and provided an astonishing 873 million meals to the hungry and 167 million nights lodging for the homeless. It remains today as a stunning example of public/private partnership.

In 1985, *Project Hometown America* was led by Elizabeth Kelly, one of United Way of America's most able senior vice presidents. A promotional marketing effort by the former legendary American Express marketing guru, Jerry Walsh, provided for a portion of each credit card charge to be used for grants to local communities for innovative projects. Over $3 million were ultimately distributed.

To enhance the technology of information sharing, Mutual of America and United Way of America joined together in 1985 to develop a nationwide communications system known as the *Human Care Network*. Its purpose was to make human service databases available to local United Ways as well as provide immediate electronic mail communication with United Ways across the country. Mutual of America's interest was in making available pension and other information to the United Way movement, one of its largest constituencies.

THE SECOND CENTURY: A PROGRAM FOR THE CENTENNIAL

In 1986, the national organization began to formulate its plans for the centennial to celebrate the founding of the "first" United Way in Denver, Colorado in 1887. For many years, Aramony had considered not doing anything. He thought that it would be a distraction. However, he became convinced that the event offered an opportunity to look to the future, "while giving a nod to the past." With James D. Robinson III, chairman of the American Express Company and new chairman of the Board of Governors assisting, all things were possible.

The *Second Century Program* was launched in order to "make a quantum leap" by doubling the number of volunteers and the amount of money raised in five years (1987 through 1991).

It had two major goals:

1. To make a dramatic leap forward in service by building a United Way system that is even more open and caring five years from now than it is today; and
2. To double United Way capacity in volunteers and financial resources over the five-year period.

It was supported by five key strategies:

1. *Community Problem Solving*—increased assessment of community needs and increased leadership by United Ways in bringing public and private leaders together to solve community problems;
2. *Inclusiveness*—involvement of people of all races, ages, and sexes in United Way activities, along with a re-emphasis on reaching out to United Way affiliated agencies;
3. *Single Community-wide Campaign*—an extra effort to center the local United Way campaign as the principal *and only* campaign in the community;
4. *Fund Distribution*—an emphasis on setting aside some funds for new ventures, and providing a greater opportunity for donor option; and
5. *Year-round Communications*—a concentration on informing people about the United Way year around, particularly in the workplace.

The five core strategies depended upon six supportive programs in order to achieve success. These six programs included:

1. Professional development;
2. Volunteer development;
3. Management assistance programs;
4. Information and referral, government relations, agency relations and outreach;
5. Strategic planning and management; and
6. Research and information processing.

A NATIONWIDE GALA USHERS IN A NEW ERA OF CARING

The Second Century Initiative became the programmatic focal point of 1987 and beyond. The movement hoped to accelerate efforts to solve major social problems such as illiteracy, hunger and homelessness, AIDS, teenage pregnancy, children in crisis, alcoholism and drug abuse, aging, and child care.

The commemorative activities were showy, extensive, and innovative. They were organized by Sheila Plank, a very creative vice president. For the first time, for example, a young leaders conference was held in conjunction with the Volunteer Leaders Conference. It drew 600 young people from all over the country. Nancy Reagan addressed the gathering.

Other "firsts" marked the celebration. A commemorative stamp was issued in honor of the centennial. Young musicians from 100 communities marched in the Tournament of Roses Parade in Pasadena to salute the "spirit of voluntarism." Sixty volunteers were given the Alexis de Tocqueville Society Award at a stunning ceremony in two of the main theaters at the Kennedy Center in Washington, D.C.

In the program area, community assessment activities were accelerated. For example, IBM sponsored the first ever United Way Marketing Conference, the Executive Committee approved of the welfare reform measures proposed by then governor of Arkansas Bill Clinton and New York governor Mario Cuomo, and workplace programs emphasizing year-round information and referral and communications services for employees accelerated dramatically.

Six million dollars in corporate and foundation money was donated to help finance the celebrations and launch a number of selected programs which included assistance to community development foundations in five cities to help them manage housing for low- and middle-income people; recruiting and training minority volunteers and professionals for the United Way system; and stimulating fund-raising and other resource development activities. A new theme was adopted: *"United Way—It brings out the best in all of us."*

MOBILIZING A CARING AMERICA: PRINCIPLES FOR THE 1990S

By 1990, United Way had begun to decrease its emphasis on the Second Century Initiative due in part to its obvious failure to double its nationwide fund-raising objectives in five years. However, many United Way staff did not consider the Second Century Initiative a failure because the goals it set, although unrealistic during a weak economy, put pressure on local communities to increase their efforts.

"Mobilizing A Caring America" was first presented by Aramony to the National Professional Advisory Council in 1989:

1. "United Ways must help donors understand the urgent human service needs and social problems of our country, while, at the same time, confront and deal with the issue of donor choice."
2. "Just as United Way would treat donors as customers, United Way must also consider people in need as their ultimate customers."

Seven principles were eventually articulated to focus on United Way's role for the future. I've listed them in some detail because in many ways, they represent a culmination of Aramony's thinking over a 20-year period and generally indicate what was happening in United Way organizations:

Principle One: Providing Leadership on Urgent Needs—United Way must speak forthrightly on the nation's and local communities' most serious social needs and on the value of people helping people.

Principle Two: Supporting Self-Sufficiency—United Way must lead and support special efforts which have promise of measurable success to help those most at risk of becoming disconnected from society to achieve and maintain self-sufficiency, while supporting services to all people who need help.

Principle Three: Building Coalitions—United Way must forge inclusive coalitions of voluntary organizations with the private and public sectors to concentrate attention and resources on urgent needs and to solve community problems.

Principle Four: Exploring New Forms of Access—United Way must expand the concept of inclusiveness by exploring new ways for health/human development organizations to participate in the community campaign.

Principle Five: Empowering People with Knowledge—United Way must provide people with information to act effectively and to become personally involved in meeting the needs of their community.

Principle Six: Providing Choice—United Way must further citizen involvement and support in meeting community needs by developing the donors' understanding of those needs, by ensuring the right of donors to direct their gifts, and by carrying out donor's wishes.[27]

After the publication, a seventh principle was added:

Principle Seven: Investing in Results—We must respond to changing community needs by distributing funds flexibly. We must invest in agencies for the achievement of agreed-upon results and emphasize monitoring requirements that focus on those results.

All of the mentioned programs described in this chapter, although primarily developed nationally, have always been "processed" by the field. That is, drafts of programs are sent out for comment, discussions occur at relevant committee meetings, and finally, Board action and approval finalizes the process.

Principle Six of the mobilizing program portends the enormous impact of the one issue which has always been the most difficult one for United Ways to resolve—"donor choice." This issue strikes at the basic core of United Ways' mandate to unify community fund raising and to distribute funds based on need. Because of its importance, this issue will be discussed in greater detail in Chapter 8.

In the late 1980s, United Way of America adopted a Canadian program, CAN-DO, which had been developed by Bob Meyers, the former president of the United Way/Centraide Canada. It consists of an intensive on-site campaign analysis for each participating community. These efforts have resulted in these communities achieving much better fund-raising results.

United Way of America also undertook to promote the "Success by Six" program pioneered in Minneapolis. It is directed at identifying and responding to the needs of at-risk pregnant women and their children from conception through preschool.[28]

In early 1992, United Way of America published a booklet, *The Quality Challenge: A Primer for United Ways*. Working with IBM's market-driven quality initiative program, it outlines steps United Ways need to take to be customer sensitive, including adopting the use of a number of assessment forms.[29] In his departing remarks, interim United Way of America president Kenneth W. Dam described the issue of quality as part of a key process for providing a framework in which United Way could become more responsive to its key constituencies and a significant way to measure and evaluate the impact of its services.

CONCLUSION

Bill Aramony's contributions as summarized above were prodigious by any standard. It is inconceivable that any more could have been tried or accomplished. Moreover, not all the programs are listed or described. There were additional national initiatives to combat illiteracy and ensure "affordable housing." In recent years, a common theme echoed by United Ways was that United Way of America was imposing the "program for the week," or "program for the month." Toward the last days of Aramony's tenure, he had focused his energies and those of the staff on a long-term, 20-year program to "save" America's children. By that time, many United Ways had begun to be numb to *any* new initiatives from the national office. Most were concerned about how to raise money in an increasingly difficult economy.

REFERENCES

1. Rosemary Higgins Cass and Gordon Manser,"Roots of Voluntarism," *America's Voluntary Sector* (New York: The Foundation Center, 1983), p. 11.
2. *Giving U.S.A.: The Annual Report for Philanthropy for the Year 1991* (New York: AAFRC Trust for Philanthropy, 1993), p. 10.
3. *The Importance of Charity and the Voluntary Initiative* (Washington, D.C.: Independent sector, 1992), p. 1.

4. Waldemar A. Neilsen, *The Endangered Species* (New York: Columbia University Press, 1979), p. 251.
5. *Giving U.S.A.*, p. 24.
6. James Joseph, *The Charitable Impulse* (New York: The Foundation Center, 1989), p. 3.
7. Richard W. Lyman, "In Defense of the Private Sector," a speech before the general session of the 1974 Annual Conference of the National Association of Independent Schools in San Francisco, March 21, 1974.
8. *A Brief Interpretive History of America's Voluntary Sector* (United Way of America: Alexandria, 1978), p. 12.
9. Phyllis J. Day, *A New History of Social Welfare* (Englewood Cliffs, NJ: Prentice Hall: 1989), pp. 204–205.
10. Thomas J. Sullivan and Kendrick S. Thompson, *Introduction to Social Problems [2nd edition]* (New York: Macmillan, 1991), pp. 39–40.
11. C. Wright Mills, *The Power Elite* (New York: Oxford Press, 1956), pp. 3–4.
12. *The Business Roundtable on Corporate Philanthropy* from a statement issued March 26, 1981.
13. Day, p. 205.
14. *Rebirth and Renewal: Proceedings of the Annual Meeting of the Trustees in Dallas, Texas on December 3, 1970* (Alexandria: United Way of America, 1971), p. 13. Reprinted by permission, United Way of America. United Way of America does not endorse the opinions or conclusions expressed herein.
15. *People & Events—A History of the United Way* (Alexandria: United Way of America, 1977), p. 2.
16. *Rebirth and Renewal*, p. 3.
17. *Ibid*, pp. 17–23.
18. *The Spirit of Voluntarism . . . United Way of America: A Progress Report* (Alexandria: United Way of America, 1972), p. 2.
19. *People & Events*, pp. 4–5.
20. *The Spirit of Voluntarism*, pp. 16–17.
21. *Ibid*, p. 16.
22. *People & Events*, pp. 4–5.
23. *Ibid*, p. 7.
24. *United Way Annual Report—1977*, p. 4.
25. William Aramony, *The United Way—the Next Hundred Years* (New York: Donald I. Fine, 1987), pp. 42–43.
26. Selected excerpts from United Way of America annual reports, 1978 and 1980.
27. *Mobilizing a Caring America: Principles for the 1990s* (Alexandria: United Way of America, 1990). Reprinted by permission, United Way of America. United Way of America does not endorse the opinions or conclusions expressed herein.
28. *Mobilizing America*, United Way of America Annual Report, 1990, p. 9.
29. See *The Quality Challenge: A Primer for United Ways* (Alexandria: United Way of America, 1992).

CHAPTER 3

Aramony's Leadership Style: A Problem of *Hubris*

> The United Way's goal is no less than to make modern man whole again—by giving him an opportunity to relate to others by giving him a chance to give, serve, and receive; by paying homage to the unity of the individual man and the unity of the communities—in every program we undertake, and in every organizational activity.
>
> William Aramony, 1972[1]

I memorized this particular phrase by Bill Aramony because I found it to be so inspiring. It reminded me of some of the great speeches by the Kennedys or Martin Luther King, Jr. Oratory skill was one of his personal virtues. In order to understand the impact of the activities of the spring of 1992, you must come to know the personality of the United Way's leader for over 20 years. In this chapter, we will examine Bill Aramony's leadership style and techniques. It was both his extraordinary abilities, which gave rise to the modern United Way, as well as his fatal flaws that brought about his downfall and the near collapse of the movement he led for so long.

WHO IS BILL ARAMONY?

Bill Aramony, a first-generation son of Lebanese parents and the youngest of five children, had risen to the top of his field. He told me that he would have become a lawyer by choice, but his family could not afford the cost. Following graduation from Clark University in Worcester, Massachusetts, he entered the Boston College School of Social Work and graduated with a master's degree in 1951.

Following a stint as an Army social worker in Texas (where he provided counseling services to homosexuals, according to his own account), he went into the family clothing and manufacturing business. He said that he wanted to do more with his life than spend his days determining how many patterns of a specific design could be cut from whole cloth. Prophetically, this became a paradigm for a series of events which ended his career.

That Bill Aramony was a leader no one questioned. But like the heroes of Greek tragedies, he had flaws which eventually proved disastrous to himself, personally, and to many of his associates. The greatest of these faults was what the ancient Greeks referred to as *hubris*, or what we, in more modern times, call arrogance or pride. As with Oedipus, the tragic Greek character who blinded himself when he realized that the fates had done him in, Bill Aramony had in fact lost sight of how his actions could be perceived by important United Way constituencies. One writer put it well when he wrote in an editorial in the *Chicago Tribune* on March 9, 1992, that "hubris blinded him" when Aramony apologized only for his lack of sensitivity to perceptions of what he had done rather than the reality of his actions.

This phenomenon is no better put than by Philip B. Crosby, author and management consultant, in an article entitled "Managerial Arrogance" which appeared in *Across The Board* in October, 1992:

> I have been trying, so far without success, to think of a business failure that was *not* caused by the specific arrogance of an individual or the cultural arrogance of a group. . . . They overexpand, they try to force their customers to obey, they consider themselves to be above the system. When people will not listen to others, when they are in love with their own knowledge, when they abuse power, they are arrogant. Such people make life miserable for those beneath them. They ruin companies; they take first place teams and drag them into last.[2]

There were numerous causes for the United Way crisis, but Aramony's leadership style was clearly a major contributing factor to what went wrong and why. He moved proudly through two decades of American history, drawing thousands to his vision of serving people. Most who met him were soon converts, some dismissed him as mostly "hype," but no one doubted his zeal in promoting the cause of the United Way.

THE PAST AS PROLOGUE

Before he came to the national office, Aramony had built a substantial reputation in the United Way movement as a dynamic and creative thinker, as well as an outstanding poker player. In many ways, the risks of the game mirrored his life. One long-time Aramony observer remarked that he had "campaigned" for the national job all of his life. Following each fund-raising season, he could be seen "making the rounds," arranging poker games, visiting his colleagues, and sharing his ideas. In the 1960s, when he received a contract from the U.S. Office of Economic Opportunity, he frequently hired people for short-term assignments. In this way he was able to build up personal "IOUs." These relationships served him well in the future. He was always a strong supporter of the national association and served on many of its committees. He envisioned the United Way as the premier voluntary organization in the community—as important as government and big business and more important than any other charity. Above all else, he believed that raising money was not the problem. The problem was education. Once people knew and understood the needs in their communities, they would give and give generously. Fund raising was only the means. The end was service.

He firmly thought that the most important role the United Way could play to contribute to the well-being of society was to use its centrist position in communities as a catalyst to bring people together to help solve local problems. He called this *the community table*. This concept of getting community representatives from all different sectors working together to help solve social problems was based on Aramony's own successful experiences. It also reflected his innate ability to succeed in close political infighting and in totally overpowering small group meetings with his visionary rhetoric. He was clearly the Rocky Marciano of social work.

For example, when the South Bend, Indiana Studebaker plant shut down in 1963, he joined other community and business leaders to move quickly to provide counseling and job referral programs to the older workers who were being let go. He worked closely with John Brademus, then congressman from South Bend, to secure emergency federal funding. It was called Project ABLE. As it turned out, the program was "able" to place over 3,500 people in new jobs over a three-year period.[3]

As the chief professional officer of the Columbia, South Carolina United Way, he helped bring together the Richmond and Lexington

County school districts, long divided along class lines, into a common program to provide a school lunch program.[4] In Dade County (Miami), Florida, he worked with top political figures and business leaders to build an effective coalition of prominent citizens who undertook studies in everything from public transportation to garbage collection.[5] It was said that there was no decision in the community (major or minor) which was not made without his participation.

HIS PERSISTENCE WAS HIS TRADEMARK

Aramony's operating style was honed in the local communities in which he served. It was in Miami, though, where he hit his stride. The community fit his personality like a wet suit on a diver. When he left there, he received the Chamber of Commerce's "Man of Action" Award. Through his successes there, he had became even more convinced that a small, elite group of powerful and influential political and economic leaders, essentially operating in secret, should and could make important decisions for *their* community. I attended one of these elite meetings with him at an exclusive club in a local hotel. It was obvious that he reveled in and was particularly good at this close wheeling and dealing. He saw it as a way to cut through red tape and bureaucracy and to achieve required results quickly. In this particular meeting, local Jewish leaders were seeking his advice on some matters relating to Israel, a far cry from local issues. As a Lebanese by heritage, he was justly proud that he was trusted by the Jewish community wherever he had served.

Aramony told me that his local reputation was enhanced when he managed to recruit M.M. "Mike" Brisco, then president of the International Petroleum Co., Ltd., to head his first fund-raising campaign in Dade County. Other local leaders had told Aramony that Brisco was the most influential businessman in the community. At first he would not see Aramony or return any of his phone calls. Aramony decided to go directly to Brisco's office and simply sit and wait until he agreed to head the fund-raising drive. He spent several hours cooling his heels. Brisco's staff said he was too busy to meet with him. Aramony waited until Brisco left his office for the day. He followed him out to his car, explaining that he would not stop bothering him until he agreed to head the annual campaign. Brisco finally agreed, and that year Dade County turned in one of its best campaigns ever.

His persistence paid off in other areas as well. He told me that the chairman of Lums, then a fast-food chain based in Miami, would not contribute to the local drive. Aramony convinced Harry Hood Bassett, then chairman of the Board of the United Fund of Dade County and chairman of the First National Bank of Miami (then the community's largest bank), to make a personal call on him. The fast-food chief was so impressed that this banker believed in the United Way so strongly and had taken time out of his busy day to pay a personal visit to him that he agreed to participate.

The other kinds of pressure Aramony used were not so subtle. His campaign research team discovered that a company, which consistently refused to even answer phone calls from his campaign staff, had a strong connection to Eastern Airlines, which was based in Miami. The airlines had been a longtime United Way supporter. This company manufactured movable stairs for the airline industry and Eastern was one of its largest customers. With one phone call from Eastern, the company immediately bent over backwards to participate in the campaign.

The Tasmanian Devil and Florence Nightingale

To the casual observer, and even to some who were more involved, United Way of America appeared to be a smooth-running, highly efficient organization headed by a charismatic leader. Although Aramony was recognized as having some quirks, these were considered by most as adding to the character of the man, and by some as unimportant by-products of an essentially dynamic and effective personality. After all, don't great people have strange habits? Isn't that part of what makes them great?

James D. Robinson III, chairman of the American Express Company and former chairman of the board of United Way of America, called Aramony "a cross between the Tasmanian devil and Florence Nightingale." This statement is very true and provides an important insight into Aramony's complex personality.

Riding the Roller Coaster

Working at United Way of America, especially at the upper management level, could be compared to riding a giant roller coaster every day of the year. If you were asked to work on a special project, you could go on many different "rides" in the same day. You could experience enormous highs and equally intense lows. These extremes were often reflective of Aramony's moods. If you wanted to get the go-ahead on a program, you had to learn to read his mood for that day—something the long-timers were particularly good at. If he was in a bad mood, the decision would be the opposite of what you wanted because he would be angry with everyone who crossed his path. Since he often appeared to be irrational during these times, he would forget what decision he had made and become even angrier if he found out later you had carried it out.

One poignant example I remember well happened a number of years ago when John Yerger, a senior executive, had given Aramony a paper prepared by one of his staff. Aramony called Yerger into his office and with a barrage of expletives told him to "fire his ass" for writing such an "idiotic report." Yerger did an about-face, left Aramony's office, and immediately discharged the person who had prepared the report. Several days later, Aramony asked where the person was who had written the report. He was shocked when he was told the individual had been fired. Aramony had never meant for that to happen. His mood at the time had been taken literally. In a less dramatic way, it was often difficult to obtain a "rational" decision from him on any regular basis.

On the issue of staff "firings," Aramony often asked me and others to fire staff he didn't like. Unless the offense was very serious, I could usually hold the line. If I made a strong case for the person, he would not press the issue. However, should this person ever screw up at a later time, the pressure to discharge the individual would increase. In one case, he asked me to dismiss an overseas employee who was extraordinarily capable, but very blunt and honest. He was afraid that he could not control "her mouth." Also, she did not fit the image of the more feminine, obsequious types he preferred. She stayed, and Aramony eventually developed a high level of respect for her.

Actually, the popular perception of Aramony as a tough, unrelenting manager who fired people at will is simply not true. He could never personally fire anyone. I recall once when he had to let a secretary go. He could not face her the whole day and went to and from his office by a circuitous route. He personally agonized over *anyone* who was fired, even though the dismissal might have been justified. When I discussed this issue with him once, he seemed embarrassed that he didn't give the impression of being tough in this regard, yet he couldn't think of anyone he had personally fired. Considering the size of the staff, very few were let go, and always the hatchet was wielded by others. This attribute is one facet of his complex personality.

He was especially proud of the fact that in his long career, he had always met payroll. Staff never had to wait even one day for their wages. "People have families, and they depend upon that regular pay-check," he often said.

Organizational structure was also subject to Aramony's whims. You could also arrive at work on any one given day and find that your whole staff had been transferred to another division. In one case, one-third of senior vice president's Bobbi van der Voort's staff had virtually overnight been removed from her supervision and split up among several other executives.

In another case, a strong, effective work group was broken up simply because it was so successful and so loyal to its management staff. Aramony could not accept loyalty or enthusiasm for anyone but himself, even within the company. Often job descriptions would be redefined suddenly or projects terminated after months or weeks of work. Aramony relished these reorganizations because he wanted to keep people "off guard" so that they would not become too complacent. Nothing could be taken for granted.

The emotions one experienced on a regular basis could range from complete disgust and hatred to excitement and empowerment. He seemed to revel in these chaotic situations, which mirrored his own volatile personality.

Aramony's personal interaction with others was usually centered around what he had done and accomplished. Practically every conversation would end with, "Isn't that great, Glaser? Aren't I a f--king genius?!" On occasion, I would brag to him this same way to tease him. He would tell me that I shouldn't boast like that about my accomplishments.

Only when Aramony was out of town could the staff begin to do productive work. When he was in town, the frenetic activity immobilized many who worked closely with him. We had to work around his often bizarre and self-absorbed behavior. Virtually everything of substance I was able to accomplish over the years, particularly in the international arena, I did in spite of him, not because of him. That is why so many of us worked such long hours. We had to achieve something that gave us our own feelings of self-worth and accomplishment even if we had to work overtime.

Yet when you were alone with him in a relaxed setting, he could be very warm, generous, humorous, and great fun. I often enjoyed immensely the many hours I spent traveling with him.

It was his leadership style that caused the problems. Everyone ultimately paid a terrible price as a result. He had created a national organization that was often out of sync with the United Way system it was intended to serve. The impact was devastating on the volunteers and staff who served the movement and, at least in the short-term, on the thousands of beneficiaries served by United Way supported charities.

UNDERSTANDING THE ACADEMICS OF ARAMONY'S LEADERSHIP STYLE

Over the years, I've attempted to place Aramony's leadership style within an academic framework in order to more fully understand him. This framework will hopefully provide you, the reader, with a better understanding of what went wrong and why.

Enter the Human Service Entrepreneur

When Aramony arrived at United Way of America, he immediately began to develop a working style and staff structure which, over the years, gradually began to serve his own needs instead of those of the organization. He brought in entrepreneurial skills seen more in the corporate community than in the social welfare field.

These skills were critical in the early days of his tenure. Entrepreneurs have been described as achievement-oriented people who dislike repetitive and routine work. They have the ability to take a simple idea and mold it into something that can be visualized and implemented. Their enthusiasm is highly contagious, and they can provide an organization with a sense of mission, excitement, and momentum. However, a darker side to Aramony's entrepreneurial personality gradually emerged that created major problems for the national association in particular, and the United Way movement in general.

Manfred Kets de Vries, a keen observer of dysfunctional management styles and organizations gone awry, describes what he calls the *entrepreneur's theater* within which the entrepreneur performs. He identifies several personality features characteristic of entrepreneurs whose companies have failed.[6]

Aramony's Need to Control Dominated Decision Making

A significant theme in the personality of the entrepreneur is the *need to control*. They fear that their grandiose ideas will get out of hand and be at the mercy of others. One of the more concerned people I interviewed had worked for Aramony for over a decade. He saw the "control issue" as central to everything that went wrong and believed that the need to control was absolute to Aramony's overall operating style. Many worthwhile efforts were discarded because Aramony could not control the outcomes.

Kenneth W. Dam, the interim president of United Way, and others pointed out that Aramony failed to recognize the changes in society that required greater participation in decision making, not top-down management. Aramony is constitutionally incapable of acceding to a participatory management style if the decisions from the process diminish his control or prevent him from doing something he wants to do. Participation, by his definition, was essentially a ruse to let people think they were involved in shaping policy and programs. He would frequently agree to minor modifications which were insignificant to the basic project, but the essential nature of the project itself could never be challenged.

An example is a major marketing effort which was undertaken some years ago. Effective marketing requires a sensitivity to the needs of customers which is usually determined by opinion polls, focus groups, and surveys. Aramony routinely opposed such efforts. Some believe that Aramony saw them as a major threat to his authority to lead and impose his own vision on the United Way.

The control issue makes it very difficult for any entrepreneur to work within a structured situation unless he or she created the structures and all the work is done only on that individual's terms.

He Valued Few of His Advisors' Opinions

Kets de Vries states that "people who are overly concerned about control also have little tolerance for subordinates who think for themselves."[7] Aramony did not suffer fools gladly. Yet he willingly took ideas from others without giving them credit. It would only be later that you might be talking to someone who would inadvertently mention that they had suggested the idea to Aramony. The ideas behind many of United Way's programs and procedures were borrowed from others. For example, the *Can-Do* Program, an important program for increasing and helping communities develop their fund-raising potential, was originally developed in its most successful form in Canada, albeit with some early input from the U.S. staff. United Way International was the idea of Bernardo Benes, a volunteer in Miami who was a close friend of Aramony. Long-range planning was originally suggested by Jack Hanley, chairman of the Monsanto Company when he first joined the United Way Board.

Several of my contacts indicated that they believed that Aramony never listened to anyone after the death of Paul Akana in 1978. He was one of the United Way's legendary "thinkers" who had built up a formidable reputation in the areas of human service planning and accountability. He was several years older than Aramony and was highly respected in the field. After he died, his friends named an annual United Way golf tournament in his honor. Most importantly, he had a level of self-confidence, temper, and persuasive personality as strong as Aramony's.

Undoubtedly, the issue is much more complicated. For many years, however, Aramony had surrounded himself with several key professionals who were able to exercise *some*, and only *some*, measure of balance to his activities. These people included retired admiral Fred Bennett, who was the chief financial officer in the early 1970s; retired general Leo Benade, the staff legal counsel; George "Gus" Shea, the much beloved and respected executive vice president; Richard "Dick" J. O'Brien, who came from the field, succeeded Shea following his death, and was extremely well liked by many United Way professionals; Roberta "Bobbi" van der Voort, a highly creative and effective senior manager; and John Garber, who competently managed many of the critical internal functions of the organization. If Aramony listened to anybody, he listened to these people. But he didn't listen to them very often!

Some believe a major change for the worse in Aramony's behavior occurred when he was reportedly diagnosed with an incurable disease in the late 1980s. Nevertheless, Dick O'Brien, the last of the people to whom he would sometimes listen, had departed months before the crisis took place. Aramony had gone down surrounded by a top staff who asked few questions and who did his bidding without question. The few who objected to his policies at that time were sent to the purgatory of nonpersonhood and rarely consulted for advice or asked to attend meetings—in effect, "shunned."

Early On He Became Obsessed With Stress Reduction

For many years, Aramony had practiced Transcendental Meditation (TM) at the suggestion of Jack Hanley. It was a way for him to manage stress. He practiced it religiously for over two decades. A few years ago, staff members had remarked to him that the organization was under tremendous stress on a daily basis. They did not get the response they expected! His reply was to invite teachers of TM to address a regularly scheduled senior management meeting so that the staff could learn to cope with stress as he had. Even though senior management meetings were held weekly, this is the only one, as I recall, that Aramony stayed at for the duration. Regularly scheduled TM sessions followed for interested staff. Some were appalled by this; others who participated in the voluntary follow-up sessions found TM to be helpful.

In recent years, he discovered New Age philosophy. The books *Emmanuelle—A Manual for Living Comfortably in the Cosmos* and its sequel *Emmanuelle II* became the "bibles" which he carried with him virtually everywhere. Their passages brought him great comfort.

At least on one occasion, his experience with meditation came in handy. Fred Lee, a wealthy Chinese businessman who was on the Board of United Way International, sponsored a sojourn in the United States of one Master Huai-Chin Nan, a mentor of Lee's and reputedly a leading expert on the ancient Chinese philosophy of Tai-chi. Aramony, his son Robert, and I spent many hours learning how to meditate. One time, Lee rented an empty room for us in the Old Town Holiday Inn in Alexandria. I remember the look on the faces of the hotel staff when we asked for a dozen pillows. For an empty room? they wanted to know. There we were on the floor in lotus position, meditating for the evening. At the same time, Robert Aramony was sitting with needles sticking out of him, receiving acupuncture treatment for a bad knee.

My main goal was to cultivate Lee so that he would donate money to United Way International. Unfortunately, the United States Securities and Exchange Commission launched an inquiry regarding purported "insider trading" involving the Morgan-Stanley office in Hong Kong and a young employee at their New York office who eventually went to prison for his role in the affair. Lee left the country, and his assets were frozen, including the lavish home he had established for Master Nan in McLean, Virginia.

He Played Out the Historic Myth

Another characteristic of this type of entrepreneurial style as described by Kets de Vries was the need for "applause." Will Rogers once said, "We can't all be heroes, because someone has to sit on the curb and clap." Aramony told the press that he never played to the crowd. However, virtually his entire human environment and existence centered around the crowd he continually sought to impress. No one accuses Aramony of humility in this regard. The "crowd" could be anyone or anything. "Sometimes the monument is an imposing office building or production facility," Kets de Vries cites as a manifestation of this need for applause.[8] Aramony built two major office buildings during his tenure, testaments to his "crowd-pleasing" needs.

"The common heroic myth," says Kets de Vries, "begins with the hero's humble birth, his rapid rise to prominence and power, his conquest of the forces of evil, his vulnerability to the sin of pride, and finally, his fall through betrayal or historic sacrifice." He goes on to say that "The myth helps us explain why quite a few entrepreneurs live under a great amount of tension. They feel they're living on the edge, that their success will not last (their need for control and their sense of distrust are symptomatic of this anxiety) but they also have an overriding concern to be heard and recognized as heroes."

These types of entrepreneurs try to steer a course between their fear of success and their fear of failure. They are not sure that success will last. Unconsciously they wonder if they, too, will suffer the dreaded fate of the mythical hero. This tension provokes enormous anxiety and drives them into action, "even if it is impulsive and thoughtless, without considering facts."[9]

Entrepreneurs, like Aramony, have a strong sense of distrust of the outside world. Several independent sources told me that Aramony had installed electronic eavesdropping equipment in offices in the first office building in order to overhear staff conversations (who knows how this information was used, if in fact it ever was). In the early days of his tenure, he had told me, "People will never appreciate what I've done. When I'm down and out, even my friends will piss on me." These words turned out to be very prophetic.

He Was Unmovable in His Sense of Dedication to the Mission

As a leader, Aramony met much of the criteria required for an effective manager. But as Peter Drucker, possibly America's most quoted management consultant, states, the overriding consideration for any leader, especially that of a nonprofit organization leader, is to think through and define the mission.[10] The United Way was stated in an all too familiar quote: *"The mission of the United Way is to increase the organized capacity of people to care for one another."* Aramony articulated this mission as the central purpose of the United Way movement for over two decades. It was printed on all publications of the national association and it was as prevalent as the union symbol that was placed on all printed material.

Virtually every speech given by anyone connected with the national association would mention the mission at least once. In recent years, Jim Robinson discussed with Aramony the possibility of changing it. He suggested eliminating the words "organized capacity" and substituting something simpler. Aramony would have none of it. The mission was sacred; it could not be changed.

Aramony Required Planning for Everyone But Himself

All strategic planning for any organization should be derived from its stated mission, thus setting the background from which that organization is able to develop its goals, objectives, and, ultimately, its programs and activities. This planning should be related to the needs of what the business community calls "customers" and what the nonprofit sector calls "clients." In the case of the United Way, "clients" could mean "donors" as well as "beneficiaries" of service.

In the mid-1970s, long-range planning became a major national thrust of United Way of America (later called the Long-Range Strategic Planning program and then just Strategic Planning). "Strategy," says Drucker, "converts a nonprofit institutions's mission and objectives into performance"[11] and "performance is the ultimate test of any institution."[12] All local United Ways were encouraged to develop formal strategic plans. Most did, with the exception of the national association itself. Aramony did not want the United Way of America to be constrained with anything that smacked of permanence, especially something called strategic planning that could saddle him to a specific course. Aramony thought only in the short term; the more PR value, the better.

To Aramony work was often a game. It didn't matter whether or not other groups were doing the same programs as United Way of America. Building coalitions with other organizations around common issues was done out of necessity, not to avoid duplication of effort. After all, he assumed that under his leadership United Way of America could do anything better than anyone else anyway. The goal was to "work" the system to achieve short-term gains if it meant that he and the United Way could achieve credit and exposure through his leadership.

However, on a less formal basis, goals were set, reviewed, and revised on a regular basis. Senior managers also recognized that they must keep staff time and resources available to handle new program directions coming from Aramony. Frequently, his new initiatives overwhelmed preexisting programs. This situation required the staff to carry out not only ongoing program activities, but the new ones as well. These activities were rarely, if ever, effectively tied to performance and less frequently to budget.

He Spent Much of His Time Wooing Board Members

Aramony's ability to function effectively as a leader depended entirely on how effectively he was able to cultivate the members of the Board. Without their imprimatur, nothing was possible; with it, everything could be achieved. He sought to convince the Board that United Way of America was not a "typical," poorly run social welfare organization, but a true, businesslike operation managed by a fellow entrepreneur. He hoped to overcome the perception that charitable organizations were run by a group of "goody-two shoes." He would later tell reporters that he did run United Way of America like a *Fortune 500* company ". . . because that was [sic] results."[13]

He spent large amounts of his working time with Board members, especially the influential ones. Everything relating to the Board was micro-managed—agendas were timed to the minute, all Board presentations would be written and approved beforehand. Invariably, they would be accompanied by high-quality graphic slides or other visual aids. Discussion at Board meetings was minimal. However, any suggestion, usually of a very minor nature, would be greeted as being very insightful. In any given meeting, only a handful of Board members ever expressed themselves. Most measures were rubber-stamped with minimal discussion. This is not to say that complicated subjects were treated superficially. They were not. Hours and hours were frequently spent by staff and volunteers changing and revising programs prior to their presentation to the Board.

All seating at Board meetings would be carefully reviewed by Aramony. Members would be seated next to other members who could influence their thinking if there was any doubt about their wholehearted support of an issue. He never knowingly seated people who didn't like one another across the table so they would be forced to face one another for several hours.

The Board volunteers believed that everything Aramony did was in the best interests of the organization. C.C. "Cliff" Garvin, former chairman of Exxon and past chairman of United Way of America's Board of Governors, told Aramony that he should not serve on corporate boards. Aramony was the "conscience" of the business community, and serving on such boards would compromise him. Overall, however, his eccentricities were overlooked and his excesses only rarely questioned. Of the hundreds of volunteers who worked with him, almost no one I know of has ever called him on any of his often bizarre behaviors. I recall one recent incident, though, when someone did. Aramony wanted each Board member to "commit" to the "Mobilization for America's Children" program by standing up and signing a large chart in the board room as a symbol of their support for the program. This request was too bizarre for the chairman, John Akers, so he and the others rejected the opportunity.

Aramony would often say about his board volunteers that "the top guys love me. I can tell them anything. I'm relaxation for them. Their people can't talk to them the way I can. They welcome someone like me from outside the company telling them what to do."

He constantly visited Board volunteers in New York and elsewhere, just to touch base and maintain contact. He continually flattered volunteers by telling them how indispensable they were. Every volunteer arriving for a board meeting or attending a national conference would be met by a staff person with limousines (in the case of conferences) or a staff person's own car if arriving for a board or committee meeting at the national office. The volunteers believed in Aramony. They loved him and rarely questioned his judgment. But, ultimately, they denied him when they perceived that he had failed them.

His Attitude Towards the Pros in the Field Was Completely Different

His approach to United Way chief professional officers was far different from that of the Board members. Don Plambeck, founder of the National Academy for Voluntarism and former senior staff member at United Way of America, said that during the first ten years Aramony sought to control the national association and, during the last decade, to control the field. He referred to the concept of a national/local system working together in harmony as a great myth.

I have often used the word "movement" to describe the United Way field as a whole, even though some do not believe that the national association and its affiliates were ever a movement per se. Aramony's basic attitude, particularly in the last years of his reign, was a barely disguised contempt for what he perceived in most cases to be the lack of creativity of United Way professionals and their often lukewarm acceptance of his initiatives. Many times he would tell me that no one in the country could do the job he could do, so he might as well stay. Preferred executives, that is, those who enthusiastically carried out his initiatives, would be given choice committee assignments, the most prestigious committee being the National Professional Advisory Council.

Many United Way chief professional officers were put in an ambiguous position relative to their careers. Advancement in the field typically occurred by moving from a smaller city to a larger one every few years. They perceived that if they objected to any of Aramony's initiatives or programs, they would be sitting in one community the rest of their professional lives. It was important to Aramony that "acceptable" people be placed in the larger communities in order to ensure maximum dues support for the national association and to carry out national programs. However, because of the independence of United Way members, it was not possible for him to completely control this process. He would often review the list of candidates the Human Resources Department submitted to a local community, but he had no real ability to select any particular candidate. Aramony once told me that Jack Hanley suggested that his success be measured on nationwide fund-raising results. "OK," said Aramony, "if you see to it that I control all of the placements of United Way professionals in local communities."

ARAMONY AND THE ATTRIBUTES OF LEADERSHIP

To ask if Aramony was a leader is like asking if the sky is blue. However, leadership takes many forms. Will he be remembered as a "great" leader? Only time will determine the answer.

In my opinion, there are only a few great leaders, like France's Jean Monnet, father of the European Community, who worked tirelessly behind the scenes for many years, never taking credit but giving it to the politicians. In the social welfare field of which I have been a part most of my life, I know of two people who fall into the mold of Jean Monnet, although they represent widely divergent parts of the voluntary sector. One is Jack Schwartz, past president of the American Association of Fund Raising Counsel, who in my judgment has contributed more to strengthening the voluntary sector in this country and received less credit than anyone I know. He founded the Coalition for the Public Good, an early antecedent to the Independent Sector, singlehandedly raised over $2 million to finance the research of the Commission on Private Philanthropy and Public Needs (the Filer Commission) in the mid-1970s, and was the first to publish comprehensive statistics on philanthropy in the United States.

Another great leader, in my opinion, is Pablo Eisenberg, Princeton graduate and president of the Center for Community Change based in Washington. Eisenberg has devoted his life to championing the cause of the society's poor and disadvantaged, eschewing perks and privileges along the way. He conducts the organization he leads as *primus inter pares*, first among equals. His group operates as a committee of the whole with key individuals at all levels participating in major decisions and taking responsibilities for outcomes. His annual reports include no letters and no personal self-promotion. In contrast, at United Way of America, *every* publication produced by the organization was required to have Aramony's picture and a note from him on the first few pages.

Dr. Warren Bennis has spent a major portion of his professional life studying the basic qualities shared by recognized leaders. I've used these attributes he has enunciated in *On Becoming a Leader* as guidelines in understanding what went wrong and why with Aramony's special style of leadership.

A Guiding Vision

The leader has a clear idea of what he wants to do professionally and personally—and the strength to persist in the face of setbacks, even failures.[14]

Aramony spoke endlessly about vision and his concept of the best of all possible worlds—a world of "people helping people. He created a vision of a better future by concentrating his speeches and addresses on the ends, not the means. Ultimately, he could not distinguish the difference between being a preacher and a visionary. His focus was always on meeting human needs. He avoided mentioning social agencies in his comments unless he was speaking directly to that particular audience.

Yet, Aramony was clearly aware of the possible failure of some of his programs. His solution was to cut his losses fast and never mention them again, as if they never existed. The Second Century program is a good example of this. Its goal was to double fund-raising results between 1987 and 1991. But the result was only an increase of about 18 percent in dollars raised and less than 2 percent when adjusted for inflation (or in real dollars). This program was dropped as soon as Aramony realized that the goal was unachievable. No one was ever held accountable for its failure. Several former and current staff members have indicated that his credibility in the field began to decline with the launching of this program. It was considered an intrusion of the national association on local responsibility. When you asked about its failure, "the economy" was often given as the reason.

Negative thinking was not a part of Bill Aramony's public persona. He often reacted very harshly to anyone, especially staff, who were not as enthusiastic as he was about an idea. When Board members criticized his ideas, he usually figured out ways to work around them to achieve the ends he sought.

Passion

"The leader who loves what he does and loves doing it[15]" has the "capacity to motivate, "[16] John Gardner states in his book *On Leadership*. "I miss the passion," one staff member told me nearly a year after Aramony's departure from United Way of America. Aramony's enthusiasm was indeed contagious. He was passionate about everything, and everything excited him. He was also passionate about helping out staff members who were experiencing difficulties. He once called on Sears to donate furniture to a financially strapped but valued worker he had brought from New York. He would loan money to someone at the slightest inkling that they were in trouble. He could be unbelievably kind and generous. When Harold Edelston, a senior staff member, died suddenly in California, Aramony spent the night on the phone trying to cut through red tape to have his body returned to his family immediately because Harold was Jewish and Jewish law requires burial the next day. Aramony succeeded. Everything he did and touched was done with energy and excitement.

To those outside his immediate circle, this passion was most demonstrated by his rhetoric. After 23 years in the United Way, I never tired of hearing his words, despite the repetition. Indeed, it was not the words as much as the passion in which they were delivered that made the difference. When written out later, they often made little sense. He rarely received a standing ovation because he never fully understood the need for pace and timing when speaking to larger audiences. His skill lay more in *how* he said things, not what he said.

In the early 1970s, I wrote many of his speeches. Aramony spent hours polishing them and, much to my dismay, rarely used the words I had written for him. In the early days, when I mentioned that he might do better without notes in the first place, he said he needed them to feel secure and that essentially he felt uneasy and uncomfortable when speaking in public.

After years of practice, the prepared texts disappeared, and he believed himself to be a great orator. He bragged that a top speech instructor, one who trained corporate executives, had told him that his gift of eloquence is what she seeks for her clients. He believed that he was so skilled that he could carry any audience, regardless of its size.

Up until a couple of years ago, he would speak to a thousand-plus volunteer audience at the annual volunteer leaders conferences with a "walking mike" and without the use of notes or a podium. With a walking mike, he would not be "separated" from his constituency by a podium. In one case, he had the stage area extended well out in front of him. In later years, staff members prevailed upon him to speak behind a podium like everyone else. It seemed to work better. Yet his forceful ability to communicate his message, particularly with individuals and small groups, remained the same. He was electrifying.

Integrity

Integrity is *self-knowledge, candor,* and *maturity* according to Bennis. A great leader knows himself, his strengths, his weaknesses, and his essential assets. He is able to work all of these into a sense of self. Candor provides the individual with the ability to face himself honestly and to never compromise principles for the sake of expediency. With maturity, one understands that leading is not just pointing the way or issuing orders. A leader must be capable of learning from others by listening, observing, and working with them. Understanding this, he or she can impart these qualities to others.[17]

Above all, Aramony was a "born salesman." He often carried several projects on widely divergent topics when he was making a pitch for funding, like the old-fashioned snake oil salesman who would pull open his coat to display the different kinds of tonics available.

Yet the rhetoric was often far different from the reality. For example, in my association with him for over two decades, I never knew him to volunteer for anything. He espoused in virtually every forum he faced that everyone should do some direct volunteer work to make our society a better place. He enjoyed citing the example of his chairman at the time, Donald Seibert, chairman of J.C. Penney, who personally washed dishes every Sunday at his church. In order to obtain commitment to the "One-to-One" program, a tutoring activity which was being promoted nationwide by the Bush administration, he suggested at one point that everyone on the national staff be assigned a student to tutor. I asked one of his personal staff at that time if he was also going to tutor someone. "He's too busy," was the response.

Bill Aramony always believed that he knew the best approach to issues and problems. He considered his own intelligence unassailable. He could be persuaded otherwise only by the powerful or the famous. Sometimes he could be convinced to drop an idea if someone could describe negative or embarrassing consequences to United Way of America and especially to him personally. The reasons for changing his mind were therefore often not rational, but strategic or tactical; not necessarily because he believed he was wrong.

All of the programs discussed in Chapter 2 underwent modification. Changes occurred not because Aramony necessarily agreed with them or wanted to achieve a consensus, but because he had to modify the program in order to obtain ultimate acceptance from either volunteers or local United Ways. For example, in the early 1970s, the standards of excellence underwent an exhaustive review process by local United Ways and numerous reviews by committees of volunteers and staff. The reader may argue that many excellent managers achieve acceptance of ideas in this way. The difference is that Aramony invariably knew the "truth" and held onto these beliefs, even though they may not have been widely shared. Once a program had gained acceptance by being installed in several communities (and this is true of virtually every program), it would be moved from a high priority to a low one, and frequently forgotten. The challenge of wheeling and dealing to sell a particular program drove him more than the content. As in his speeches, his daily conversation was frequently laced with *how* he sold ideas to others, rather than *what* was sold.

Aramony readily agreed with his top volunteers if they objected to some program or other. But he would simply come back at it another way. For example, when John Akers wanted to slash the dues paid by United Ways to the national association, Aramony spent a great deal of time trying to figure out how he could sell *other* programs, which would raise the same amount as the dues which were being lost.

This quality extended as well to his benefits. He had asked one of his top board members if he thought United Way of America could buy him an apartment in New York. The volunteer advised against it. Aramony then had a spinoff purchase the apartment anyway, as later reported by the press.

Trust

If an individual possesses integrity, trust follows. Trust is a quality which can't be acquired; it must be earned. It is a critical quality of leadership imparted to a leader by his followers so that both can act together for their mutual benefit and those they serve.[18] But when the crisis hit, Aramony's reservoir of goodwill had dried up. He lost the trust of many of his staff members through a number of misjudgments and poor management techniques. A few examples follow.

Not a Democracy. For many staff members at United Way of America, Aramony could do no wrong. People hung on his every word and, regardless of the nature of the request, carried out his wishes/orders. These people were the true believers. Other staff, particularly newer staff, often fell into the trap of questioning a decision or commenting on a presentation Aramony was making on a particular program only to be told, "This is not a democracy; don't ever forget that!"

He listened to senior staff, particularly the most articulate ones. It was often the quality of one's presentation rather than its content that mattered most to him. In many cases, Aramony would make decisions based solely on the need to cultivate and enhance the positioning of some staff member at the expense of others. His penchant for playing people against one another caused stress, tension, and low morale and was often not in the best interests of the organization.

Planned Chaos. In his article entitled "Skilled Incompetence" in the *Harvard Business Review,* Chris Argyris of the Harvard School of Education explains how a manager who sends mixed messages can create considerable "chaos." He states that these mixed messages often create problems. For example, a manager might say, "Be innovative and take risks, but be careful." If one asks for more information, it would be seen as a sign of immaturity or inexperience. Also, one could not ask for clarification, because that would indicate that the one who delivered the message was somehow duplicitous. A manager might also send an ambiguous message on purpose, rather than dealing with the situation head on.[19]

Aramony would often make promises to important people because he wanted to please them. When they had departed, he would tell the staff responsible for the program, who were frequently present during the conversations, to "f--k 'em, don't do anything." Then it was up to the embarassed staff to tell the party at some later time that we weren't able to do what Aramony told them we would.

Demeaning Staff. United Way of America held annual retreats. Aramony always spoke to the entire staff and was invariably spellbinding. These retreats were devoted to dealing with critical issues and obtaining staff input and support. However, Aramony was rarely seen after his speeches, and it was always left to other staff members to interpret what he had said. In addition, it was clearly recognized that it didn't really matter what anyone thought anyway. Nothing would be approved, let alone implemented, without Aramony's *precise and very clear* imprimatur. At one particular retreat around about 1981, when the strategic planning process was being discussed and its direction defined, Aramony suddenly informed the staff, "I know what the issues are," and out he walked.

Aramony irritated staff by rarely holding a scheduled meeting on time. Staff members were almost always kept waiting, or meetings were canceled or changed at the last minute. All staff members were expected to be available at a moment's notice whether or not they were in the middle of appointments or on their way to them. United Way of America secretaries were expected to recognize his "Where the hell is ---?" If they asked who was calling, his response would often be something like, "Mickey Mouse—who the hell do you think it is? Get him/her for me, NOW!" He would rarely identify himself, leaving secretaries (as well as spouses) terrified that they might not recognize his voice.

A few years ago, I was on vacation in Haiti in the West Indies where I had worked many years before. I received a message that there was an urgent phone call for me at the front desk. I raced to pick up the phone. "Glaser, what the hell are you doing?" Aramony's familiar voice vibrated over the phone lines.

"I'm on vacation."

"Do you know who I have in my office?"

"No, who?"

"Rosendo." (Rosendo Gutierrez was on the Board of United Way International.)

"He wants to know what you're doing with such-and-such a program. Here, I'll let you talk to him."

"I was visiting Washington and stopped by to see Bill," Gutierrez slowly mumbled with evident embarrassment. "I was asking him about the program, and before I knew it he had called your secretary and asked her to find you. I didn't even get the chance to tell him it could wait!"

Aramony would never hesitate to do things like this to show that he could find anyone anyplace in the world and that staff could be interrupted for any reason on or off vacation, day or night. He called me one Thanksgiving Day to go for a walk to discuss matters which happened to be on his mind. Regardless of where he was in the world, his personal secretary had to give him a wake-up call from Alexandria, which sometimes meant that she had to get up in the middle of the night. The more courageous of his personal staff, especially those with families, bought answering machines, which irritated him immensely. Most of the staff believed that neither their opinions nor their privacy was respected. By and large, they were correct. In many respects, he felt he "owned" people because of the high salaries he paid them.

Know Thy Place. Aramony believed to his core that he was a very special human being by virtue of his success. He attributed to himself superior intellect, creativity, and an obvious ability to inspire others to believe in what he believed. He articulated this superior attitude to his closest staff. One of his aides tells the story that she had decided not to order a car for him because he was staying at a hotel and it would be easy to find a cab. She was severely berated by Aramony for not recognizing that he was a special person and required a special pickup.

It was well known that he used rental or chauffeured cars when he traveled, particularly in New York City where he was under contract with a company to make certain his favorite driver, Charlie, was available on call. When he discovered that one of the heads of a spinoff had on one occasion ordered a car for himself and his own staff, he was severely chastised for assuming prerogatives reserved only for "the boss." What people read in the press regarding abuses applied with almost no exceptions exclusively to Aramony.

Anger. Possibly his most egregious quality was the "put-down." Staff members were regularly intimidated in front of volunteers and other staff through a barrage of verbal abuse. Over the years, I was a recipient of this invective on several occasions, as were many other employees. One of the worst times was in front of the professional chairman of United Way International's Advisory Committee who had complained to him that I was not seeking his advice or input on the international program. Within minutes, Aramony was at my office, screaming in front of everyone for me to come into the hallway immediately, even though I was briefing a new employee at the time. I realized later that his behavior in this case was due to the fact that the next chairman of the Board of United Way of America headed a national company located in the same town as this individual.

George Wilkinson, a former senior staff person, tells the story of listening outside of Aramony's office while he was waiting to see him. Aramony was yelling at his public relations staff for not ensuring that he was included in an article in a recent magazine which had featured outstanding managers in the nonprofit sector. It didn't include him and he was enraged.

In his exceptionally beautiful work, *Love and Profit: The Art of Caring Leadership*, James A. Autry, a former corporate executive, describes the dangerous characteristic of anger:

> Anger as a weapon frequently leads to humiliation, and humiliation is one thing no employee will ever forgive you. Think about it: Of the long-time grudges or ill feelings you may still personally harbor, aren't they really about humiliation?
>
> . . . *you cannot act properly when you act in anger.* So mine is a business decision: You cannot afford to do something with such long-term negative impact. It will come back to haunt you more than you'll ever believe.[20]

"Amen," I say. Aramony rarely held a grudge even if his anger concerned a substantive matter (except in matters regarding perceived disloyalty). Two minutes after the incident, it would be as though nothing happened. Yet, the object of his anger was not so easily mollified. However, if Aramony was angered because an individual failed to show proper respect, the sin could be fatal. On one occasion, at a major conference, Aramony was explaining a program before a group of executives seated at his table. A senior staff person from United Way of America indicated his disagreement with Aramony in a way that could be construed as being disrespectful. Aramony jumped up, walked over to him, and, pointing his finger, unleashed a barrage of invective. The employee was asked to leave the organization shortly afterwards.

A Lesson in Loyalty. Once, when attending a meeting in England with Aramony, I reminded him that I was leaving a couple of days early to attend a retirement party for a dear friend and colleague with whom I'd worked closely on many projects for many years. The conversation went as follows:

"You're what?"

"I'm leaving tomorrow for New York to go to the farewell dinner for J.S. Remember, I mentioned it to you before. We're done here anyway."

"You're not going anywhere. We have this meeting Friday and I want you to attend. If I'm here, you're here."

Aramony had taken my affection for a close colleague as a betrayal to him. Arguing was futile. During a sleepless night, I had made up my mind that I was going to leave anyway. By disobeying Aramony,

I fully expected to get fired. The next morning, Aramony lectured me in the back seat of a cab as it barreled along from the suburbs towards central London. The day was particularly gloomy, even by London standards.

"Listen to me, Glaser, and don't say anything. Just be quiet," he said, stabbing my leg with repeated jabs of his finger. "Loyalty is the most important thing there is. It's more important than competence. Don't *ever* forget that."

The meeting on Friday was canceled. There was no more discussion and I left England in time for my friend's event. Aramony returned himself the next day.

Kets de Vries points out that when fantasies of unlimited power, success, and brilliance are cut short, certain types of CEOs may experience feelings of rage and anger and act vindictively.[21] It was in providing personal favors and obligations, not by example or adhering to specific standards, that Aramony achieved intense loyalties. He related to others much more like a ward boss than a chief executive.

Requisite Adulation. Many of the people who held senior positions at United Way of America, especially in the later years, as well as many of his personal staff were slavishly devoted to him and "dedicated to giving him *glowjobs*," as described in *Esquire*, referring to the needs of this type of manager. The article cynically describes how to excel at being an office sycophant. A couple of these techniques bear mention because they are descriptive of the actions typical of some on the national staff and by others who recognized that this was the only way to get anything done:

"Flatter him: But only about the things he is proud of, for only those will he believe. Consult him: Make him feel he's captain of the team, even if he's totally superfluous."[22]

Shared Madness. In some cases, the enormous amount of energy directed at appeasing the boss can result in a kind of "shared madness." In recent years, Aramony failed to recognize that many of his programs were being rejected by United Ways or given only lip service, although most of the senior staff at that time continued to share this unreality.

Kets de Vries notes "how contagious the behavior of a senior executive can be, and how devastating the effect on his subordinates and his organization."[23] He refers to this behavior as similar to a psychiatric disorder. He says:

Where elements of *folie à deux* seep into organizations, conflict be-

comes stifling, creativity is discouraged, and distrust becomes the prevailing attitude. Instead of taking realistic action, managers react to
emergencies by withdrawing or scapegoating. Fear will be the under-
current of the overall organizational climate. As ends and means become indistinguishable, the organization will drift along losing touch
with originally defined corporate goals and strategies.[24]

There are four basic ingredients that leaders must possess in order
to instill the necessary ingredient of *trust* in a lasting relationship with
his or her subordinates, according to Bennis. Based on my experience,
I've ranked Aramony using the letters A to E (A representing the highest score and E the lowest):

1. *Constancy*. Leaders never create surprises for the group.
   Aramony score: D
2. *Congruity*. There is no gap between the theories espoused by
   the leaders and the lives they lead.
   Aramony score: D
3. *Reliability*. Leaders are there when it counts; they are ready to
   support coworkers when it really matters.
   Aramony score: B
4. *Integrity*. Leaders honor their commitments and promises.[25]
   Aramony score: B

Curiosity and Daring

Aramony referred to his lifestyle as that of "dodging bullets." He
would be the first to admit that the last one hit him between the eyes.
"That's life," he nonchalantly said to me afterwards. These qualities—
curiosity and daring—are evidence of Aramony's need for risk taking
and his nonacceptance of failure. It is these qualities for which Aramony is best known. One needs only to contemplate his amazing career
to realize that most people would never be willing to take the risks he
took (first, to initiate his programs and second, to keep them going to
the point that the United Way would become the preeminent organization in the nonprofit world). The lightning changes he made in his
first 200 days galvanized the United Way. In a very short time, he had
succeeded in changing the name of the movement, creating a new mission statement, reconstituting the board, completely revamping the
staff, and building a new headquarters. Impressive programs, which
dramatically changed the United Way forever, had followed.

Aramony correctly realized that he had but a small window of opportunity to make changes of this magnitude. "I have just a short honeymoon to get everything done, after that it's too late," he would say. He cut his losses quickly. He never looked back, only forward—often driving himself and his staff at breakneck speed. In doing so, he left key constituencies in the dust, a factor which contributed to his downfall. Although some of my former colleagues might disagree with such an extreme conclusion regarding the leadership of the national office, I suspect that those most likely to disagree have been part of the problem.

Kets de Vries and Danny Miller, in their seminal work *The Neurotic Organization*, describe five dysfunctional types. Many feel that the firm they characterize as *"The Dramatic Firm"* may well describe United Way of America, especially in its later years.

> Dramatic firms live up to their name in many respects: They are hyperactive, impulsive, dramatically venturesome, and dangerously uninhibited. Their decision makers live in a world of hunches and impressions rather than facts . . .

> Boldness, risk taking, and diversification are the themes. Instead of reacting to the environment, the top decision maker, often an entrepreneur, attempts to enact his own environment.

> *On Structure.* . . . far too primitive for its broad product market scope. First, too much power is concentrated in the entrepreneurial chief executive. Second, the absence of an effective information system top executives . . . prefer to act on intuition rather than facts. Finally, the striving for dominance by the leader obstructs effective internal communication, which is mostly in a top-down direction. Upward and lateral communication is scanty.[26]

> They are likely to surround themselves with sycophants, obsequious yes-men who are all to willing to provide accolades and worship on a regular basis. . . .[27] The leader's overconfidence and their desire for recognition make them prone to undertake large and risky ventures. These can make heroes out of them, since their dramatic nature will capture the attention of a broad audience.[28]

Those who have worked for the national association as well as many United Way professionals will find each one of these statements a truism.

Some scholars consider the dysfunctional styles described by these authors as typical of an addictive, co-dependent situation. In their book

The Addictive Organization Anne Wilson Schaef and Diane Fassel have taken these types of organizations and compared them to the addictive personality.[29]

CONCLUSIONS

This chapter has described the environment in which Aramony's autocratic leadership style was allowed to flourish, a description of that style, and the type of organization it created. You could question why I've spent so much time describing how Aramony ran the organization. I can only respond by stating that the contagion produced by his operating style affected the entire United Way movement. The volunteers, as well as the staff, were perceived by him as extensions of his will. The cost to the private lives of many of the professional staff was severe. Although Aramony was considered the leader who drove the organization, for the most part, the national staff basked in his "glory" and willingly carried out his directives, often against their own better judgment. In doing so, they failed not only themselves but the movement they served.

The next chapter will describe some of the ways Aramony's powerful personality actually worked in relating to his closest staff and through various United Way constituencies to achieve his goals, and hence the goals of the United Way movement as he perceived them.

REFERENCES

1. *The Spirit of Voluntarism . . . United Way of America. Rebirth and Renewal:* A Progress Report (April 1972), p. 12. Reprinted by permission, United Way of America. United Way of America does not endorse the opinions or conclusions expressed herein.
2. Philip B. Crosby, "Managerial Arrogance" in *Across the Board* (October, 1992), p. 32.
3. William Aramony, *The United Way: The Next 100 Years* (New York: Donald I. Fine, Inc., 1987), pp. 107–111.
4. *Ibid*, p. 105.
5. *Ibid*, pp. 106–107.
6. Manfred F. R. Kets de Vries, "The Dark Side of Entrepreneurship," *Harvard Business Review* (November–December, 1985), p. 161.
7. *Ibid*, p. 162.
8. *Ibid*, p. 163.
9. *Ibid*, p. 165.
10. Peter F. Drucker, *Managing the Non-Profit Organization-Principles and Practices* (New York: HarperBusiness, 1992), p. 3.
11. *Ibid*, p. 99.

12. *Ibid*, p. 139.
13. For example, *The New York Times* "Ex-Chief of United Way Vows to Fight Accusations" (April 10, 1992).
14. Warren Bennis, *On Becoming a Leader* (New York: Addison-Wesley Publishing Company, Inc., 1989), p. 39.
15. *Ibid*, p.40.
16. John Gardner, *On Leadership* (New York: The Free Press, 1990), p. 51.
17. Bennis, pp. 40–41.
18. *Ibid*, p. 41.
19. Chris Argyris, "Skilled Incompetence," *Harvard Business Review* (September–October, 1986), p. 76.
20. James A. Autry, *Love and Profit: The Art of Caring Leadership* (New York: Avon Books, 1991), pp. 114–115.
21. Manfred F. R. Kets de Vries and Associates, *Organizations on the Couch-Clinical Perspectives on Organizational Behavior and Change* (San Francisco: Jossey-Bass Publishers, 1991), p. 253.
22. Stanley Bing, "The Strategist—I've Always Loved You, Mort" (*Esquire*, April, 1988).
23. Manfred F. R. Kets de Vries, "Managers Can Drive Their Subordinates Mad," *Harvard Business Review* (July–August, 1979), p. 126.
24. *Ibid*, p. 130.
25. Bennis, p. 160.
26. Manfred F. S. Kets de Vries and Danny Miller, *The Neurotic Organization: Diagnosing and Revitalizing Unhealthy Companies* (New York: HarperBusiness, 1984), pp. 31–34.
27. *Ibid*, p. 84.
28. *Ibid*, p. 86.
29. See Anne Wilson Schaef and Diane Fassel, *The Addictive Organization: Why We Overwork, Cover Up, Pick Up the Pieces, Please the Boss & Perpetuate Sick Organizations* (San Francisco: Harper 1988).

CHAPTER 4

The Followers

Service is the rent we pay for living. It is the very purpose of life and not something you do in your spare time.[1]

Marian Wright Edelman, President
Children's Defense Fund

In Chapter 3, I discussed how Bill Aramony's leadership style, for better or worse, impacted dramatically on the workings of United Way of America and its constituencies. He presided over both its explosive growth and its image-shattering decline. The end results were inevitable because Bill Aramony answered to no one but himself. He held few people in awe, although he had a strong predilection for the company of the "great" and the "near great."

However, it would be unfair of me or anyone else to blame Aramony alone for what happened. Equal, if not greater, fault lies with those who supported him in every way and believed that he could do no wrong or that if he did, it was somehow "okay." These were the professionals who worked on the national staff, the local United Way chief professional officers, and the volunteers who served on the Board of Governors. There were a few like me who had been with him for many years and knew how to work around him to carry out program goals irrespective of his imprimatur. Because his personality was so expansive and because he was "larger than life," his influence spread to other constituencies touched by the United Way as well. While I have discussed only issues related to Aramony's leadership style up to this point, we must now consider why so many believed in him, followed him, and then suffered enormous guilt for what they knew, yet failed to act. How Aramony sought to control his environment and *his* people is another important factor in understanding what went wrong and why. This chapter will focus on a quality all too many in the United Way possessed, that of unquestioning "followership."

POWER CAME FROM RESTRUCTURING THE NATIONAL STAFF

The national staff existed essentially as soldiers whose purpose was to carry out the initiatives of its leader-general. They became instruments which enabled Aramony to exert his will towards constituencies outside the organization.

The national staff, as well as United Way professionals, were kept off balance and "on the ball" as we have seen by frequent restructuring as a major way he chose to exert his control. This restructuring occurred at least once every six months and caused considerable anguish among staff members, since only a few of the most senior staff were usually consulted and the reasons for the changes were rarely explained. It was impossible, under these circumstances, for senior managers to empower people whom they literally weren't sure would be working for them from one day to the next.

However, all these restructurings frequently had a positive side as well. Aramony was a proponent of making structure subordinate to the abilities of each staff person. At least for part of their time, staff professionals were always doing what they did best—whatever that happened to be. He often caused positions to "make a fit" between abilities and assignments. This flexibility, which affected primarily the program staff, created among them an expectation that they would have to adjust quickly to new initiatives. It also kept the staff from getting into a rut.

Flexibility and responsiveness by the national staff were also assured by the lack of uniform enforcement of standards for most internal functions, particularly in the personnel area. Although personnel practices and senior staff salary ranges were set by the Board, Aramony exercised wide latitude within those parameters. Financial rewards were a major way of exercising his control. The salaries at United Way of America were relatively high compared to other charitable organizations. There seemed to be no limit. For female staff members in particular, it often appeared that raises and perquisites were increased in direct proportion to their attractiveness. If Aramony needed to justify a higher salary for a particular staff member, they became "profession-als" overnight.

As in most companies, staff were generally divided into what is called "support" and "professional." Support staff are considered those individuals who provided critical clerical and administrative ser-ices to the professional staff for whom they worked. Thus, when one became a "professional," that person usually employed his or her own support staff. Aramony generally did not concern himself with special qualifications for professional status. If he said someone was a "pro-fessional," "poof," they became one immediately. But if a staff member happened to commit some act that Aramony didn't approve of near the time he or she was to be considered for a raise, it would likely not be granted, even though during the rest of the year that person might have performed well. It would be very difficult for that individual's superior to reverse such a decision (unless Aramony for one reason or another wanted to appease the person who had interceded on behalf of the subordinate). This unequal application of salary policies at the senior level created considerable morale problems.

Petitions by staff for redress of various grievances over the years were dealt with politely, particularly if presented by lower-level staff. (One of these incidents was cited in the *Regardies* article in February, 1992 which refers to a lawyer hired by staff to represent them before the United Way.) From this quarter, they were perceived as nonthrea-tening. Sometimes minor concessions might be granted. However, su-pervisory staff were often hauled on the carpet if their staff participated in such petitioning. For example, once while I was serving on his pro-fessional staff, Aramony burst into my office, with obvious anguish on his face. He accused me of being a "traitor" because my assistant was involved with a group peacefully attempting to redress their griev-ances. It was only after considerable explanation that Aramony under-stood that my assistant had been asked for her advice, and, as I had explained to him, had actually helped keep the peace among a very irate group of support personnel. The group had intended to march unannounced into Aramony's office to present their complaints di-rectly to him. This act, if carried out, would have had disastrous con-sequences for the individuals involved.

INTIMIDATION HELPS MAINTAIN THE STATUS QUO

Although it is clearly possible to lead through fear and intimidation, it is obvious that this approach does not provide lasting loyalties. It would be patently unfair to say that Aramony held the organization together exclusively through fear and intimidation. But it would be fair to say that he certainly did not encourage a participatory process where individuals were respected for their ideas or for their contributions. In significant ways, even positive change was seen as a threat. Take the following event as an example.

For many years, United Way of America's national volunteer leaders conferences had been "top-down" affairs. A major purpose of these conferences was to provide a platform for national initiatives. Considerable funds were expended on multimedia shows, slide presentations, and training well-respected volunteers and local United Way staff to present the national program in a first-class manner. Participation from the audience was minimal. For the first time, a senior vice president had succeeded in opening up the process at a national conference which took place in Los Angeles. Emphasis had been placed on workshops and smaller groups, where volunteers had a genuine opportunity to participate and actually express their opinions on a particular program under discussion. In addition, the senior vice president involved large numbers of the national staff in the process, creating a bottom-up enthusiasm that had never before existed. Staff had great discretion in working with the volunteers within an open process which had significantly boosted morale.

"What do you think you're doing?" Aramony yelled at the senior vice president following the conference. "If you think you can use your relationship with the staff to get *my* job, you've got another thing coming!"

The staff people were never thanked for what was a highly significant contribution, and the format was never used again.

This senior vice president, who once was touted as a successor to Aramony, also related to me a time when Aramony wanted to exert his control over the senior vice president's staff. The individual had refused to fire someone Aramony didn't want around anymore. During a meeting shortly after the senior vice president's refusal, Aramony showed the person a napkin scribbled with the individual's name that he wanted dismissed, drawn under a sketch of a tombstone.

During this time, Gifts in Kind America, an early spinoff, had just received recognition in the *Nonprofit Times,* a major trade journal for charities in the nation. It cited the organization as having the lowest fund-raising costs and second-lowest administrative costs of all the charities in its national survey. Aramony, who was volunteer president of Gifts In Kind America, asked his general manager to call Susan Corrigan, then the *de facto* chief executive. It is unclear whether or not he was to act as a liaison to the Board from United Way of America (replacing Dick O'Brien, who had left United Way of America), or whether he simply misinterpreted Aramony and was to become president—over Corrigan. In any case, the latter interpretation was the one understood by him. The phone discussion went something like this:

> GM: Aramony has just named me as president of Gifts in Kind America. I would like a full briefing on the organization immediately. Bring all financial and other information to my office now.

> Corrigan: Mr. Aramony has not mentioned anything about this to me. Our president is appointed by the Board. Let me discuss this with Bill and I will get back to you.

Corrigan then called the office and spoke with Aramony's secretary.

> Corrigan: "What does Bill have in mind? Is [the general manager] new liaison to the Board? Did he not understand his role?"

> Secretary: Aramony did not mean that [he] was president. I will talk to Aramony and he will talk to him.

United Way of America's general manager continued to make unreasonable demands. Eventually, Corrigan told her chairman, Thomas D. Hutchens, a senior executive at the J.C. Penney Company, that the situation was out of hand and that the oversight by the General Manager was entirely unnecessary. Hutchens apparently spoke with Aramony, who shortly thereafter resigned as volunteer president and recommended that Corrigan become president. She was appointed to that position *by her own board* in September 1991.

Aramony possibly reasoned that it was best to take a tactical retreat since W.R. Howell, chairman of J.C. Penney, was scheduled to be chairman of the Board of United Way of America in 1992.

In December 1991, Gifts in Kind America was recognized by *Money* magazine as the "most efficient" of the top 100 charities in the nation.

These are just a few instances in which Aramony exerted his will to retain power through intimidation, in this case over a spinoff, even though he had not been active in the organization since its inception—and even though the chief executive was doing an outstanding job.

INCONSISTENT TRAVEL POLICIES ALSO LOWERED MORALE

Travel policies, as well as personnel practices, at United Way of America were not enforced equally. No one could hire a car and driver except the president; certainly no one could fly anything but coach class unless express approval was granted by the president. I recall one particular case where an exception was granted. A senior staff person was so heavy that he could not fit into a coach class seat and was given permission to fly first class routinely. United Way International staff were permitted to fly business class when traveling overseas. If a staff member were traveling *with* the president, all prerogatives accorded the president were accorded any traveling companion. He would never permit the traveling staff to sit in coach class while he flew business or first class or allow the person to stay at a less expensive hotel than he would stay at during a particular business trip. Frequently, the traveling companion would put charges, particularly meal charges, on his or her corporate card so as to not overburden Aramony's personal travel budget. For all other staff traveling without him, any "reasonable" expense was justified as long as coach travel was used. Meal charges were limited to $25 per day when traveling alone. However, with a bona fide guest, this amount did not apply. All expense accounts were vetted by United Way of America's accounting department.

A problem of morale occurred because staff was aware of Aramony's extravagance and often had to fight for even small raises for their own staffs as well as protect their program budgets from being raided.

"LINE OF SIGHT" MANAGEMENT WAS AN OCCUPATIONAL HAZARD

Frenetic activity was most pronounced when Aramony was back in Alexandria, particularly when he returned from a trip (this was most of the time). The atmosphere in the office became electric, particularly for the executive staff on the top floor. Suddenly, meetings would be called and everyone would have to drop whatever they were doing to handle whatever Aramony wanted done that instant. He would be so energized from his trips and so full of new ideas that he couldn't be bothered with the status quo. Often the focus of previously scheduled meetings would be changed so that he could expound on these new ideas which might or might not be related to anything that was current. Sometimes, unfortunate staff members who happened to be on the elevator with Aramony on his way back from a trip would be given an assignment on the spot and asked to come to the meeting that was about to begin just because they had happened to be on the elevator at that particular moment. One could never not accept these assignments. The ultimate sin would be to say, "I'm too busy." The command was clear, period. "Line of sight" management was an occupational hazard.

Staff members were often diverted to carry out assignments of questionable value. For several days in the mid 1980s, six staff people, including Aramony and myself, as well as a volunteer and a professional writer spent several days at Fripp Island, a seaside resort in South Carolina, drafting his book *The United Way—the Next Hundred Years.* He justified this exercise and expense as necessary so that his philosophy about the United Way could be promoted more widely.

ARAMONY'S IMPORTANT STAFF MEMBERS WERE HIS PERSONAL "GROUPIES"

Aramony had a small group of senior and mid-level staff members whom he relied on for everything. They were his own personal "groupies." He tended to play the remainder of the senior staff against one another. He carried out his policies through these top and mid-level staff members in a variety of compensatory and informal ways. These people met his personal needs and provided him with the psychological support he evidently required to function at his peak. Some of the descriptions below are composites.

The CFO

The most important role was that of the *chief financial officer.* This person had to be trusted completely. The first CFO at United Way of America was Fred Bennett, a retired Navy officer, who developed our initial accounting system in the early 1970s. He exuded integrity, which was especially important for an association trying to establish credibility in its early days. For a few years in the mid-1980s, one CFO was recruited from the outside by professional headhunters. However, by that individual's own admission, the job was over that person's head, and the individual left under pressure to pursue another career. It is said that the selection was actually made by Aramony's trusted administrative assistant against the advice of experts. In subsequent years, the CFOs were either closely supervised or consisted of Aramony's friends and long-term associates who rarely, if ever, questioned his expenditures.

The Office Wife

Another important role was that of the *office wife*, a term I first heard from Aramony when I was hiring his personal staff. This was the role most often played by his administrative and/or professional assistant, depending on which one he wanted to travel with him. She was Aramony's constant companion wherever he went and was expected to be on call 24 hours a day. Aramony required this kind of continuing support day in and day out, much like most people need water or air. She was someone off whom he could bounce ideas, seek advice for his personal problems, and gain relaxation from the stress of the job.

These women were well paid for their work. They were always attractive females whom he considered to possess exceptionally perceptive and brilliant minds well beyond their years. Since Aramony related to these women in public as friends and companions, rather than as professionals, considerable speculation and rampant rumors about the true nature of their relationships became a favorite topic on the United Way grapevine. It also didn't help that at conferences, they sometimes sorted his laundry and occupied a room connected to his suite. Aramony seemed to relish this "macho" mystique and rarely sought to discourage the loose talk by changing his behavior.

It was this particular practice that created additional morale problems among his immediate staff who worked closest with him. I confronted one of these administrative assistants, whom I had been responsible for hiring, with the impression that this behavior was creating. I explained that the behavior was not directly relevant to what might actually be going on. My concern was with the morale and the problems of perception that were being created with other staff, volunteers, and United Way professionals who were concerned and embarrassed by what they observed. She became very emotional and told me never to talk that way to her again.

The Bagman

The third staff role I'll discuss is what I call the *bagman*. This individual handled Aramony's private finances and investments, as well as unpleasant jobs like discharging unwanted employees. Paid by United Way of America, this individual spent much of his or her time working on Aramony's personal matters. Aramony justified this position because it freed him of those burdens and allowed him to concentrate on activities related to the job. For two years, I went in to the office almost every Saturday morning myself to balance his checkbook and pay his personal bills. When I left his office, I had him sign a document which exempted me from any responsibility for checks I had signed on his behalf.

The Court Jester

Then there is the *court jester*. In medieval days, this person was known as the "King's Fool" and was considered by historians as an important supporting role to the king. (In some ways, Aramony saw this role as one he personally played in relationship to his own corporate volunteers.) This was an individual who could tell Aramony anything with impunity—argue with him, tell him his ideas are stupid, or call him pejorative names without any fear of retribution. Many times I heard such a person tell Aramony that he, Aramony, was full of shit and didn't know what he was talking about. No other person could talk to him that way but the "court jester." This person had top-level program responsibilities as well, but that was not his primary job. Indeed, it didn't matter whether or not the primary job was done well or not. His (the person was always male because of Aramony's additional need for "male bonding") responsibility was to keep Aramony company when he wanted to enjoy his favorite pastimes—dining, gambling, and going to the racetrack. This individual was also on 24-hour call.

The Golden Boy/Girl

Last, but not least, is the *golden boy/girl*. New top management staff would frequently be recruited from the outside. Each was heralded as being "the answer" to all kinds of management and program issues and problems. This new person would find him or herself overburdened with enormous responsibilities as soon as he or she walked in the door. Within a year, this person would be so overwhelmed that failures were inevitable. At that point, the person would be stripped of responsibility and "hung out to dry." If the individual did anything to err in any way, the slide of *golden boy/girl* would be greater and faster.

Kets de Vries has this to say about the phenomenon: " . . . just as inevitably, the president's infatuation with his latest recruit would soon exhaust itself and disappointment would set in."[2]

These personality styles, perhaps appearing of minor importance to the reader, were highly significant supporting roles acted out every day for the 23 years I was associated with Aramony. Without them, he could not operate effectively.

WHY DIDN'T ANYONE COMPLAIN?

If you're wondering why no one complained, you are not alone. Aramony seemed to hold everyone and everything in check.

No one complained because there were no valid avenues of appeal. Higher-level staff (either the legal counsel, personnel director, or executive vice president) were under Aramony's powerful influence and would do nothing that they thought would irritate him. All problems were referred to this staff. Board members were off limits, because they, too, would always defer to Aramony. There was no recourse but to like it, lump it, or leave it. Sometimes appeals could be made to one's immediate boss, but success through that avenue was usually fruitless.

Many individuals, such as "golden boys and girls," simply left when they realized that they were no longer in favored positions, a process which often took several years.

Allegations of sexual harassment were never brought to the fore because staff members who were allegedly harassed would never make formal complaints. In my capacity as his assistant for many years, only two women actually came to me with complaints of sexual harassment and abuse, although I had heard of many other instances. One woman insisted that I not say anything because she was afraid of losing her job. She told me that Aramony later apologized to her. Another woman was a very naive but attractive individual whom Aramony had transferred to his office staff from another division. It came to my attention that Aramony had allegedly seduced this young married woman after heavy drinking at a local restaurant the night before . . . on a convertible sofa in the sitting room next to his office. She was hysterical because she had also told her husband and father about the incident. She quit shortly thereafter. No formal complaint was levied, and under pressure from her family, she left on her own. I confronted Aramony about this incident later when we were alone and asked him how he could do such a thing. I told him that he might have destroyed her marriage. He simply shrugged.

Other staff members were much more forthright than I was about his behavior with women. One reportedly told Aramony that he could lose his job or go to jail. Temporarily, at least, these revelations would scare him. But it never lasted long and the behavior would continue. One senior executive reportedly lost his job when he confronted Aramony on issues related to perceptions concerning his behavior with women.

It was very clear to me that the incidents brought to my attention of alleged sexual harassment by Aramony were basically power trips exercised over much younger, insecure support personnel who believed him when he told them how brilliant and effective they were and how much they could "learn" by being associated with him. There were never any such charges or hearsay regarding women who were his professional peers.

Marty Payton, a management consultant who appeared on the "Today Show" on October 6, 1992, offered some guidelines that potential harassers might ponder before they act. One, don't do anything you wouldn't want replayed on the "Today Show," and, two, don't do anything a videotape of which you wouldn't want in the hands of your spouse's divorce lawyer, or to be described in a best-selling book.

"BUYING" PEOPLE: THE ROLE OF OUTSIDE CONSULTANTS

The use of outside consultants by United Way was particularly abused in my judgment. Of 16 questions put to one of my assistants by the investigating attorneys regarding activities of United Way International, nine dealt with the role of consultants. They felt that they had uncovered an area of abuse. One *very* part-time consultant on my payroll was paid a few thousand dollars per year less than I was. When I complained to Aramony that the conditions of his contract could be met with a few days of work, he responded that the consultant was a responsible individual and would be available for other assignments. Another consultant, related to one of Aramony's former aides, was put on the United Way International's payroll following a luncheon meeting without asking my advice as to whether he was necessary. A European consultant, whom Aramony had retained to supposedly protect our interests, struggled personally to come up with something to do. One well-placed consultant was asked to lobby to have Aramony awarded the Presidential Medal of Freedom, the country's highest civilian honor.

Aramony was president of United Way International and had every right to hire people over my objection or without seeking my advice. I should add that many of the consultants worked hard to the best of their abilities. However, this is not the point. There were serious opportunity costs associated with these decisions. That is, the funds spent on most consultants were imposed upon the budget. Those funds could have been used to carry out United Way International's mission better and more economically by employing people with more relevant skills, or redirected towards other areas, or not spent at all. Aramony firmly believed that he needed to hire people to obtain their advice, loyalty, prestige, or influence.

The area of consultants and consulting costs illustrates an important aspect of every staff member's relationship with Aramony. Staff people like me could say "no" some of the time, but not all of the time. He asked me on numerous occasions to hire someone who was the granddaughter of a famous president. Her name brought instant recognition. He wanted to say that she was on his payroll. I never did hire her because there was nothing she could contribute. She was always available to give free advice anyway because she was a good person. She had even provided me with her home phone number in case I ever needed to reach her on short notice.

WHY WE STAYED

What were the motivations for people working in such a situation over an extended period of time? Why did the staff put up with Aramony and his ways? I believe that there were a number of reasons why so many good people kept their mouths shut, took their lumps, and stayed on.

1. *The staff perceived that they were part of a "winning" team.* Aramony always had the complete support of the great majority of board members. Face it, this was the most powerful voluntary board in America. It *was* America! For the most part, they venerated him and his idiosyncrasies. "Well, no one's perfect, and look what he's doing for human services in America," sums up how most people felt about him. Aramony spent much of the time cultivating people he perceived to be important on an individual basis. In this way, he developed deep personal relationships, one on one, *mano a mano.*

In addition, despite occasional griping, Aramony was widely supported by the majority of United Way professionals. As a United Way of America staff person, you were perceived as a "winner" by just about everyone connected with the United Way.

2. *United Way of America staff members were in a position to do a great deal of good for society.* In my case, that good could be achieved at the international level as well. There are very few opportunities in the human service area outside of United Way of America for highly motivated people to be able to have as much influence in "doing good" in

the world. For me, in particular, this was a dominating theme as well as an excuse for tolerating the questionable behavior I experienced for so many years.

3. *The financial rewards and the perks were among the best in the human service field.* These benefits included an excellent fully vested pension plan paid by the company; a choice of first-class medical plans supported by the company; a generous expense account, providing you could show a business purpose for dinner meetings and entertainment; a relatively luxurious work setting with free parking; and, for those who lived in northern Virginia, few commuting hassles because of United Way of America's suburban Alexandria setting.

THE PSYCHOLOGICAL DANGERS OF WORKING FOR A CHARISMATIC LEADER

Schaef and Fassel point out in *The Addictive Organization* that workaholism is symptomatic of an addictive type of organization whose pattern is set by its leader. It is an addiction that can be extremely destructive to oneself and one's family. Yet, in American society, workaholism is often tolerated because it is so socially useful and supported by the ever-present Protestant work ethic.[3] Workaholism was clearly valued throughout the organization. Aramony fully expected his staff to be on call nights and weekends and to work constantly, at the expense of friends and family. Nothing was more important than loyalty to him and to the job. He loved the workaholics in the organization because they were so productive, *but* there is no evidence that he *respected* them. However, those who worked excessive hours *directly on his behalf* were often handsomely rewarded. For example, the communications staff who handled the crisis of the organization with the press and public (one of whom kept a sleeping bag in her office) were both promoted by Aramony. However, his personal staff, that is, those most closely associated with him, were expected to work only when he worked and play only when he played.

Some students of the subject believe that people follow charismatic leaders because they are fulfilling a pathological need. These individuals, it is reasoned, are trying to resolve a conflict between who they are and what they wish to become. This dynamic causes followers to develop strong emotional attractions to such leaders and to seek to comply with their wishes.

Recently, other students of the subject have also moved away from this more pathological interpretation. Social psychologists and organizational researchers have come to believe that subordinates of charismatic leaders work for them because of identification with their abilities, particularly the qualities of "strategic insight, unconventionality, dynamism, an ability to excite, and other traits so extraordinary that subordinates are strongly attracted to them." Some subordinates may even dream of becoming charismatic leaders themselves by acquiring some of these traits.

Organizational behaviorist Jay Conger cites numerous studies which show that followers of charismatic leaders are usually more highly committed and motivated and ". . . will exhibit willing obedience to the leader, high trust in the leader and attachment to him, a sense of empowerment, and a greater sense of group cohesion around shared beliefs as well as less internal group conflict."[4]

This emulation may not necessarily take the form of imitation of the leader's style, behavior, and mannerisms, but only the internalization of some key values. "They learn to trust him because of his self-confidence, his strong convictions in the organization's mission, his willingness to undertake personal risk, and his history of accomplishment." From this approval comes a sense of empowerment and self-confidence. The high-pressure atmosphere created by such leaders creates an even greater need to succeed since failure to deliver could mean the failure of the mission and a fall from grace.[5]

What occurred at United Way of America reflects a highly ambivalent love/hate type relationship. The trust that derives from working for an individual like Aramony is due to this enormous emotional and financial dependence and need for approval. Since Aramony's leadership style was often so essentially self-centered, controlling, and always unpredictable, he fostered a climate of uncertainty and stress. As a result, most staff members expressed profound ambivalence about their work at United Way of America. Despite it all, most staff stayed over the years, some were fired, and a few left voluntarily. But many were not happy.

NOT EVEN THE LOCAL UNITED WAY PROFESSIONALS WERE SPARED ARAMONY'S LEADERSHIP STYLE

Many hundreds of professional United Way staff members throughout the country wanted to be a part of the national organization. United Way professionals who joined the staff from the field considered it a promotion of which they were very proud. They were often the envy of peers. And they would find that when they came to United Way of America, enemies became friends, and strangers everywhere looked up to them because they were part of United Way of America.

Professionals affiliated with the United Way system came from a variety of disciplines. Only some were social workers (even though many of the professional founders of the national association were social workers). Some were practitioners of community organization, one of social work's subdisciplines. The major United Way training schools were Boston College, Ohio State, and the University of Pittsburgh.

Under Aramony, the focus changed from recruiting social workers to recruiting those with business backgrounds to the United Way. He believed the future of United Way depended upon its identification with business, and not social work. To put it more bluntly, its future lay with its identification with power, not "pussyfooting." Business leaders were society's leaders; social workers were not. A number of selected individuals, myself among them, participated in a specially designed master's of business administration course at the University of Miami while other professionals took a course for several days at the Harvard School of Business Administration. These courses were established by United Way of America in cooperation with the institutions involved. This latter course was particularly popular because of the prestige attached to Harvard.

There were very few Ivy League graduates in the United Way. Most of the practitioners were from a widely diverse pool of people; historically, there were few women and minorities. Aramony and his human resources staff went to great lengths to rectify this imbalance. Academic background was of no importance to Aramony whatsoever. One of his chief financial officers, who held that job for many years, never even graduated from college!

As part of the national staff, you could bask in the glory of Aramony. You were treated with respect in local communities as his personal representative. Aramony's great strength lay in his ability to handle his powerful constituency for over 20 years in ways that ensured the continued flow of dues, while at the same time preventing them from coalescing against him. With thousands of professional United Way staff in local communities and staff members spread across the country, there was always the possibility that groups of them would get together, withhold dues, and in this way seek to "dethrone" him. This never happened.

There were a number of coup attempts, but loyalists throughout the system informed him of these threats and worked with him to pre-empt any effective revolts. He did this by granting prestigious committee assignments to those whose help he needed or with whom he wanted to ingratiate himself.

His closest colleagues continued to be his peers who held the best assignments and who were placed in what were considered the best towns. Some served with him on the Board and its committees of Mutual of America, the pension insurer, where they were paid expenses and compensated for their time. Through this perk, some were able to increase their personal income by $20,000 a year or more. There was also a group of *young turks* (or YTs as they are sometimes called within United Way) who were tested in a variety of ways. Mainly, they had to "look good," be quick, articulate, and creative, and be slavishly devoted to implementing the continuing barrage of national program initiatives. Few YTs were willing to do this for long. A few years ago, a YT was "selected" to be trained as Aramony's replacement and was to join the national staff for on-site training. When he realized that Aramony simply wanted to mold him into his own image, he decided to stay in his own community. One YT, who headed a United Way in a Western state, was dapper and well-dressed and always made a decidedly good impression. He was the favored person for many months, until it was discovered that he had substantial problems with his staff and was charged by his successor with "overreporting," that is, reporting higher campaign results than had been achieved.

Another achieved YT status by copying Aramony's maverick style with new ideas and new initiatives. However, he, too, was unwilling to subordinate his own ideas to Aramony's personality.

Essentially, no one could win. No one was ever as capable as Aramony. It was always clear that Aramony wanted to control the selection of his replacement so that he could continue to control the organization essentially forever.

WHY THERE WAS NO WIDESPREAD DISAFFECTION

No group or subgroup ever mounted a serious or realistic attempt to undermine Aramony's authority. I believe this was due, in large measure, to the many positive contributions he was recognized as having made to the United Way movement. He had believed in the movement to which they belonged, he had taken the risks which they never would have taken, and for a long time "it worked." He had recruited a top-level Board of Governors from leading corporations and labor unions of America. It served as a model for their own United Ways from Santa Clara, California to Portland, Maine. Their own Boards were upgraded with local versions of the national corporate board.

Mainly, he affected the pocketbook. Top boards support top salaries. "A cardinal rule," Aramony once told me, "is that you never put anyone on your Board who makes less than you do. The more your Board members make, the easier it will be for you to be well compensated."

Aramony firmly believed that the voluntary sector, in general, and the United Way, in particular, provided indispensable contributions to the betterment of American society and that its professionals should be compensated to reflect the true worth of that contribution. United Way was fundamentally a product of the business community, and it is these values, he believed, that would result in community acceptance and hence support. Chief professional officers in the movement benefitted enormously from his never-ending battle for high salaries and perks, of which his own served as the best example. Clearly, those who serve the public good deserve to be paid well. They take care of many problems most members of society would rather not face. These were Aramony's beliefs.

Aramony would not be identified with a movement of self-flagellating, self-pitying, and nonpragmatic, idealistic martyrs who found empathy and common cause with those they served. Linda Grant correctly wrote in the *Los Angeles Times Magazine* that "Aramony hated the image of poverty that social workers project, working in shabby offices surrounded by borrowed furniture."[6] He was clearly not of the Jane Addams school, whose devoted followers went to live among the poor. It was the elite, he would say, particularly those who served on the Board of United Way of America, who not only knew what was best for the country, but had the ability to do something about it through the United Way.

HOW ARAMONY WORKED WITH THE BOARD OF GOVERNORS

Although conventional wisdom would attribute great qualities of leadership to the corporate chieftains who served on the Board of Governors of United Way of America, when it came to exercising their responsibility, they were for the most part followers. Although many members of the Board worked exceedingly hard to carry out the pro-grams as designed and initiated by Aramony, they were drastically remiss in addressing operational questions.

In the earlier years, John "Jack" W. Hanley, then chairman of the Monsanto Company and A.W. "Tom" Clausen, the president of Bank-america, headed long-range planning efforts. James E. Burke, chairman of Johnson & Johnson, was also a strong supporter of the national as-sociation and had participated on several key Board committees. Ex-citing leaders like Hanley, a warm and generous individual as well as one of America's great salesmen, provided outstanding leadership in "selling" long-range planning and personnel development to the United Way movement in the 1970s. His easygoing, friendly protegé at the Monsanto Company, Earle Harbison, also a member of the Board after Jack Hanley retired, raised many substantial questions about the program areas he was asked to lead. Aramony often expressed consid-erable concern about Harbison's continued questioning but still gave him high-profile assignments because of his considerable ability.

James D. Robinson III, chairman of American Express, devoted both time and money to a wide variety of program areas. Although initially negative about United Way, he became a devoted supporter of its programs and services and has been a powerful player on the Board ever since his election to it in 1980. John J. Phelan, Jr., former chairman of the New York Stock Exchange, virtually singlehandedly researched and developed United Way of America's Donor Choice pol-icy paper after visiting numerous local communities.

Top corporate leaders always treated the staff at United Way of America with the utmost respect. These were individuals who had "ar-rived" and had few axes to grind. I recall receiving a personal letter from the late John D. de Butts, chairman of AT&T, who wrote to me in response to a request I had made of him. I remember a note from Jack Hanley telling me that he was going to deal with me, not Aramony, because I was going to be doing all the work anyway! And Earle Har-bison and I still share laughs over the time his wife "disappeared" beneath the head table dais at which she was sitting when it slowly began to separate at a major conference event. Frank Sullivan, former head of Mutual Benefit Life, with whom I had worked closely on a "personalization" project, was one of the most down-to-earth, warmest people I had ever met. These are a few of my memories of people at the top. Aramony may have a different view of those individuals.

Aramony's success was due in large measure to his ability to con-trol the environment and the circumstances in which he might find himself with his volunteer leadership. Nothing was left to chance. Although he understood the need to set priorities, he involved himself in some of the most excruciating detail in such areas as furniture arrangements in his and in other offices. He was a master at not only setting the stage for a performance, but making sure everyone understood their respective roles. Yet, it was his attention to detail that often produced amazing successes. Again, it demonstrated his need to control outcomes as much as was humanly possible.

An example of setting the stage had to do with the all-important area of impressions, especially regarding something most of us would never consider—seating arrangements. Empty seats were anathema to him. If a board member were to leave a meeting early, he would signal one of the many staff members sitting in the back to take that person's seat so the table always looked full. Staff who arranged meetings of any kind (except Board meetings where attendance was tracked up until the last minute) were required to always "underseat," that is, provide fewer chairs than the number of people attending. His intent was to create the impression that there was such a high level of interest in the meeting that more people came than were "expected." Extra chairs were always kept ready to pull out as soon as these "additional" people walked in. This kind of activity may seem trivial, but more staff were hauled on the carpet for arranging a meeting with empty chairs than anything else I can think of.

His preparation was greatest when top volunteers were involved, especially for Board meetings. He was exceedingly good at reading the drift of meetings with these volunteers and knew when to back off, move ahead, or just outright level with a volunteer if he disagreed. Debriefings followed important meetings, and responsibilities were laid out for staff follow-up. But most of the volunteers were followers who raised few questions concerning *how* United Way of America did its business. After all, Aramony was the expert on social welfare, the best in the nation, or so he and they (the Board members) believed, and United Way of America was very fortunate to have him as its chief executive. Thus, they not only considered him the expert, but impugned to him all of the noble virtues of those who spend their lives serving others. Complaints to the Board by the staff, if they ever heard them, were ignored. After all, staff in all bureaucracies, corporate or others, complain about working conditions and grumble about authority. Aramony was no different than they were in this respect—a leader with all the problems of any big *corporate* organization.

He created an environment in which these leaders found great comfort. The February 25, 1992 issue of *The Chronicle of Philanthropy* quoted me as saying that I supported Aramony's lifestyle because corporate America was comfortable with it. What I said was that I never heard any volunteer complain about the relatively luxurious surroundings of United Way of America. Although other human service leaders might have had some qualms about building a headquarters as impressive as the national office building, Aramony had no such problem. He believed in the deepest recesses of his being that the work accomplished by the United Way was critically important to American society and deserved a symbol which would demonstrate respect, if not awe.

THE COMMUNITY, THE NATION, AND THE WORLD HAD BECOME ARAMONY'S OYSTERS

Thus, Aramony was able to build a stage which allowed him to perform before the country and the world. He was able to do this because of the commanding and decisive influence of United Way of America over the local United Way professionals in 2,200 communities, and, most importantly, over the Board of Governors. For the latter, he was their conscience, their four-star general in the efforts of corporate America to show the nation that it was an ardent supporter of the war against the ills of family disintegration, drug abuse, latchkey kids, and youth crime. Together with the unions, the United Way was admirably positioned as the handmaiden of America's power structure to solve national and community problems through voluntary action.

It was this great vision that he relished. Aramony felt that he was so well suited to sell it to corporate and union America that he had no competition. He was quicker, brighter, and sharper than most of the people with whom he dealt including his own volunteers. Indeed, in my long experience with him, I rarely saw him "one upped" by anyone.

He was very uneasy with cause-related and grass-roots organizations which steadily chipped away at United Way's virtual monopoly of community-wide fund-raising process. However, this attitude did nothing more than reflect most corporate thinking as well. Corporate leaders were uncomfortable with anything that rocked the status quo. The corporate goal of increased profits depended on community stability. Thus, when minorities, including women, demanded equal employment opportunities, or lawyers advocated the rights of the poor and disenfranchised, or mothers with children demanded day care at their place of work, the corporate community became uncomfortable.

Robert Bothwell, the long-haired (until recently) president of the National Committee for Responsive Philanthropy, was the most articulate spokesperson for this diverse constituency of organizations not generally supported by the United Way. One of the key senior vice presidents at United Way of America said that Bothwell's long hair was an asset to United Way because of the negative image it created in the corporate mind. He hoped that he would never cut it. Aramony recognized the value of Bothwell as a focal point around which he could galvanize support. That is, Aramony could point to Bothwell's activities as a warning that there were individuals and groups who wanted to erode United Way's monopoly over workplace solicitation and distribute funds for charities outside the United Way allocations process. In this way, he could use Bothwell as leverage to gain acceptance of his various programs that he felt were important for United Way organizations to adopt. Aramony once told Bothwell, when he met him by chance on an airplane, "Bob, you've contributed more to helping me get long-range planning programs in local communities than anyone I know!" To that, Bothwell reportedly replied, "That's great, Bill. Why then don't you give me your Alexis de Tocqueville Society Award?"

Aramony believed that his role was clear—to use his skill to bring leaders together to help solve the problems of people. He believed that America could be saved, and with himself as *de facto* leader with the help of corporate America and organized labor. Power was the "name of the game." As we have seen, he felt deeply that society and communities could be healed when the business and political leadership at the national and local levels could meet and discuss problems through the mediating efforts of the United Way. This point of view, a barely disguised elitism, was part of his basic ideology. Those in power, and those who had achieved it in the economic and political arena (with himself as the great enabler), were uniquely qualified to help solve the ills of society.

He believed that the great majority of professionals in human services did not have the vision to even begin to think in those terms. There were very few exceptions, with Frances Hesselbein, former national executive director of the Girl Scouts of the United States of America, and Lane Adams, former executive vice president of the American Cancer Society, being among his notable exceptions. He always recognized that social agencies, for the most part, did "good work." But, he had little patience with the problems faced by charities and for their generally depressed outlook on community problems and attitudes of hopelessness. Aramony's message was always emotional and upbeat, looking ahead and never behind. And when it came to solving the major problems facing the nation, the concerns and parochial interests of charities had a limited role because, according to him, they did not understand the "big picture" or have the influence to do anything about it, even if they did understand it.

With his business and labor constituency behind him and an operating style which had brought him great success, Aramony was equipped and able to bring the movement into the national spotlight. The corporate leaders of America had made access possible, and a quick perusal of the Board of Governors was usually enough to ensure credibility, especially in recent years when the organization was led by Jim Robinson of American Express and John Akers of IBM, at their peak probably the most respected business leaders in America.

Aramony was justifiably proud of his relationships with top political figures as well, and his office was filled with mementos of himself together with the past few Presidents and First Ladies. His enormous respect for power was based on this appreciation of the tremendous effort it took to achieve a measure of success and greatness in life, his own humble beginnings serving as an example. Name-dropping was a habit he had acquired, particularly if the individual said something positive about the United Way that he could relate to the impressionable. He once remarked very proudly following a meeting with John Gardner, founder of Common Cause and chairman of the Urban Coalition, some years ago that Gardner had told him, "You've done for social welfare what I did for the political process."

Contacts had always occurred with the federal government (it was inevitable with a movement as large as the United Way) since Calvin Coolidge became the first President to kick off a United Way campaign at the national level. With the Reagan administration, Aramony found a high level of acceptance. The President had participated in previous United Way campaigns as a private citizen and as governor of California. Nancy Reagan had served as National Chairman of the Women's Committee from 1969 to 1971 for what was then called the United Community Campaigns of America. She also inaugurated the production studio at the new office building. Aramony was a frequent visitor to the White House and, in recent years, was beginning to develop a potentially productive relationship with Louis Sullivan, then Secretary of the Department of Health and Human Services.

Aramony was intensely well liked and well respected by the power structure whom he know how to please through his quick intellect, talent at flattery, and ability to articulate "win/win" situations. When dealing with outside constituencies, Aramony was able to parlay two important attributes of United Way—the possibility of financial resources, at least on a joint basis, and the tremendous network which extended, at least in theory, to over 2,200 communities across the nation. The assumption of others was that United Way could *demand* implementation at the local level. Aramony did little to dispel this notion. Since all local United Ways were autonomous, any new program had to be aggressively sold to local leaders. In later years, local United Ways had become so overwhelmed with United Way of America (that is, Aramony's) initiatives that it was difficult to deliver on those commitments.

When Fred Ryan, President Reagan's executive director of the Office of Private Sector Initiatives, moved into the international arena, Aramony saw another opportunity to position himself on the world stage. An offer by Aramony for United Way International to manage and run this initiative for the White House was never fully accepted. However, both Aramony and/or I participated in the private sector conferences held in England, France, and Italy. President Reagan's efforts to export voluntarism through public/private collaboration as occurred in the United States, although somewhat superficial in its penetration, was generally well received overseas.

Aramony, as representative of the United Way, was seen by the voluntary sector power brokers in Europe as a leading representative of charity in the United States, on par with foundation directors. The common experience of charities overseas was that each one raised its own funds through aggressive solicitation or was heavily endowed like foundations. United Way, a self-liquidating charity (that is, all the money raised is distributed) based on concepts of "community" and public/private efforts to advance the public good, was not well understood overseas. However, Aramony tended to see most foreign cultures through American glasses. He is a true believer in all that America stands for.

One of the most successful ventures in the international area was the conferencing function. Aramony held great stock in conferences which provided a forum at which he could present his ideas to a large and often new group of people. He loved to attend them; rarely for the content, but for the exposure it afforded him. These forums also presented opportunities to make contacts. He also believed, and probably correctly, that the main purpose of these conferences, especially the elaborate ones sponsored by United Way International, was to bring people together in order to create a shared experience and sense of mission. Thus, general sessions were expected to be elaborate affairs consisting of multimedia productions, sound and light shows, choruses, elaborate signage, and the like.

Rarely did he attend the working sessions at any conference, preferring to shop, dine, gamble, and play the horses if they were available. Indeed, it often took considerable effort to track him down to make sure that he showed up for major events at which he was scheduled. At a conference in Budapest a few years ago, he had been asked to chair the last session of the day with a panel of three presenters. He was aware that a shop at which he wanted to purchase some rugs would be closed by the time the session was expected to conclude. Before the last presenter could speak, he announced, "Helmut, you don't have anything to add, do you? We're all tired. It's been a great conference. Let's go home. Thank you all for coming." Vintage Aramony!

Aramony spent all the time it took to cultivate key people he needed on his side. He did this largely through informal conversations over lunch or dinner. Although he had the appearance of being somewhat loose and informal in style, in fact he was quite compulsive and left little, if anything, in his work or life to chance. He understood that everyone likes to go "first class." Money was no obstacle in order to create a proper, comfortable environment. It invariably worked, and until the spring of 1992, it worked well for both the United Way and for him, personally.

REFERENCES

1. *Washingtonian* (December 1992), p. 58.
2. See Kets de Vries, "The Darker Side of Entrepreneurship," p. 165, for a discussion of this syndrome.
3. Anne Wilson Shaef and Diane Fassel, *The Addictive Organization: Why We Overwork, Cover Up, Pick Up the Pieces, Please the Boss & Perpetuate Sick Organizations* (San Francisco: Harper, 1990), pp. 126–127.
4. Jay A. Conger, *The Charismatic Leader—Behind the Mystique of Exceptional Leadership* (San Francisco: Jossey-Bass, 1991), pp. 127–128.
5. See Conger, pp. 126–134, for a general discussion of this concept.
6. Linda Grant, in "Acts of Charity," *Los Angeles Times Magazine* (September 13, 1992).

CHAPTER 5

The Fallout

"Was John Akers asleep at the switch?"

IBM employee in the Northwest

O ne day a few years ago, Bill Aramony rushed up the spiral staircase which hung suspended from the second floor in the atrium of the national office building. Aramony himself had suggested this architectural design. He liked open spaces and big vistas. The stairs poured off the second floor like a waterfall. As it cascaded downward, the steps twisted slightly as they became larger and larger, flowing out on the bottom floor to face the front door and welcome people in. The meeting of the Board of Governors had just finished. His face was lit up with excitement, his eyes popping.

"I did it! I did it! I nailed him," he explained to those who happened to be standing around, repeatedly pounding his right fist hard into his left hand.

He was referring to John Akers, the chairman of IBM, whom he had just recruited to help the national association design a marketing program. Akers was quite possibly the top corporate leader in America. To have recruited him for the United Way in the first place had been a major coup. He hoped to use the renowned marketing expertise of this great company to revitalize the United Way movement. Aramony looked, of course, beyond that role for this then well-regarded corporate leader. He looked forward to the day in 1990 when Akers would be persuaded to become the chairman of the nation's largest voluntary organization. Later, regrettably, Akers would preside over the tragic events of 1992 and within a year after that, find himself no longer head of IBM. The executive committee and/or the board of United Way of America had always approved Aramony's salary, expenses, and virtually everything else he had done. They had also approved the establishment of the spinoffs, with the exception of Voluntary Initiatives/America. It became an unfortunate situation for Akers that the events of the spring of 1992 happened on his watch. But it could have happened on anyone's watch.

The reaction to the press reports was widespread and affected all of the constituences associated with United Way of America. Not only did all of the major networks pick up on the story, but newspapers, editorial writers, and cartoonists had a field day highlighting the abuses. One of the most talked-about cartoons was by Bob Rogers of the *Pittsburgh Press*. It showed a hand reaching out from a stretch limousine asking an apparently destitute citizen, "Pardon me . . . Care to give to the United Way?" These and other graphic images aggravated the perceptions of abuse of charitable dollars by United Way of America's president and, by association, local United Way organizations and the charities they served as well.

DAMAGE CONTROL BECAME TOP PRIORITY

"There is no odor so bad as that which arises from goodness tainted," said Henry David Thoreau, America's great loner, over a century ago.[1] The fallout from the events of the spring of 1992 were dramatic. John Akers and his staff, including Kenneth W. Dam, the interim president, immediately began the process of damage control. The first step was to continue the ongoing investigation. The second step was to take any measures which would regain immediate credibility. To achieve the latter, Dam immediately cut back on all perquisites. The two company cars used by senior staff, including Aramony's, were sold, and special parking places for select staff were eliminated (Aramony had two reserved places, one outside the building and one in the garage); first-class travel, as well as travel on the Concorde (euphemistically called "supersonic craft!"), was forbidden; expense accounts were brought under control by and entertainment expenses subjecting travel to increased review procedures; and the use of hired cars and limousines was discontinued. Most of these changes were announced at the Volunteer Leaders Conference in March of 1992.

Unfortunately, the impression given, I presume inadvertently, was that these so-called "abuses" were the general practice at United Way of America and that Aramony's perks were available to other staff as well. All of the abuses listed in the newspaper, with rare exceptions, were enjoyed *only* by Aramony. At least one of the national staff was reduced to tears upon hearing the reports because she thought her colleagues in the field would think she had also abused their trust. It was also reported that Coopers & Lybrand, a major accounting firm, was retained to review all records to determine what amounts, if any, were owed by Aramony to United Way of America. One of the very first steps taken by United Way of America's interim president was to cut out all nonessential consultant services and contracts, including support for United Way International.

The major problem facing the national association was a financial one due to the cutoff in dues by local United Way organizations. Burgeoning legal and accounting fees required Board members to pitch in and establish a special fund to cover these costs. One way he hoped to alleviate the financial problem was by reducing staff. Dam offered an incentive package of three additional months for anyone who resigned prior to June 16. By August, the staff had been reduced by a third, from 275 to 185.[2] Some staff felt that they had to resign because the organization was going bankrupt, and they had better get out while they could with the best possible deal.

For five months, Dam traveled extensively throughout the country, especially to the larger United Ways, to listen to their concerns. An estimated 6,000 volunteers and professionals attended these sessions, where the overriding sentiment was a demand that the national office be more responsive to the dues-paying locals. Early on decisions were made to include local volunteers on the national United Way of America board to ensure that local and regional interests would be addressed in future decision-making meetings.

Virtually everything Aramony practiced, believed in, and stood for for 22 years was revised, overturned, and eliminated in five short months. Was the baby thrown out with the bathwater? It's too early to tell, but the focus of concern had clearly shifted from the center to the periphery. Local United Ways now exert more control over matters of policy than the national organization. The Board of Governors still retains its top corporate leaders, none of whom resigned, but also created 15 spots for local volunteers. Wherever possible, Aramony's special programs were brought under the control of the national association. Their fate would be considered in due time.

UNITED WAY AFFILIATES ACROSS THE COUNTRY
MOBILIZED TO LIMIT THE DAMAGE

The reaction from local United Ways was far from uniform. Many expressed pent-up frustrations by attacking Aramony. Suddenly, the emperor they had accepted and idolized for so many years had no clothes. Many local United Way members responded immediately by distancing themselves from the national association. Some affiliates, like Milwaukee, Wisconsin, disaffiliated from the national association. Local board members and staff called the press and sent out press releases highlighting their differences from the national office. Time and again, they explained that money collected locally was spent locally, that the national office was supported by only one percent of the local funds raised, *but* that payment to the national association was temporarily being withheld pending a resolution of the reported allegations.

In addition, they reassured the public that no such abuses occurred among the United Way members in their community *and* that controls would be instituted to make sure that there was no opportunity for abuses to occur in the future. Salaries, membership fees to local business clubs, and company cars would all be reviewed to make sure that they were brought into line with public expectations. If the crisis, they reasoned, could be isolated to the national organization and to the excesses of one person and his close associates, then the impact on local communities would be reduced.

Aramony, of course, was blamed for everything. He had to be the scapegoat (as Ted Koppel had so eloquently put it), sacrificed if the national organization as an institution was to survive. It was reasoned that, although Aramony had abused his power, the system itself was above suspicion. It had served the people of America well and would do so in the future. The fundamental concern of most United Way members was to demonstrate that the local organization was completely different and independent from the national association and that such abuses did not occur in their community. This was often difficult to do because, in many cases, local salaries were relatively high as compared to salaries paid to local officials. (Often, the local United Way executive was paid more than the mayor or the local university president. In the larger cities, cars or car allowances and club memberships were common.)

Reporters were asking a lot of questions they had never posed before. Now, the entire community would know about the high salaries, the perks, and the problems. A newscast in Ohio, for example, juxtaposed the stately home of the chief professional officer with scenes from a homeless shelter. It was open season on any United Way official. The media had become a battleground for both attacking and defending the United Way.

The Washington, D.C. United Way placed a local advertisement making the point that it may use the same logo as the national association, but that it was a very different organization. Cleveland distributed printed flyers making the same point. United Way of America was in effect a trade association, while their local United Way affiliate raised funds to meet local needs.

Most social welfare organizations which depend upon public donations for their livelihood realize how fragile the public trust can be. The slightest incident, whether true or not, can profoundly affect giving. Although it may be possible to foresee the consequences of reduced giving because of a poor economy, losses due to a breach of confidence by the public in charities is much harder to foresee, or plan for.

Since the time of the Great Depression, United Way organizations have always known how to make a strong case to get people to give despite the hard times. However, this situation was different. It struck at the basic core of what the United Way was about—safe stewardship of the charitable contribution to be used to meet the most important human needs of the community.

PROTECTING THE "IMAGE" MEANT EVERYTHING

Overnight, the stewardship, in the guise of the president of United Way of America no less, was seen in the worst possible light. Instead of children playing ball at a YMCA, or senior citizens being fed at the neighborhood center, or drug addicts receiving counseling at the halfway house, what they saw instead was the leader of the organization flying the Concorde, riding in limousines, and buying apartments with hard-earned charitable dollars. No one remembered the pictures of the happy kids, satisfied seniors, or reformed drug addicts. No one cared that for over two decades America's favorite football players, many selected because they or their families had personally benefited from United Way services, had sincerely touted the wonderful job the United Way and its associated charities had done to help people in need. *No one* wanted their contributions to be used in such a way.

The success of local United Way organizations are measured to the second decimal place, that is, in terms of dollars and cents. Thus, the possible loss of funds because of the crisis could be devastating. Professional United Way executives could lose their jobs; so could the heads of charities.

My cousin Mollie is an active volunteer in a small United Way in Pennsylvania. One of its attention-grabbing activities is the use of a large stuffed teddy bear as their chairman (they admit having difficulty getting a real person to take on the job). This bear comes to all events. After the scandal broke, one of the volunteers innocently used a limousine from his company to transport the bear to a solicitation meeting. Before an explanation could be made, people asked if their money was going to hire limousines!

Aramony's lifestyle was well known to anyone even remotely associated with him. This group included many local United Way professionals in communities across the country. It was something most of his associates accepted because it improved their own standard of living, even though many of them recognized that much of his behavior would not be tolerated if it were ever made public. Most United Way professionals, in fact, credit Aramony with elevating their status by identifying the United Way organization with business rather than with social work.

PERKS WERE THE FIRST TO GO

The first level of casualties in this war were the perks that had been accrued by local United Way chief professional officers. They wanted to make certain that they did not fall into any "bad" categories indicated by the press. First to go, for example, were the company apartments, club memberships, and frequently the company cars. These seemed to be initial items of concern by the local press and Board members.

SALARIES BECAME PUBLIC KNOWLEDGE

Salaries were carefully reviewed to make certain that they were in line with local norms. But I know of no salaries which were reduced even if they were considered to be out of line. Betty Beane, the president of Tri-State, the United Way which covers parts of New York, New Jersey, and Connecticut, asked her Board to review her salary and benefits totaling $263,000. Ralph A. Dickerson, Jr., the president of the United Way of New York City, was forced to give up his United Way–supported in-town apartment.[3] Not only had the press climbed all over

Aramony's back, but it was hounding the locals as well. All too many local United Way chief professional officers assumed a "holier than thou" attitude as though the excesses were a complete surprise.

THE LOCALS WERE PUT ON THE DEFENSIVE

The impact on the local United Ways was immediate. Some communities established ad hoc response teams of staff and volunteers, often using an emergency phone number to handle calls from the public. Virtually all local United Ways developed information and materials for not only the press, but their corporate and labor constituencies and the general public.

Many local United Way professional officers came under fire for many of the same reasons that affected Aramony, especially in the areas of salaries and perks. Many perks, such as club memberships, were taken away. Due to overwhelming public pressure, several hundred United Ways eventually withdrew their dues from the national association. I conducted a short written survey among over fifty of my friends and acquaintances in the field regarding the impact of the crisis and what their communities had done about it. About half responded. Typical of the reaction to the drowning flood of negative news accounts about the United Way of America were the steps taken by John Rush, president and chief executive officer of the United Way of the Ozarks:

1. Within 24 hours, the Board held a special meeting;
2. Dues were cut off immediately and a news release issued;
3. Key constituencies were contacted; and
4. Board representatives attended the Volunteer Leaders Conference with the specific purpose of determining the scope of the crisis at United Way of America.

Before the crisis, it was a badge of honor to local United Way professionals to be part of such a great organization. Now any involvement with United Way of America became a mark of shame. The organization to which they had been proud to belong was under constant fire. In reality, social welfare professionals in any human service area suddenly became accessories after the fact, not just local United Way professionals. They, too, suffered the consequences of this tragic event. For many local United Way chief professional officers, it was the first time they had ever been put on the defensive by the community they served.

THE VIEW FROM UNITED WAY OF AMERICA

Although the Board had given Aramony a resounding vote of confidence on February 3, with the continued public exposure, new measures had to be taken. On March 2, John Akers, chairman of the Board, informed the investigative team, who thought that they had completed their work, that they had only just begun. He wanted a thorough investigation that would leave no stone unturned in getting at the truth. The "people" had spoken and Akers wanted to get to the bottom of the matter but at the same time protect his own reputation and that of the Board he headed. He possibly rationalized that if blame could be placed on Aramony, it would mitigate the responsibility of his board members. The reactions of these Board members could be characterized as follows:

1. They were not unaware that any of these abuses were happening.
2. They believed that Aramony had known what he was doing when they had approved the measures he had proposed and that therefore it was okay.
3. They wanted to get to the bottom of things.

One Board member was heard to say, "We thought we had a Babe Ruth; who we really had was a Pete Rose."

DAM STEPS IN TO MAINTAIN ORDER

It was clear that Akers wanted a complete accounting and that he wanted to make it public regardless of what the investigation found or where the chips might fall. The lawyers and investigators proceeded accordingly, unearthing things that probably were never intended for public viewing. As Kenneth Dam told me, "If everything gets exposed now, then anything else that might leak out later would be anticlimatic." He believed that it was better to "let it all hang out" at once, rather than let it dribble out slowly. It was only in this way, he reasoned, that United Ways could get these events behind them and move on.

Dam stated to me and others that the problem was not so much the failure of the Board to act, but its structure or lack of it. It was apparent that he saw this as a failing of Aramony and not the Board's failure to create the proper structures. There were virtually no committees dealing with internal controls such as finance (even though there was an audit committee headed by Board member Larry Horner), personnel practices, and ethics.

Dam saw the clear need to restore credibility and to supervise the now continuing investigation. At least one leader in the voluntary sector told me that even though Dam was a very credible individual, his appointment was widely seen as a "whitewash." Dam, an IBM employee, would be expected to protect Akers and the Board. If this would be the case, then there would be no accounting to the public of the Board's responsibility. But this leader believed that half of the blame for what happened should be placed with the Board. (Others I interviewed mentioned to me that two-thirds of the blame rests at the Board level.)

Jonathan Powers, a retired IBM executive, became the chief financial officer in March 1992, filling a critical position in an area of the organization that needed to reestablish credibility. Powers was familiar with the United Way since he had been on loan to board member John Phelan, who had conducted the Donor Choice study. Powers played an important role in bridging misunderstandings between United Way and IBM personnel because he was familiar with and respected by both cultures.

Concerned about the deteriorating dues situation, United Way of America was forced to borrow money, as well as seek additional funds to cover the mounting legal and accounting bills. As part of this effort to restore credibility and recoup the dues, Dam spent considerable time explaining to the press and public what United Way of America was doing to investigate the issues which had arisen. Although about 20 percent of the United Way members continued to hold out dues payments, by year end, Dam was able to bring the financial situation under control. It was said that IBM was pressuring local United Ways to pay their dues in communities where their local operations contributed funds.

As soon as it was known that there would be negative press on United Way of America in general and Aramony in particular, United Way of America's communications staff moved into high gear. Well before the news articles appeared, United Ways were being kept informed. Aramony, until he left permanently on February 28, dealt with the communications staff directly, bypassing the senior vice president who was in charge of communications.

The Communications Department Digs In for the Media Barrage

On February 7, Sunshine Overcamp, senior vice president in charge of corporate communications, and Tony deCristofaro, vice president, sent out a list of questions and answers asked by Charles E. Shepard, *The Washington Post* reporter. The questions and answers dealt with the structure of United Way of America and its relationship to local United Ways, the services provided by the national association, and Aramony's accomplishments as its leader, etc. It mentioned that when the allegations first surfaced in mid-December, the Board and Executive Committee, acting at Aramony's request, undertook an independent investigation. It indicated that Aramony was in no way involved in directing the investigation. After reviewing the information which had been provided up to that point in the investigation, the Executive Committee gave Aramony a "resounding vote of confidence."[4]

On February 10, a memo was sent out dealing exclusively with the Jack Anderson article of February 12. It again described the new structure of United Way of America (268 national staff members, down from 300; a 2.9 percent decrease in the national budget to $28.4 million in 1992; and that dues were at 82 percent of the budget).

In regard to the spinoffs, the information stated that their major purpose was to reduce costs to social agencies. In discussing consulting work, it stated that any staff member is prohibited from receiving outside compensation without written approval from the president. It also said that Charities Funds Transfer did not convey funds to United Way of America as alleged. The memo stated that the Board of Governors set the compensation for the president and salary ranges for staff. The relationship of the NFL to United Way of America was described and Aramony's attendance at the Superbowl game justified as a legitimate cost of doing business.[5]

On February 13, following the Anderson article and just a few days before the first Shepard article, the communications staff alerted the field that all communications should be sent to them by telefax and, if that was not available, by first-class mail. Overcamp provided all staff members with her own and her assistant's home phone numbers. This information also said that the *Regardies* magazine article would be on the stands on February 21. To add to the woes, it said that a demonstration may occur in the next few days at United Way of America by the Queer Nation protesting the stand by the Boy Scouts of America, a charity supported by most United Ways, for not admitting homosexuals as scout leaders.[6]

The first Shepard article (February 16) was faxed to all United Ways, accompanied by six and a half pages of suggested responses to the press. It reiterated many of the items already discussed, but concentrated more on the perks and spinoffs as follows:

Partnership Umbrella: Its $900,000 in initial funding came from a "marketing royalty payment" and was *not* from contributors' money. The discount program was made available to 40,000 charities.

Sales Service/America: After a Board-authorized study concluded that United Way of America would no longer be a provider of sales/catalog items, an inventory of products and payments due were valued at $2 million. These were "sold" to Sales Service/America in exchange for a secured loan. It is repaying the loan at market rates and the first year's principal had been paid in advance. In 1991, the principal and interest payments paid to United Way of America were $600,000.

Professional Travel Systems Loan Payment: This company, which provided discounted travel services to nonprofits, closed in 1988. Partnership Umbrella absorbed its travel functions, including the repayment of a loan of $148,962.

The New York Apartment: In a meeting in which Aramony abstained from the discussion, Partnership Umbrella decided to purchase an apartment for him in New York for Partnership Umbrella and United Way of America business, thus saving "thousands of dollars in lodging costs annually."

The employment of Thomas J. Merlo, the chief financial officer, was also discussed. His differential in pay, the memo said, was due to additional responsibilities, such as overseeing the building services function and the management information system. His housing and commuting allowances were in lieu of relocation expenses. It concluded that his work resulted in substantial cost savings to United Way of America. Merlo was handsomely rewarded with an annuity worth $427,000 which had been purchased for him by United Way of America. As of this writing, the U.S. District Council had decided in a suit brought by Merlo not to grant it to him.

The point was also made that Partnership Umbrella had saved charities $7 million of the retail prices of products and services purchased. Also, it stated that Aramony received no compensation from any of the spinoffs and that he used a car service in New York and other cities and paid for these services by the hour.[7]

On Monday, February 24, with the publication of the second and more devastating of the articles by Charles E. Shepard, considerable additional information was sent to local United Way organizations, along with the following statement to *The Post*.

> United Way of America wants to be open and forthright with *The Washington Post* and the public.
>
> We have reviewed your request for financial information concerning Partnership Umbrella and Sales Service/America. As we have previously informed you, we believe it is inappropriate for those companies to disclose proprietary information to you. They are tax-paying, independent and proprietary businesses.
>
> However, we recognize your concerns and those of our constituencies about that position, and *a solution to the problem of disclosure of proprietary information in a competitive marketplace is being actively sought.*

Suggested responses to the press were also included. In addition to those already stated, it said that the apartment in Miami was bought with Voluntary Initiative America funds, a nonprofit spinoff, to be used as an office for United Way International for its Latin American program. The press release also described a personnel program to benefit charities which would be run by Anita Terranova under Partnership Umbrella.

In addition, it included a full description of the Mutual of America grant which established the "William Aramony Initiatives in Voluntarism" fund previously discussed, as well as the establishment of Voluntary Initiatives/America, formed as a nonprofit organization in 1990 in Florida. In 1991 and 1992, Voluntary Initiatives/America received grants of $202,883 and gave away or committed to give away $131,100.

The release also included a paper called "The Nonprofit Enterprise" by Russy Sumariwalla, United Way of America consultant. It stated that the economic conditions, as well as government cutbacks, had created severe financial problems for nonprofits. Other methods were required to raise necessary funds, such as profit-making subsidiaries.

This situation resulted in the search for alternative sources of income, an increasingly important survival activity for many charities. Sumariwalla wrote:

> Setting up appropriate autonomous corporations (for-profit or nonprofit) provides flexibility and focus otherwise unachievable within a

large, multi-division, multi-function, and complex organization. The single focus allows the entity's management to *concentrate* on one thing, be more innovative, make quick decisions as opportunities arise and in short, use the entrepreneurial spirit to get the job done with dispatch and at a lower cost. This approach has allowed United Way of America to focus on direct services to members, remain unbloated, and provide leadership to the sector on major issues confronting it and society.[8]

Additionally, a "fact sheet" on each of the spinoffs was sent.

REACTIONS BY UNITED WAY–SUPPORTED CHARITIES AND OTHERS

United Way–supported charities were probably the least supportive and reacted to events very strongly. To some extent the reaction could be considered normal, as there is always ambivalence between the donor and the donee. On the one hand, the recipient is very grateful for any support that is received which enables the organization to deliver services to people in need. On the other hand, there is often resentment because the amount is never perceived as being enough, and it usually comes with conditions, such as strict accountability on how the money is spent, as well as some prohibitions against other fund raising. But these were only the basic reasons. Aramony essentially believed that most health and human service organization leaders were a barrier to progress, not leaders for change as he was. If he could have gotten away with it, he would probably have had the United Way movement bypass the United Way allocation system altogether and give to organizations which reflected his own program thrusts. He always felt that he knew what was best for people.

He met regularly with the largest national agencies, known as the Top 17. He had done this for years, usually in places like Miami, Puerto Rico, and Las Vegas. He believed, often correctly, that if he developed a close personal relationship with the leaders of the major charitable organizations, he could convince them to achieve his own program goals, or at least neutralize them and keep them from resisting his initiatives.

This approach had always worked well for him in the past. It had worked with the age-old dispute with the American Cancer Society, which had resulted in bringing them back into the system, albeit on a contractual basis, outside of the normal allocations process. Lane Adams, its former executive vice president, had become one of his closest and most trusted friends. The same approach had also worked to a somewhat lesser degree with the American Heart Association. However, in recent years, the leaders of the major charities consistently stated that Aramony rarely listened to what they were saying, often left important discussions to make phone calls, or would simply leave meetings for long periods of time. These executives felt that *they*, not the United Way, were on the frontline of serving people. Many felt that the United Way had misinterpreted its own mission. United Way was in fact a fund-raising organization, not a service one. And they believed Aramony fundamentally lacked respect for what they were about.

Most would agree with David Liederman, president of the Child Welfare League of America, who said that those who choose to go into the social welfare field have an enormous sense of responsibility to uphold the public trust. This trust is violated when social welfare organizations lose sight of their mission and adopt perks and prerogatives not consistent with a life spent serving others. Because the United Way was so large and set an example for the sector, the impact was even more devastating.

Brian O'Connell, president of the Independent Sector, said that he had personally refused increased compensation because it would not be acceptable to broad and diverse membership.

The Reverend Tom Harvey, executive director of Catholic Charities, provided an example of an incident at a Top 17 meeting. Following a particularly exasperating attempt to explain that a program being espoused by Aramony was not on target, he simply told Bill that he did not know what he was talking about.

Andy Miller, general of the Salvation Army, said, "What Tom Harvey is trying to tell you is that what our, what his people, need out there is some support. Knowing that what they are doing is important and appreciated. I tell my people," he said, "that they are doing the work Christ wanted them to do. This reassurance is very important to them. It allows them to continue to work under very difficult conditions."

Then Carmi Schwartz piped in. "I never thought I'd come to appreciate Jesus Christ!" Schwartz was president of the Council of Jewish Federations and Welfare Funds.

They continued to meet with Aramony because these sessions were one of the few opportunities available for the leaders of America's major charities to share common concerns and problems head to head. Although many of these leaders personally liked Aramony (it was hard not to like him as a person), they deeply resented the presumption that he, and he alone, always knew what was best. There were not many tears shed for him other than on a personal level, although there was tremendous concern that the events he had set in motion could affect the income of their charity and therefore their ability to deliver services. Life in the nonprofit sector would never be the same.

The Alternative Fund movement, consisting mainly of organizations not funded by United Ways and represented mainly by Pablo Eisenberg, a member of the board of the National Committee For Responsive Philanthropy, and Bob Bothwell, its president, were much less charitable. This group began in the mid-1970s in response to the failure of the Commission on Private Charity and Public Needs to initially focus on beneficiaries of charitable activity. Aramony had always been anathema to their efforts to open up the corporate solicitation process and expand the franchise of the Combined Federal Campaign to advocacy and minority organizations, including environmental causes. United Way–supported organizations actually served far more minorities, just because of their size and scope, than the advocacy groups even though they may not have had a "minority name" in their title.

Bothwell recognized that Aramony had convinced corporate America that United Way was "motherhood and apple pie," bigger and better than any other charity, and that he fought tirelessly to keep alternative funds out of the local campaigns. Since United Way was considered so successful, the corporate community readily accepted Aramony's thinking. Bothwell claims that Aramony could easily have "co-opted" the alternative funds movement in the mid-1970s and early 1980s when they were weak by encouraging their participation in the local United Way–run campaigns. Now, the alternative funds movement, he claims, will not accept United Way domination of the fund-raising process, particularly in determining eligibility regarding who can participate. They will insist on a partnership arrangement, similar to what has evolved in Milwaukee and San Francisco with alternative funds in those communities.

Now "the bloom is off" and corporations will consider other options and will open their companies to his organization's constituent groups. Because of Bothwell's success and the successful effort which broke open the Combined Federal Campaign to virtually any charity, his organization's budget has risen dramatically. From 1991 to 1992, it increased over 20 percent in this one year alone. Some blame Bothwell and his group for being primarily responsible for United Way's troubles, but in my opinion, they were probably one of many causes, but certainly not *the* main cause.

COPING WITH THE ATTITUDE OF THE DONOR— THE CRITICAL CONSTITUENCY

The donors, as a class, were the most surprised by all these revelations about the United Way. They expected something different from the largest and, possibly, the most respected charity in the nation. Whether or not many of the allegations involved violations of law was not relevant. Such behavior was simply not expected of a charitable organization which was supposed to husband charitable dollars with the greatest of care. They called the talk shows, wrote letters to newspapers, and canceled their pledges. Although the "average" citizen was willing to tolerate high salaries for sports and entertainment figures without so much as a wink, for staff of charitable organizations it was unacceptable. The salary issue alone, which had been publicized in other places at other times, would probably not have made a stir. However, together with over $4 million in pension benefits, flights on the Concorde, large numbers of trips to Las Vegas and Miami, apartments and condominiums, and allegations of cronyism and nepotism spread all over major newspapers, it was just too much.

There was also the issue of *coercion*. The United Way movement has always been opposed to coercion, and many of its local members had specific policies against it. These events gave some people the excuse they needed not to give.

Information provided the public by United Way of America states that "United Ways realize that coercion creates animosity, hinders communication and understanding, and eventually leads to less support." Peer solicitation is recommended rather than solicitation by management. A United Way of America training document says that any kind of pressure violates United Way operating standards. While pressure sometimes works in the short run, it "invariably results in long-term losses." United Way of America had developed a policy against coercion many years ago. It states:

> The Board of Governors of United Way of America believes that the most responsive contributors are those who have the opportunity to become informed and involved. A well-planned campaign with an effective communication program, conducted by committed volun-

teers, will ensure responsible contributors. While we have always been unalterably opposed to coercion, we do recognize our responsibility to state our beliefs formally, as freedom of choice is a basic tenet of our democratic society.[9]

One hundred percent giving in a company, that is, when every single person gives something, is not considered an acceptable goal; it means that there are undoubtedly many who are being forced to give because of fear of job security or for other reasons. The goal is to get those who want to give to give more. When 80 percent of the people in a company give, that is generally considered good participation. United Way organizations rely on education and communication of the services they finance through their affiliated charities to make their "case" for funds. They do this through films, videotapes, and meetings with small groups of employees. During the campaign period, meetings with employees often take place around the clock, especially where there are multiple shifts.

Aramony distinguished between pressure and coercion. "Pressure," he would say, "is what happens at church. When the plate is passed, people feel obliged to give. This is pressure, not coercion." He applies the same analogy to United Way. In some companies, incentives are offered in terms of gifts and winners of contests, but it is considered inappropriate to use coercion by threatening job security or promotions for those who did not want to give or did not give what was deemed a "fair share." ("Fair share" is a company's standard for the "right amount to give." "Fair share-plus" programs are implemented for those who want to give more.) Pins and plaques are presented to those who give the recommended amount of money. The special beauty, as well as the success, of payroll deduction occurs because the voluntary contributions are deducted regularly *before* donors receive their paychecks, just like taxes—except it's voluntary. Also, a recommended deduction is based on a percentage of salary (say 1 percent every pay period), not on an absolute amount (for example, $5 per week). Using a percentage eliminates the need to ask for increases of an absolute dollar amount. Percentage figures never change, but the amount raised every year increases automatically because of annual salary increases among most working people. This seems obvious. However, new United Way members, especially those overseas, often opt for absolute amounts, which they then have to increase every year.

The types of donors described above, primarily the working men and women of America, contribute most of the money raised by United Way. For the rich (euphemistically called "high net worth" individuals), there is the Alexis de Tocqueville Society. Their reaction to this crisis was even more bitter. *The Chronicle of Philanthropy* quoted Walter H. Annenberg, a major contributor to the Society, as saying that he would stop giving to United Way until he was convinced "that a thorough housecleaning had been undertaken."[10]

Others, it seems, saw nothing wrong with what Aramony had done since it reflected their own corporate culture, where such perks were commonplace.

In November and December of 1991, prior to the crisis, United Way of America had commissioned an independent research firm to conduct a survey of 1,512 charitable contributors. It was designed to help develop a positioning strategy for United Way by "examining donation behavior and familiarity, factors affecting the donation decision, relative performance of United Way, preference for designating or not designating to a specific agency, and benefits of the allocations process."

The key results were as follows:

1. United Way ranked *second* in the number of contributors (49 percent); behind church and religious organizations (73 percent); followed by the Salvation Army, a United Way–funded agency (46 percent); the American Cancer Society (38 percent); the March of Dimes (35 percent); and the American Red Cross (23 percent).

2. The *most important* decision donors make when deciding whether or not to donate to a particular charity is "where the money goes," that is, the services provided by the organization.

3. Ninety percent of respondents said that the most important factor in making a donation decision was to "make sure the money you give is well spent." The second most important donation decision was based on giving to "an organization you can *trust*" (87 percent).

4. At the time of the survey, the United Way was not distinguished in a positive way from other organizations. It ranked either on par or lower than corresponding ratings of other charities.

5. Half of the respondents said that they preferred to give directly to a specific charity if they had only one method of choice; 31 percent said that they preferred their gift to the United Way to be distributed by it to other charities.

6. About 40 percent of the charitable contributors reported that they would be much more likely to give an undesignated gift if they knew the United Way was assuring the accountability and the quality of service of those charities that it funds.[11]

THE AFTERMATH

From April 9 to April 21, 1992, a little over a month after the heavy news coverage, a survey indicated that the public's favorable feelings toward the United Way had decreased from 80 to 70 percent since October 1990, while negative feelings had risen from 14 to 25 percent. The most frequent concern to the public was how the contributed funds are managed. The study indicated that current donors would continue to give at the same or greater levels *if* corrective action was taken. The most frequently mentioned action to be taken was to provide more information to the public, specifically showing how the money is used. More disclosure of wrongdoing was cited by only 1 percent of the sample.[12]

In July, five months *after* the crisis broke, United Way of America commissioned another survey of 1,000 randomly selected individuals who worked in a company in which a United Way campaign took place (or their spouse worked in such a company). The donor situation seemed to have improved:

1. Ninety-eight percent of donors who had recently seen or heard media stories about United Way would continue to give *if they believed corrective action had been taken* to respond to their concerns. Sixty percent of those who had heard or seen something about the United Way had additional suggestions for corrective action. Ranked in order of most to least strongly favored (or frequently proposed), these suggestions included positive public communications actions, more information about United Way given to the public, monitoring of spending, improved staffing, distribution of funds to those in need, publication of finances, and reduction in spending. Three-fourths said that future corrective action should be taken by both the national office and the local affiliates.

2. Forty percent thought that their United Way was independent from the national association; over a third did not know; and one-fourth thought it was managed by the national office.

3. Most people (63 percent) who had been exposed to recent news stories about the United Way said that they planned to give the *same amount* to the fall campaign as they had in April, while 9 percent said that they would *give more*. Twenty-three percent said that they would give less (down from 32 percent in April).

4. When those who said they would give less were asked why, 13 percent said that they would give less because of the news stories. An

additional 6 percent said they would give less both because of the stories and the economy.

5. Of those who had been exposed to media stories, 28 percent said
that they would give the same as last year if corrective action was taken
based on their recommendations, 16 percent would take a "wait and
see" attitude, while 13 percent said that they would give more. Only 2
percent said that they would give less.[13]

These surveys are very important in understanding the impact of
the crisis on people, particularly on the donors. They reflect donors'
perceptions of the United Way before and after the events. The perceptions show how seriously the donor viewed the violation of ethical
standards. However, these surveys strongly indicate that people have
a short memory, particularly if they believe corrective action has been
taken. The ultimate test in terms of how seriously the public views the
crisis will be determined by the success of subsequent campaigns. As
of this writing, United Way campaigns have shown an average loss of
2.2 percent. This is attributed roughly to the following factors, in order
of importance: the economy; the generally negative atmosphere toward
institutions; national-local problems, particularly regarding the Boy
Scouts not permitting gay leaders; and, lastly, Aramony. Among the
several knowledgeable people with whom I spoke, their gut reaction
was that the Aramony situation was of less importance than the economy for the poor campaign results.

THE SPINOFFS GOT THE HEAT

Most of the commentary describing the spinoffs is from press reports
and the Investigative Report produced by the lawyers hired by United
Way of America. I, of course, had no access to be able to confirm the
facts particularly in the report. There are errors of which I am aware
as well as those pointed out by others. In addition, serious questions
have been raised, as pointed out by Suhrke and Hopkins and others,
regarding the conclusions derived from the information as presented.
These reservations will be discussed later.

However, the report indicates the intricate web of relationships
among the spinoffs, and among the volunteers and staff charged with
oversight and implementation responsibilities. Virtually none of the
arrangements described could have been implemented without Aramony's extensive involvement in the decision-making process. What

emerges is a pattern of manipulation of the spinoffs to achieve both the bona fide program goals he sought and to serve his own interests. In at least three instances, these activities appear to violate New York State laws (where United Way of America is incorporated) regarding permissible activities by charitable organizations.

The immediate reaction of the spinoffs was to hunker down. Partnership Umbrella and Sales Service/America, the two for-profit organizations, responded to the press only sporadically or not at all. Both were pressed to disclose their financial information. Charities Funds Transfer, a nonprofit, charitable spinoff, had never had a complete financial audit!

The general public probably had no idea what spinoffs were. The very name has a derogatory connotation and trivializes the often very good reasons why they were established in the first place. The impression was that these spinoffs were somehow wrong and that they were an attempt to hide something from those whose responsibility it was to exercise oversight and financial accountability.

The establishment of so-called spinoffs is perfectly legal and in fact may be an appropriate management decision, depending on whether or not its purpose is consistent with the parent organization's mission and goals. As Henry Suhrke, editor of *Philanthropy Monthly* magazine, pointed out, an organization such as the United Way is unique by virtue of the fact that it is the largest, oldest, and best-known federation of its kind. Its varied activities encompass an enormous range of activity touching the lives of millions of people and thousands of institutions. It would be virtually impossible, and most likely unwise, to absorb all of the functions currently performed by the spinoffs into the operating structure of United Way of America. As he pointed out, if United Way of America did this, it would undoubtedly be accused by its critics of being even more avaricious and monopolistic.[14]

The key issue here is that the Board *must* be clear about the mission of the organization, and then must decide how to, or how not to, accommodate the many opportunities presented to it by its board members, its corporate and labor constituency, and the public. The decisions on how to structure these spinoffs and whether or not to remove them from United Way of America were largely determined by Aramony himself, even though they were formally approved by the Board. Aramony's expansive view of life made him susceptible to wanting to be all things to all people, and to accommodate as many ideas and activities as possible. His first instinct is to say "yes," not "no." "If I were to toss a thousand balls into the air, some of them will land and produce results," he would say. It seemed to him to make good sense to provide opportunities for some functions to be performed independently, unfettered by what would be insufferable if these functions resided within United Way of America's bureaucracy. Interlocking directorates created the best of both possible worlds, freedom *and* control—freedom so that they could function with minimum bureaucracy, and control so that they would not stray from their intended purposes.[15]

Gifts In Kind America, Charities Funds Transfer, and United Way International

Three of the major spinoffs were nonprofit (tax-exempt) organizations—Gifts In Kind America, Charities Funds Transfer, and United Way International. Gifts In Kind America and United Way International were the only spinoffs that had broad-based Boards. All the other spinoffs were closely held corporations by Aramony and a few of his very trusted staff and volunteers, who were also very close friends. Gifts In Kind America felt very little heat. It had a broad-based, active board and had been competently run for several years. It also had been publicly recognized as an effective charity and, most importantly, Aramony had little interest in it after it had been established. Charities Funds Transfer had been closely allied with Partnership Umbrella, with Steve Paulachak originally heading both organizations. He worked at Charities Funds Transfer as a volunteer, working one-fourth time. Both organizations shared a townhouse near Old Town Alexandria, about a mile from the national office. Paulachak is paid as head of Partnership Umbrella, which is a Virginia nonstock company, that is, it has no stockholders and any profits are required to be reinvested or given away. Partnership Umbrella gave a general-purpose grant of $25,000 for general operating purposes to United Way International a few years ago, its only recorded donation. It took one phone call from Aramony and the check was "in the bank."

United Way International, the international service arm of the United Way movement, was incorporated in 1974. It is the oldest of the spinoffs and it was the most severely affected by the events. When the contracts with the consultants were terminated, other "unnecessary" contracts were terminated, including those with United Way International. Eighty percent of United Way International's funding depended on the United Way of America. The rest came in from overseas, principally Canada.

I ran United Way International on a part-time basis until 1986 when Terry Colley Benshoff was hired as a full-time associate and I devoted all of my attention to the effort, instead of half of my time to Aramony and half to the international effort. Until April of 1991, United Way International was housed at United Way of America, where it received free rent, phones (except for overseas calls), heat, and utilities as well as other services of an in-kind nature. There was always considerable resentment among some staff at United Way of America over the international program. Many felt that it was superfluous to the primary mission of United Way, which was to service to a domestic constituency. The international program, it was reasoned, diverted this effort.

United Way International had always received a direct grant of various amounts from United Way of America, but until recent years, the organization received little moral support other than personally from Aramony, who also served as its unpaid president. When it moved its offices from the United Way of America building, it was free to enter into contracts outside of United Way of America, whose services were in significant respects considerably inferior and more expensive than what could be found on the open market. Bureaucracies, whether in the public or the private sector, do not tend to be as responsive as contractors functioning in a highly competitive environment, whose livelihood depends upon providing consistently high-quality service at all times.

United Way International did much better outside of United Way of America. Its goals were clearly acceptable to most who understood the organization as promoting one of America's most viable exports. However, in a weak economy with pressing domestic needs, it was viewed as being trivial by most United Ways. Its U.S. constituency has always been small, but its overseas constituency, from Asia to Africa to the former Soviet Union, has held it in the highest regard.

One incident is worth reporting. The day after the teleconference on February 27 at which Aramony "retired," he and his son asked that a portion of United Way International's space be made available as an office for Aramony. Aramony himself called the chairman of United Way International, James F. Mulvaney, as well as Cheryl Wills-Matthews, the former chairman, to ask them if it was okay. Both thought it was a fine idea. Mulvaney was ecstatic that Aramony would be located at United Way International and be able to devote all of his time to the international program. This total lack of perception about what this would mean to United Way International, already compromised by Aramony's travel revelations, was astonishing. Aramony did not resign as president of United Way International until March 30, over four weeks after he left United Way of America. That Friday afternoon, his son arranged for his furniture to be moved into United Way International. On Saturday morning, Aramony called me at home and told me that he had changed his mind because he didn't want to compromise United Way International. On Monday, the furniture was moved out.

Charities Funds Transfer's movement to a separate spinoff was agreed to by a committee of United Way professionals. Its purpose was to facilitate the movement of funds between headquarters of companies to United Way organizations in communities in which their plants and facilities were located. Since United Ways across the country where subsidiaries are located depend upon these corporate donations, local professionals who run these United Ways have a strong interest in assuring that this transfer of funds works well. In retrospect, it may have been a mistake to overlap the staffing of Charities Funds Transfer and Partnership Umbrella simply because it looked inappropriate. However, such overlap is common, and at the time it appeared to be a reasonable, cost-saving decision.

The board of Charities Funds Transfer, which consisted of a few local United Way professionals, began to question Paulachak about how the organization was being run, since it had never had an audit. Paulachak had said that the "right" accounting firm, which could do the job properly, hadn't been found.

Partnership Umbrella and Sales Service/America

The press stories and the Investigative Report came down hard on these spinoffs. The primary focus was on the for-profit spinoffs, particularly Partnership Umbrella, an organization which provided discounted services and merchandise to charitable organizations. Partnership Umbrella (as well as Sales Service/America, the other for-profit spinoff) refused to make its financial statements available. Under the law, they were not required to do so.

Why Partnership Umbrella? Partnership Umbrella was an immediate winner. The private sector recognizes a good thing when it sees it. Partnership Umbrella, incorporated in 1986, was established at the time when income-generating activities of charitable organizations were under pressure from small business. In fact, in 1984, the Small Business Administration had published a report, *Unfair Competition by Nonprofit Organizations with Small Business*. In 1988, this same issue was on the agenda of the White House Conference on Small Business and was a subject of a special report by the Government Accounting Office to the Joint Committee on Taxation of the Congress.[16]

Over the years, the Huntington T. Block Insurance Company has offered officers and directors' liability insurance to United Way of America and its spinoffs. The policies were underwritten by Chubb, the insurance company. Partnership Umbrella began to offer this insurance to other voluntary organizations on a large scale. The advertisements in the trade publications consistently show the advantages of this service. In light of recent events, its value appears to be even more important. AT&T also recognized the central position of United Way of America's Partnership Umbrella in promoting its products. Robert Allen, the chairman of AT&T, is a member of the Board of Governors of United Way of America. He assigned super saleswoman Linda Boyd to work the United Way and its affiliated organizations. Attractive and low key, she worked well with Aramony (who catered to her constantly), his staff, and the system in a thoroughly professional manner. One of the benefits of being associated with her was an invitation to attend the Kemper Open, a major national golf tournament held in the Maryland countryside.

In 1986, United Way of America entered into a management agreement with Partnership Umbrella, which permitted access to United Way of America members for the purpose of selling products and services. Under this agreement, United Way of America was obligated to make Partnership Umbrella's services known to its membership, but not to market its products. For its part, Partnership Umbrella's goal was to establish appropriate relationships with vendors, develop marketing strategies, and deal directly with the constituent United Ways. In March 1987, the Executive Committee had approved the motion which permitted 50 percent of the proceeds from the AT&T incentive payments to be distributed to Partnership Umbrella (the balance to be distributed to United Way of America for various program activities) because Partnership Umbrella was largely responsible for reaching the sales goals. In 1988, United Way of America gave Partnership Umbrella over $930,000 derived from the AT&T incentive payments. Although the Investigative Report made an issue of the fact that "sharing the incentive payment with Partnership Umbrella was an improper allocation and use of United Way funds," this is clearly just an opinion. Considering the well-recognized success of the organization until the crisis broke, in my opinion it is not a correct one.

Although Partnership Umbrella had been extremely successful in carrying out its mission, it got in over its head by buying real estate, serving as an intermediary for the establishment of Sales Service/

America, and bailing out other spinoffs. Its problem began when it wavered from its central mission, that is, providing discount services to charities.

It appeared to be most compromised when the press reported that it purchased and furnished a New York condominium for Aramony in July 1988 for over $440,000. Six months later, it purchased its own office near Old Town Alexandria for $100,000 in cash and a $400,000 mortgage which it shared with Charities Funds Transfer.[17]

The board-commissioned Investigative Report examined, in detail, the relationship between Sales Service/America and Partnership Umbrella. Sales Service/America was approved as a spinoff in May 1990, one month *after* it had been incorporated as a nonstock Virginia company (which means it was incorporated before the Board agreed to spin it off). The sales function had been grossing $6 million per year for United Way of America. The original objective in establishing it as a spinoff was to avoid taxes from unrelated business income, downsize United Way of America (following a trend in the corporate community), and increase sales of United Way of America products.

Sales Service/America, as an independent spinoff, had been carefully positioned and established as a separate entity. One of the principal reasons for spinning off the Sales Service Division of United Way of America was to be able to purchase supplies as a "middleman" at a 30 percent discount, savings which would have been passed on to United Way members through lower prices. The Advertising Specialties Institute, which regulates such matters for the industry, did not permit nonprofit organizations from serving as "middlemen."

In addition, two separate studies were undertaken, which were minimized by the Investigative Report. First, a catalogue consultant was hired to determine if enough sales could be generated by the sales service function to be able to exist independently. It was estimated by the consultant that the increased benefit of creating a separate organization would be approximately $100,000 in sales. Second, a consultant was hired to determine the best software for the purposes, and whether or not existing software could be modified to accommodate the special needs of the spinoff in order to handle its inventory and receivables. In 1990, United Way of America paid Partnership Umbrella $87,000 to conduct a "feasibility study" on the transition of the Sales Service Division of United Way of America to the new entity, Sales Service/America. This study, conduct by Robert Aramony, indicated a savings of almost $200,000 in personnel costs.[18] The Investigative Report implies that this study was somehow superfluous to the two other studies already undertaken. However, the other studies, as cited above, were of an entirely different nature.

Until October 1, 1990, Robert Aramony had been employed by Partnership Umbrella, *while at the same time* serving as Sales Service/America's chief operating officer as stipulated in a Management Agreement between Sales Service/America and Partnership Umbrella. Under this Agreement, Sales Service/America agreed to pay Partnership Umbrella $150,000 per year. The Agreement was terminated in April 1991, when Robert Aramony resigned from Partnership Umbrella to immediately head up Sales Service/America full time. The termination agreement provided for a cash payment of $125,000 from Sales Service/America to Partnership Umbrella, and Partnership Umbrella was to pay Robert Aramony's salary. In January 1991, United Way of America gave Sales Service/America over $100,000 to cover "transitional expenses." The Investigative Report states that this payment "apparently enabled" Sales Service/America to make the $125,000 payment required by the Management Agreement.[18] Sales Service/America said that the funds were used for "systems software upgrades" and "extensive accounting software programming and testing."[19]

In October 1990, Sales Service/America arranged for a $500,000 line of credit and a $250,000 term loan from a Virginia bank under the condition that, in case of default, United Way of America would buy back inventory equal to the outstanding balance on the loan. No funds were ever drawn on the line of credit, according to the Investigative Report.

It gave United Way of America a five-year promissory note on November 1, 1990 for $2,174,300 at 10.5 percent simple interest for start-up purposes. In return, United Way of America took a lien on Sales Service/America inventory and receivables.

The voluntary regulatory organizations, the National Charities Information Bureau (NCIB) and the Philanthropic Advisory Service of the Council of Better Business Bureaus, were equally harsh on the for-profit spinoffs for failure to disclose their finances. Ken Albrecht, president of the NCIB has consistently supported full disclosure of all records of spinoffs which in any way raise money in the name of charity. This clearly included full disclosure by Partnership Umbrella, the most controversial of the spinoffs. The NCIB did not review United Way of America because it doesn't review national organizations of local charities; in addition, the NCIB receives some money, but much less than in previous years, from the United Way and therefore finds it a conflict of interest to evaluate the organization.

The Lesser Spinoffs

The "lesser" spinoffs also bear mention because of their relationship to Partnership Umbrella. These other spinoffs are Voluntary Initiatives America, Inc., Mobilization for America's Children, and the two travel spinoffs, Professional Travel Systems, Inc. and PTS International, Inc.

Voluntary Initiatives America, Inc. was the direct result of a gift of $1 million in February of 1987 from Mutual of America, the United Way's pension insurer, to Bill Aramony. The interest was to be used at his discretion while the principal amount would be subject to the discretion of Mutual of America. The program was called the "William Aramony's Initiatives in Voluntarism" program.

William J. Flynn, chairman of Mutual of America and a genuine humanitarian, had been a close associate of Aramony for many years. To his credit, Flynn succeeded in promoting, through his position at Mutual of America, ecumenical activities between faiths, particularly between Christians and Jews. Flynn is a close associate of Nobel laureate Elie Wiesel, who serves on the Board of Mutual of America. Flynn has helped to finance some of Wiesel's international conferences on promoting world peace and understanding the nature of hatred. Aramony immediately took to Flynn and strongly supported his friend as he built up what was then the National Health and Welfare Retirement Association (originally started by Ralph Blanchard in the 1940s) into one of the most highly rated insurance companies in America (Best's rating of A+ [Superior][20] and AA+ from Standard & Poor[21]). In December, the Board of Governors of United Way of America created the "William Aramony Initiatives in Voluntarism Fund" to manage the interest on the endowment. In April of 1990, Voluntary Initiatives America was incorporated in Florida as a nonprofit, tax-exempt organization. It received its tax-exempt status in August. Unlike the other spinoffs, there is no record that United Way of America ever approved its establishment as a corporation or explained why it was incorporated in Florida. This lack of approval is somewhat unusual since Voluntary Initiatives America received nearly $300,000 from Mutual of America by the end of 1991 based on the funding agreement.

"This fund," Aramony told me shortly after he received word of the grant, "will give me the opportunity to do something really big and important for the country. I'm not going to spend the money on just anything. I'm going to use it in a way that'll make a difference." In 1990, shortly after the first payments were received by United Way of America from Mutual of America, Voluntary Initiatives America purchased a condominium in Coral Gables, Florida for Aramony for $125,576. A year later it was sold to Partnership Umbrella.[22]

Aramony's interest in using the mass-purchasing power of the voluntary sector began during midcareer at United Way of America. The first initiative in the area, as well as the first failure, came with the establishment of Professional Travel Systems (PTS), Inc. in 1983 with a loan of almost $150,000 in working capital from United Way of America. This loan was eventually repaid by Partnership Umbrella. PTS went out of business in the late 1980s. Its assets were taken over by Partnership Umbrella. PTS International was incorporated as a Virginia nonstock corporation in April 1985, and went out of business in September of 1987.[23]

"I know what's best for America's children," said Aramony. "Everyone else has their own agenda. They don't see the big picture." Mobilization for America's Children was his brainchild. It consumed all his efforts and those of all the staff he could in any way justify in diverting to the effort, even threatening those who were lukewarm to the idea with dismissal. In the opinion of many, it needed to become a more broadly based coalition of forces. He considered this program, estimated to take 20 years to achieve its results, as the crowning achievement of his career. It was something that he could work on after his retirement as well. In the months before his forced resignation, this program dominated his thoughts and actions. It was incorporated before the Board of Governors agreed to establish it in 1991 as a separate, tax-exempt organization. Mobilization was to be funded with $1,000,000 from one anonymous source, an additional $300,000 from other anonymous sources, and $500,000 from the estimated $800,000 from savings resulting from an early retirement program. Events took over and the money was never transferred. In 1991, Mobilization received $50,000 from Voluntary Initiatives America.[24] Aramony intended to commit huge amounts of staff time and effort to this project—to the point that it threatened to overtake other programs of the organization.

The enormous fallout from the events of 1992 created major problems for the spinoffs, particularly for Partnership Umbrella, the nexus for the funding and management of most of the other spinoffs. Were it not for the purchase of the condominiums, the most visible activity of Partnership Umbrella, the public might not have cared as much.

Fortunately, the new leaders sensibly reviewed each spinoff to determine its appropriate relationship to United Way of America.

THE NEW UNITED WAY TAKES SHAPE

On June 25, 1992 the Board approved the April 2 report in goose-step fashion, just like they had approved all of Aramony's initiatives. Not much had really changed. The board had simply replaced Aramony with Ken Dam and the investigating attorneys. Such historic changes had not taken place since Aramony first articulated the 13-Point Program almost 22 years before:

> The United Way of America Board of Governors today effectively created a new United Way of America—one that will have far more direct involvement from local United Ways and a clearly defined mission to support those organizations.
>
> Marked by improved fiscal controls and management systems, the actions today put the structure that led to past problems behind us, and refocus efforts on the real mission of the United Way system. This completes the work on changes to UWA's operating structure.

These changes included a new mission focused on the needs of local United Ways "to support and serve local United Ways to help them care for people in their communities." Under pressure from national charities, this was later changed "to support and serve local United Ways to help increase the organized capacity of people to care for one another."

It was followed with a statement that said: "UWA will do for local United Ways what they cannot do for themselves: provide services at economics of scale, and provide appropriate national services such as advertising and public-policy advocacy."

The new governance included 15 local United Way representatives on a newly expanded 45-member board. The number of meetings per year were doubled.

Local United Way volunteers and professionals will comprise half the membership of six board oversight committees including nominating, budget and finance, compensation and human resources, ethics, membership, and program and services. An independent ombudsman was appointed to monitor operations and services to members, as well as compliance with a code of ethics. This person will have access to all volunteers and staff and draft reports independent of United Way of America influence or censorship.

In addition, "rigorous" fiscal and personnel controls were put into place, and a multi-tiered dues program was established which will include a base fee with additional services provided and higher levels. A formal advisory system of local volunteers and professionals, and annual regional forums will be created.

The name, United Way of America, is to remain unchanged. As for the spinoffs:

1. *Charities Funds Transfer* is to be absorbed by United Way of America;
2. *Gifts In Kind America* will enter into a cooperative memorandum of understanding with United Way of America to serve the nonprofit community.
3. *Sales Service/America* will be changed from a Virginia nonstock company to a stock corporation with all of the stock owned by United Way of America ("commercial barriers" prevent the reabsorption into United Way of America according to the report).
4. *United Way International* will receive no membership funds and will remain independent.
5. *Mobilization for America's Children* will be administered within United Way of America and all funds were transferred to a separate account. The board reaffirmed its commitment to this 20-year strategy to serve America's children. (*Note*: This program had strong support from two key board members: Jim Robinson and Earle Harbison.)
6. *Voluntary Initiatives America* is to receive no funds from United Way of America, and current funds are to be placed in a separate account and administered by an appropriate grant process.
7. *Partnership Umbrella* is not to be used as a vendor by United Way of America. Agreements remaining in force between the two organizations will not be renewed, and efforts will be made to determine if any monies are owed United Way of America by the organization.[25]

On August 19, the annual meeting of the Board was held in Alexandria under the leadership of its new chairman, W.R. Howell, chairman of the J.C. Penney Company and successor to John Akers. "As the voluntary and professional leadership of United Way, we are the ones who can help make it happen all across America," he said. It was videotaped for those who could not attend. "We have gone beyond all the issues raised," reported Ken Dam according to the press release, " and today reforged a new relationship with local United Ways so the entire United Way system will emerge stronger than ever."

Clearly the quote that introduces this chapter is true. The Board under Akers leadership had abdicated its responsibility, as had the previous Boards, mostly by rubber-stamping Aramony's decisions to establish the spin-offs without full, open, and critical discussions of the pros and cons of doing so. The board also failed to comprehend the negative impact Aramony's life-style would have on the public psyche if it became public knowledge. But mainly, the Board failed to understand the essential difference between stewardship of a charitable enterprise and that of a for-profit corporation. After the press reports, the chairman retained lawyers at great expense to do what the Board should have done in the first place. He then abdicated responsibility to them to produce a poorly developed report replete with errors, innuendos and ambiguous statements. Although the changes eventually approved by the board after the crisis were excellent by any standard, if the Board had exercised its proper oversight in the first place, these events might never have happened.

REFERENCES

1. Brian O'Connell *America's Voluntary Spirit* (New York: The Foundation Center, 1983), p. 92.
2. Report of Kenneth W. Dam, President, United Way of America, to the Annual Meeting (August 19, 1992).
3. "Affiliates Feeling Pinch of United Way Scandal," *The New York Times* (April 22, 1992).
4. Memo from Sunshine Overcamp to Chief Professional Officers, Communications Directors. Subject: Post Inquiries (February 7, 1992).
5. Memo from Sunshine Overcamp to Chief Professional Officers, Communications Directors. Subject: Upcoming Jack Anderson Column (February 10, 1992).
6. Memo from Sunshine Overcamp to Chief Professional Officers, Selected United Ways, and Metro II–IX. Subject: Urgent Media Related Information. Please Read Immediately Upon Receipt (February 13, 1992).
7. Memo from Sunshine Overcamp to Chief Professional Officers, Communication Directors. Subject: *The Washington Post Article* (February 16, 1992).
8. Memo from Sunshine Overcamp to Chief Professional Officers, Communications Directors. Subject: *The Washington Post*—Second Investigation Story (February 24, 1992).
9. "United Way Policy Against Coercion" from United Way of America Fact Sheet (August 1991).
10. "United Way: The Fallout After the Fall," *The Chronicle of Philanthropy* (March 10, 1992).

11. "Results of 1992 Positioning Research," *Market Research: News You Can Use* (United Way of America: June 1992).
12. "Executive Summary—April 1992 Public Opinion Poll," United Way of America Research Services (April 1992).
13. "Executive Summary—July 1992 Public Opinion Poll, "United Way of America, Research Services (August 1992).
14. Henry C. Suhrke "PM Annotated Investigative Report on United Way of America, "*The Philanthropic Monthly*, Vol. 24, No. 10 (December 1991), p. 19.
15. *Ibid.*, p. 7.
16. Gary N. Scrivner "100 Years of Tax Policy Changes Affecting Charitable Organizations," *The Nonprofit Organization* (Pacific Grove: Brooks/Cole Publishing, 1990), p. 133.
17. Verner, Liipfert, Bernhard, MacPherson and Hand, *Report to the Board of Governors of United Way of America* (April 2, 1992), pp. 15–19.
18. *Ibid.*, pp. 25–27.
19. Henry C. Suhrke "Spinoff Responds to Investigative Report," *Philanthropic Monthly*, Vol. 25, No. 2 (March 1992), p. 21.
20. 1992 Best's Guide to Life Insurance Companies, p. 530.
21. S&P's Insurer Solvency Review—Life/Health, p. 338.
22. *Investigative Report*, pp. 31–32.
23. *Ibid*, pp. 33–34.
24. *Ibid*, pp. 32–34.
25. Fact sheet entitled "A New United Way of America is Created: Born Out of Local Input and Redefined Values," by United Way of America (undated).

CHAPTER 6

Did Aramony Exceed the Limits?

Man did not weave the web of life;
He is merely a strand in it.
Whatever he does to the web,
He does to himself.

Chief Seattle, Washington Territory, 1854

The catchwords of the late 1980s were "downsizing," "low over-head," and "profit centers." In addition, the work force was becoming more diversified in the age of technology. The creation of more small businesses, many operated out of one's home, were growing. Changes were necessitated. The extravagant 1980s had come to an end. Aramony had already begun to act on these matters. As chairman, John Akers immediately began to press for a leaner, more economical organization. Among the most dramatic of his actions was to seek a reduction in the voluntary dues paid to the national association by the local United Way members. He believed that the United Way, like most businesses, should be cutting back. The economy was bad and not getting better; the times demanded cutbacks. The local United Ways were shocked. There had never been any particular pressure from the field to reduce dues payments. It was clear that there was nothing Aramony could do about Aker's virtual demand that dues be reduced. Nevertheless, Aramony tried to find ways to recapture the lost revenue through a number of "carrots" offered to the field which would restore the lost revenue.

Downsizing could have been achieved in a number of ways, but none were acceptable to Aramony because he wanted to do it *his* way. He had always managed to convince his volunteer leadership that it was his responsibility to manage the organization, which included balancing the budget. The work of United Way is too important, he would say. He believed that we need more money to serve the people of the country, not less. That meant more for more staff, more programs, and more volunteers. If anything, Aramony would want the dues raised, not cut back. He was not about to lay off staff—something he was constitutionally incapable of doing—reduce salaries, or eliminate programs. His personal example was not one of frugality. Rather than give up his expensive habits, he would take from other budgets within the organization.

One solution had been to spin off some functions to reduce United Way America's overhead, while at the same time create entities which, once incorporated, could function independently without the constraints imposed by United Way of America's bureaucracy. These spinoffs were not subject to United Way of America's direct oversight. This would result in his ability to control numerous functions without United Way of America Board approval. However, United Way of America Board approval was essential for the creation of such spinoffs.

This chapter will look at the law as it applies to nonprofit organizations. An understanding of the legal parameters governing his activities may provide some understanding of whether or not laws were broken.

IS WHAT HE DID WRONG?

Nonprofit organizations are regulated by state and federal law. The following information is intended merely as an overview in order to place the activities of United Way of America, its president, and the controversial spinoffs in perspective. Obviously, if laws have been violated, the proper authorities will ultimately make that determination.

THE LAWS GOVERNING NONPROFIT ORGANIZATIONS

A *law* is defined as "a rule established by authority, society, or custom."[1] In our society, federal laws apply to the entire country, while state laws affect only resident corporations and citizens. Laws regulating charity have existed since the dawn of time when people first began to live in civilized society. They have evolved over the centuries into a body of regulations and precedents which is ever changing and expanding.

One of the interesting aspects of American society is that our ethical issues usually drive our legal system. Once descriptions of unethical behavior become widely known through the press and other media, the governmental legal apparatus feels obliged to investigate these matters suddenly thrust into the public domain. Since the investigative resources of the government are limited, our society often depends upon the example set by our high-profile individuals. We expect them to receive their just due and set examples for the rest of us.

Charities and the Law: The Factor of Publicity

Since equal justice under the law is the basis of a democratic society, it is expected to be applied equally to the rich and poor, the powerful and the weak, particularly in regards to so-called "white collar" crimes. However, don't be fooled. Although the law may not be relative, it is certainly political. It is highly unlikely that the federal prosecutor for the Eastern District of Virginia would have pursued the United Way case were it not for the enormous publicity it had generated.

Public investigative resources are limited, and examples must serve to keep others from committing the same or similar violations. Indictments and convictions of famous people are intended to dissuade others from committing the same or similar offense. For example, the indictments of Charles Keating in the savings and loan scandal, Casper Weinberger in the Iran-Contra hearings, and Leona Helmsley for tax evasion all send a message to the general public: If it can happen to these people with power, money, and influence, it can happen to anyone.

The United Way of America crisis created the "perfect situation" for the federal authorities to make an example for other charities. It is by far the largest and most publicized charity crisis in American history. An example set here could have profound impact on voluntary organizations in America for many years. As soon as the revelations hit the papers, voluntary boards throughout the country immediately moved to review their personnel policies and practices, paying particular attention to salary and perks.

The general impression by the public, and indeed virtually every constituency from United Way of America Board members to on-line workers, was that the excesses of Aramony regarding his salary and perks described by the press, although probably "legal," were simply "not right." The activities of the spinoffs described in excruciating detail were even more suspect as somehow "not legal" or, at best, "questionable." When the hysteria died down and the experts were able to provide a sober analysis of the situation, virtually everything that was done to create the spinoffs was, for the most part, perfectly legal.

State Law and Charities

Every state has laws which govern nonprofit charitable organizations—how they should be structured and maintained, and what their reporting requirements should be. United Way of America spinoff activities possibly violated applicable New York state law where United Way of America is incorporated. For example, the Investigative Report of April 2 stated three possible violations of New York state law. "Under Section 176 of the New York State Not-For-Profit Corporation law, not-for-profit corporations are not permitted to make loans to corporations in which one or more of its directors or officers hold a substantial financial interest . . .' " It cited Merlo as the Chief Financial Officer of United Way of America and a director of Sales Service/America. This same violation under Section 176 is cited in regard to another spinoff, Professional Travel Systems, which received a loan for $148,962 when Aramony, Merlo, and Paulachak were officers at United Way of America and directors of the spinoff. The report also cited a local bank, Crestar, which provided a $250,000 term loan to Sales Service/America, requiring as a condition for the loan that United Way of America enter into a buy-back agreement with the bank whereby it would repurchase Sales Service/America's inventory for an amount equal to the loan balance in the event of default. "Because the Buy-Back Agreement was effectively a guarantee," the report said, "New York law may also prohibit the Buy-Back Agreement."[2] Regardless of New York state law, no concern was given to possible violations of Virginia law, the state in which United Way and all of the spinoffs are located and conduct much of their activities.

Understanding Nonprofit Organization Law

An understanding of the nonprofit organization law is essential in order to fully understand the critical issues at stake in this crisis. In his extremely informative work, *A Legal Guide to Starting and Managing a Nonprofit Organization, Second Edition,* Bruce R. Hopkins, long considered one of this country's leading authors and experts on the law of charitable organizations, discussed the philosophical and legal underpinnings of nonprofit law which have bearing on the role of nonprofit organizations in society. In order to put in perspective the events which took place at United Way in the spring of 1992, it is first necessary to understand the definition of *nonprofit* and the related doctrine of *private inurement*.

A private corporation, unlike a nonprofit one, operates for the benefit of its owners by passing on profits to its shareholders who hold equity in the corporation. This transfer of profits from a corporation to its owners is referred to as *private inurement of net earnings*. It is this important doctrine of *private inurement* which separates nonprofits from for-profits. A nonprofit organization is not allowed to distribute its "profits" to those who control or support it.

The federal law on tax exemption for charitable organizations, which has been expanded over the years, states that profits from a charitable enterprise may not be passed along to individuals in their private capacity: "Inurement is likely to arise where the beneficial benefit represents a transfer of the organization's financial resources to an individual solely by virtue of the individual's relationship with the organization, and without regard to accomplishing exempt purposes," advises the IRS in recent rulings.

Impermissible private inurement, according to the IRS, means that an *insider* may not influence the nonprofit organization in a way which results in private benefit to anyone or may not influence the organization in such a way as to confer such a benefit in violation of the private inurement doctrine. An insider in this case is defined as a director, key employer, major contributor, officer, and the like. Of course a tax-exempt organization may "benefit" individuals and groups in carrying out its exempt purpose, for example, through payments to vendors for services rendered, rent, and reasonable compensation.[2]

The purpose of the private inurement doctrine is to ensure that charitable organizations serve public interests, not private ones. When determining tax-exempt status, the IRS decides whether or not the organization under consideration is benefiting public interests or private ones, although incidental benefits to private individuals will not prevent the granting of tax-exempt status, as long as the basic purpose of the organization otherwise qualifies. A charitable organization may still conduct commercial activities to further the larger cause of its tax-exempt purpose, providing that such activity is not its *primary* purpose.

In 1989, the U.S. Tax Court (*American Campaign Academy vs. Commissioner*) articulated another rule called the *private benefit doctrine*. It is broader than the private inurement doctrine. In this instance, the court determined that the prohibition against private benefit is not limited to those situations of private inurement that benefit *insiders*. It significantly includes what the court has called an additional category of *disinterested persons*. In other words, the private benefit doctrine can be applied to those situations were there are no insiders and include a much broader class of people related to, but outside, the charity under question. In the case under consideration, students of a school that trained individuals in political campaigning violated the private benefit doctrine because they were eventually employed almost exclusively by Republican candidates. The Court defined this group as a *targeted private interest* and, therefore, not incidental to the schools tax-exempt purpose.[4]

UNITED WAY OF AMERICA AND THE LAW

During the February 27 teleconference from United Way of America, Berl Bernhard, counsel to United Way of America, clearly stated that "there was no misappropriation found, no embezzlement found, no fraud, no malfeasance in office." One of the major issues raised by the press and public, however, was Aramony's salary, perks, and pension(s). Let's see what the law states about these issues.

Compensation and What's OK

One of the key issues of the crisis was the annual compensation of $390,000 paid to Bill Aramony, along with $76,000 in benefits in 1990. The public perception is that those who work for charitable organizations should work for less than those who are employed by profit-making organizations. This perception was something that Aramony fought against most of his adult life. Was he wrong to do so? What are the facts and what is the law?

For almost 20 years, United Way of America has consulted outside experts to help in setting salary ranges. In the mid-1980s, Towers Perrin, a pension and compensation consulting firm, took over this activity from McKinsey and Company, Inc., a management consulting firm. Its charge was to recommend salary ranges for the heads of the largest United Ways and United Way of America senior staff. During 1985, when Jim Robinson was chairman, he assigned his vice president of compensation to work with Towers Perrin. In January 1986, the firm presented a report to United Way of America's Executive Committee which recommended ranges for the president and senior staff salaries. These ranges cited four survey sources upon which these recommendations were based. The ranges were eventually adopted by the Executive Committee after a review by a Board committee. It set the "midpoint" of the president's salary range as $260,000 effective as of January 1, 1986.[5]

Towers Perrin recognizes the difficulty in setting salary ranges for the nonprofit sector because of its tremendous diversity. But several issues need to be considered. The first of these issues is the determination of the competitive marketplace from which the company plans to attract and maintain talent. The second issue is how the company wants to position itself relative to that market. Do they want to pay salaries that are higher, lower, or the same?

Other considerations include the budget size. Does Aramony have responsibility for the $3 billion raised by independent local United Ways? Or is he responsible for the mere $29,000,000 budget of United Way of America? Still other considerations include length of service and number of staff members. Towers Perrin's 1992 "Compensation Survey Report of Management Positions in Not-for-Profit Organizations" included 311 trade associations (representing companies), professional associations (representing individuals), educational institutions (providing and promoting educational activities), health and welfare programs (providing and promoting public health and social welfare services), and other associations representing a total of 5,755 employees. Of 49 health and social service organizations, 13 had budgets of over $19.9 million, and seven had over 199 staff positions (United Way of America had about 275 staff positions in Aramony's day). The survey also indicated that salaries that year for a "top executive officer" of a nonprofit ranged from $56,400 to $470,000 with an average salary of $152,200.[6] Far exceeding Aramony's salary during the same period is that of foundation executives Harold Williams, president of the J. Paul Getty Trust ($509,001) and Franklin A. Thomas, president of the Ford Foundation ($422,426).[7]

By way of comparison, surveys conducted by *The Chronicle of Philanthropy* indicate that of the largest 18 charities supported by United Way, the Boy Scouts of America chief scout executive's salary is highest at $223,375. The lowest is the Salvation Army national commander and his wife, who receive about $50,000 in total benefits including salaries. The largest salary for a United Way chief professional officer is $243,333 (New York City). The average salary of the chief professional officer for the largest charities is $129,219, while the average salary of the top United Way chief professional officers is $179,648.[8]

In setting a salary for the new chief executive officer of United Way of America, what Jim Moss of Towers Perrin called "minimizing the noise level," the amount was set at $195,000, with 18 months of severance pay if termination was involuntary.

Federal law requires charities to make their information returns (Forms 990), forms filed annually which list all financial information including salary information of the top five officers, available to the public on request within regular business hours and at the place of business of the organization.

What Does the IRS Say About Salary?

The law states that all compensation, no matter how it's determined or in what form, must be "reasonable" in order for an organization to retain its tax-exempt status. These constraints are for those employees that fall under the doctrine of private inurement. Experts agree that it is very important to document how a salary was arrived at based on comparable data from related sources.

Excessive compensation is a form of private inurement that can lead to loss of tax exemption. Aramony was inclined to bestow bonuses, especially in recent years when he was concerned about increasing salaries, and therefore increasing benefits. Bonuses, usually "grossed up" to cover taxes, were a way to provide additional income for the beneficiary, keep percentage increases in salaries lower, and not saddle the organization with escalating salaries and benefits. The IRS now has developed criteria for assessing such compensation arrangements:

1.   The compensation actually paid must be reasonable.
2.   The agreement must be negotiated at arm's length.
3.   The arrangement must state whether or not the service provider participates in or has any control over the conduct of the organization.
4.   That "contingent" payments must serve a "real discernable business purpose" of the exempt organization (that is, independent of any purpose to benefit the service provider).
5.   The amount of compensation must be dependent upon the accomplishment of the objectives of the compensatory arrangement.
6.   The arrangement must state whether or not the actual operating results reveal any evidence of abuse or unwarranted benefits to the service provider.
7.   There must be a "ceiling of reasonable maximum limit" in the compensation agreement to avoid a "windfall benefit" to the

service provider based upon factors "which had no direct relationship to the level of services provided."[9]

Another important compensation issue refers to the controversial
fringe packages. Increasingly, the Congress and the IRS are looking at
the total package of salaries, perks, and fringes when making a determination about "reasonable compensation." Clearly, the IRS is concerned about such perks as country club memberships, entertainment
allowances, and golden parachutes. These perks are often interpreted
as part of one's compensation package, that is, part of the salary which
could be subject to taxation as income. It was widely reported in the
print and broadcast media that Aramony's pension arrangements are
worth $4.4 million, most of which was based on what are called *non-
qualified plans*.

The Biggest Fringe Benefits of All: Deferred Compensation Plans

Deferred compensation plans are divided into qualified and nonqualified plans. *Qualified plans* can be either *defined benefit plans* or *defined
contributions plans*. The former is the type of plan provided by Mutual
of America, United Way of America's pension insurer, to local United
Way professionals and other charities. Under a defined benefit plan,
benefits are established in advance by a formula, and employer contributions are determined within federal tax law limits and by actuaries
applying a variety of interest and mortality factors. With this plan, it's
possible to predict exactly how much a staff member will receive at
different times depending on the retirement dates. On the other hand,
a defined contributions plan, which was not made available by Mutual
of America, provides an individual account for each participant and
bases benefits solely upon the amount allocated to the participants account, adjusted by investment gains and losses and forfeitures allocated
to the account.

Nonqualified plans are used as means to provide supplemental benefits and/or to avoid the technical requirements imposed upon qualified plans. They are regulated by law and are perfectly legal types of
arrangements. In this case, the employer's deduction is deferred until
the amount attributed to the contribution is included in the employee's
income. These plans can be funded or unfunded. As to the plans that
Aramony had in mind for himself, he made certain they were funded,
and, according to the Investigative Report, used funds from the over-
funded qualified plans in order to fund the nonqualifying ones. Where

plans are funded to the employee's trust, the proceeds are taxable to the employee's gross income the first year in which they are transferred. Hence, Aramony would have to pay taxes on several million dollars he would receive the first year from his nonqualified plan were he to withdraw the total amount. One of the major issues raised by nonqualified plans is that boards often are not aware of the long-term financial obligation of the organization to fund these plans. Deferred compensation plans were made available to top-level senior staff. Other staff members could elect to participate in a range of other kinds of tax-deferred annuity plans.

UNITED WAY OF AMERICA, THE SPINOFFS, AND THE LAW

The fact is that the creation of spinoffs, either tax-exempt or for-profit, is both legal and common. Nonprofit legal expert Bruce Hopkins states that the federal law specifically provides for the tax treatment of income derived from a taxable subsidiary and flowing to its tax-exempt parent. It also provides regulations regarding the tax consequences to the parent organization if and when the subsidiary is liquidated. Moreover, a tax-exempt organization can create other tax-exempt subsidiaries. Many nonprofits have taken advantage of these rules by creating tax-exempt lobbying organizations. Several court decisions, including one from the Supreme Court, as well as numerous IRS private rulings have supported this activity. Hopkins points out that transactions between spinoffs is not only perfectly normal, but frequently beneficial to participating parties as well.

The press has indicated that millions of dollars were transferred to the spinoffs. The issue is not the transfer of funds, but *how the funds were used.* In the case of tax-exempt charitable organizations, the funds must be used for charitable purposes; in the case of for-profit spinoffs, the test becomes whether the amounts spent on capitalizing the spinoff were appropriate, and how the funds were ultimately used.[10]

The other issue relates to the fact that members of most of the boards of the spinoffs were friends and colleagues of Aramony as well as Aramony himself. This also is an acceptable practice. It is certainly not illegal. The reasoning is that overlapping directorates are considered an acceptable way to control and monitor subsidiaries. For many years, hospitals and universities, for example, have used subsidiaries as ways to carry out their mission.

Gifts In Kind America—The Model Spinoff

The basic model for the spinoffs was Gifts-in-Kind, now known as Gifts In Kind America. The first of the spinoffs to be eventually situated outside the building, it is in many ways the most successful one. It was approved at the Board of Governors meeting on December 15, 1983 and incorporated in March 1984. Its original purpose was to ensure the efficient distribution of gifts from corporations to eligible charities, provide a service to corporations by screening the recipient charities, assure accountability to donors, and act as a clearinghouse for such gifts. It also enabled companies to help the communities in which they operated, reduce inventory-carrying costs, and possibly receive some tax benefits.

In my opinion, Gifts In Kind America was established as a separate organization for the best reasons and succeeded in carrying out its mission beyond expectations. Its success is due to a number of important reasons. Among them are its broad-based Board, excellent executive leadership, and, perhaps most important of all, Aramony's lack of real interest in it after it was established. Therefore, this spinoff was never compromised. Its mission, policies, and directions were established independently of Aramony by its Board and its president, Susan Corrigan. Corrigan had been Aramony's executive assistant for a few months before being asked to work with a new Gifts In Kind program. Stephen Paulachak, who was working on the program at the time, told her she would have to find another job if she did not secure funding by January 1, 1984. Funding from the Lilly Endowment began on January 1, based on a proposal submitted by Corrigan.

The impetus for Gifts In Kind America was to create a vehicle whereby companies could contribute overstocked or obsolete merchandise to tax-exempt organizations and thereby receive a tax deduction. It first began when the 3M Company asked several charities, including the United Way, to distribute copiers and typewriters to their respective members. Donations have included office equipment, computer hardware and software, school supplies, personal care items, etc. The initial Board of Directors consisted of Aramony, Stephen J. Paulachak, and Lane Adams, former president of the American Cancer Society and a close Aramony colleague. Aramony recruited William M. Ellinghaus, executive vice chairman of the New York Stock Exchange, as its first chairman. Today, the 22-member Board is well represented by a broad selection of corporate leadership. United Way of America is represented by senior vice president Bob Beggan.

Initially, Gifts In Kind America was housed by United Way of America, paid its own rent and other operating costs. Paulachak, who had resigned from the Board, served for a while as its chief professional officer.

Aramony had served as volunteer president at the time the organization was first incorporated, although he rarely attended meetings. After several years, Eilinghaus finally asked Aramony to resign as president and join the Board. Aramony was furious and refused to do so. By that time, Gifts in Kind America had moved into separate quarters and had achieved considerable success under Corrigan's leadership.

The creation of Gifts In Kind America as a separate corporation created some dissention in the United Way field. Local United Ways had received many services as a result of its basic dues payments. Gifts In Kind America, no longer a part of United Way of America, and in need of raising its own funds to assure its independence, began to charge local United Ways to serve as its local representative (primarily as a clearinghouse). If they were not able to participate, Gifts In Kind America would often select another local partner.

Under the leadership of the current chairman, Thomas D. Hutchens, the organization has delivered over $300 million in product donations to over 50,000 voluntary organizations in 2,000 communities over the past decade.[11]

The success of Gifts In Kind America can be attributed to several factors:

1. A widely diverse and active board which was deeply committed to the mission of the organization;
2. Strong support for its able and committed president;
3. Placing the needs of the organization ahead of other considerations, including those of local United Ways; and
4. Securing independent sources of funding.

Unfortunately, the example set was not followed in the establishment or operation of any of the other spinoffs.

Partnership Umbrella

By far the most controversial of the spinoffs was Partnership Umbrella, created as a Virginia nonstock, nonprofit company. This means that it has no shareholders and none of its profits can benefit its directors. Its profits have to be either invested into the business or given away to charity since Partnership was *not* tax-exempt. Like other profit-making corporations, it pays taxes. It was presented to the Board of Governors as one of three cost-cutting initiatives which would use the buying power of the nonprofit sector to negotiate deep discounts. The example cited as a precedent was (you guessed it) Gifts In Kind America.

Other reasons given to the Board of Governors for creating a separate entity was to assist large and small United Ways and non–United Way affiliated organizations in obtaining discounts on a wide variety of products and services. (It differs from Gifts In Kind America, which receives donations from companies for free distribution to the recipient.) Since its revenues might eventually be taxable as unrelated business expenses if it were housed in United Way of America, it was reasoned that a separate entity would be best in order not to raise questions regarding United Way of America's tax-exempt status.

In establishing Partnership Umbrella, Aramony indicated that United Way of America would permit it to use the name "United Way" and to clarify the terms of its sponsorship. Its after-tax "profits" would be used to provide venture grants to United Way of America for special initiatives and to increase discounts to agencies.

Its initial Board of Directors, unlike Gifts In Kind America, consisted of Aramony's close friends and colleagues: Steve Paulachak; Lane Adams; William J. Flynn, chairman of Mutual of America, United Way of America's pension fund, and a long-term colleague and friend; and Florence Hesselbein, former chief executive of the Girl Scouts and a close Aramony colleague.

It became controversial for a number of reasons. First, it appeared to be a charity because of its mission to provide discounted services and equipment to charities, yet it would not make its audit available to the public (which is not required for a for-profit company by law). Although this may not look right, it was perfectly legal to withhold this information. Second, it loaned money to other spinoffs and purchased real estate (which is also legal, but didn't look right). Third, it had a Board consisting of Aramony's friends and cronies (also legal, but it didn't look right).

Charities Funds Transfer

Charities Funds Transfer was approved by the Board of Governors and was established in 1988 to speed and facilitate the disbursement of funds from company-wide campaigns. Thus, the funds raised by facilities in different parts of the country would be sent by the company's headquarters office to Charities Funds Transfer to be distributed to United Ways in the communities in which their plants are located. This procedure had been costly and time-consuming for corporations. Local United Ways' corporate offices in communities such as Detroit, Chicago, and New York City had performed this function, receiving income either in terms of fees from the company or interest income from the *float*, that is, the interest earned off the money held over time.

A study of the New York City system conducted by the American Express Company recommended the establishment of an entity like Charities Funds Transfer. As a result, Aramony established a special task force to develop procedures which would be approved by the National Professional Advisory Council.

Initially, the Board consisted of Richard J. O'Brien, then Executive Vice President of United Way of America; Hamp Coley, a senior vice president at United Way of America and one of Aramony's longest associates. Also included were Allan S. Cooper; Jack Costello; Calvin Green; and Joe Guise, also close Aramony associates. The Board also included Paulachak. It was funded from of the proceeds off the float. Why no corporate representatives were included is not clear. It would have seemed appropriate to involve some company headquarters people who used the service and had a vested interest in its success. However, one of the individuals involved in the initial discussions leading to the spinoff's establishment told me that if corporate people were involved, it would make it more difficult for the members of the Board consisting of Aramony's close associates to have an excuse to visit companies here and abroad.

One controversial trip by some of the above-mentioned Board members and their spouses involved a visit to the Charities Aid Foundation in London, which provided a similar clearing function for its corporate members. Was payment for this trip by Charities Funds Transfer, a charity, "illegal"? The answer is no, if there was a bona fide business purpose of the trip. The Board members might have to pay for their spouses attending as well as extra days not associated with the business purpose.

Charities Funds Transfer has just recently completed its first audit after being in business for four years. Is the failure to produce an annual audit illegal? No, not for this type of charity.

Sales Service/America

In April 1990, the Sales Service function was spun off from United Way of America as a nonprofit, nonstock Virginia corporation, similar in structure to Partnership Umbrella. Its purpose was once again to avoid unrelated business expenses, downsize United Way of America, and increase current catalog sales of products (then at $6 million) to local United Ways, which, it was believed, could be better accomplished through a separate entity.

Its initial Board consisted of O. Stanley Smith, a retired banker and businessman from Columbia, South Carolina and a close friend of Aramony's for over 30 years; William S. Ruben, former chairman of a major department store chain and previously an active volunteer from Miami; Thomas M. Hallin, former Arthur Andersen partner from Denver and close colleague of Aramony's; and Robert D. Aramony, Aramony's son. Thomas J. Merlo, chief financial officer of United Way of America, was a founding member as well as secretary-treasurer, until his resignation in February 1992. Board members were to receive compensation of $1,000 per meeting to cover expenses and time. In April 1990, Robert Aramony became president of Sales Service/America.

Is it illegal for Aramony's son, Robert, to have become the head of this spinoff? No, it isn't. Fortunately, he was well qualified for the job. But, even if he had not been, it still would have been legal to hire him.

United Way International

Jim Robinson called voluntarism America's greatest export. United Way International was incorporated in 1974 as a nonprofit, tax-exempt corporation. It is the oldest United Way spinoff. I was privileged to have served as its chief operating officer for nearly two decades, on loan from United Way of America.

Its purpose was to formalize relationships within the United Way movement in the United States and United Way organizations which had evolved in other countries as early as 1928. Services were provided to over 200 United Way organizations in 25 countries. It conducted 11 international United Way conferences and assisted in encouraging the growth of the voluntary sector in other countries. It pioneered programs in the former Soviet Union by helping the Russian Republic develop a draft of what hopefully will become its first law on charity. It had placed full-time staff there before other voluntary organizations. In Poland, it channeled millions of dollars of surplus Defense Department material to voluntary organizations through an office it supported in conjunction with the American Committee for aid to Poland; and conducted two major conferences for the newly developing voluntary sector there (the first conference was addressed by Lech Walesa) and created a United Way organization in Hungary.

Recognizing that we had neglected Western Europe, I worked closely with the European Foundation Centre and the Fondation de

France to hold the first major conference for voluntary organizations in Western Europe. Hundreds of representatives attended the two events, held in 1991 and 1992. In recent years, United Way International had supplied the ambulance service in Shanghai, China with modern emergency equipment (provided at deep discounts by vendors), saving hundreds of lives; also supplied were over 80 donated hospital beds to homes for the aged in that country. Until United Way of America cut back its funding because of its severe financial problems following the crisis, United Way International had received 80 percent of its financing from that source. It also received voluntary dues from its affiliates, particularly the United Way/Centraide Canada, and from several dozen local United Ways interested in the program.

Aramony had been president since its inception and had always taken an active interest in its activities. He had never missed a Board meeting and attended every international conference, although he rarely attended any of its sessions other than the opening and closing ones where he either welcomed everyone or said farewell. The Board consisted mainly of volunteers who had been active in United Way of America or were long-term associates, colleagues, and friends of Aramony. Other than Gifts In Kind America, it was the only spinoff with a broad-based Board. In April 1991, United Way International moved to another building where it subleased office space from Sales Service/ America. Several weeks after Aramony resigned from United Way of America, he also left the presidency of United Way International.

I served as uncompensated chairman of the Board of a nonstock graphics design and advertising company which provided United Way International, as well as another spinoff, with high-quality products at below-market prices. In this case, my Board position accomplished the goal of saving money while producing excellent results. An independent evaluation by an outside individual selected by Thomas J. Hallin, chairman of the organization's audit committee, conducted six months before the United Way events took place determined that our prices were highly competitive. Was it legal? Of course.

I recall the near hysteria of some United Way International Board members when they realized that United Way International actually bought products from Sales Service/America, another spinoff.

The "Lesser" Spinoffs

The organizations we've discussed represent the major United Way spinoffs. Others included the now defunct *Professional Travel Systems* incorporated in 1983, which offered discounts to United Ways and other voluntary organizations. Its Board consisted of Aramony colleagues, even though none of them were familiar with the travel business. As Aramony's assistant at that time, I had negotiated successful travel costs with a local vendor that had provided outstanding service. Their prices were always at deep discount rates. I had provided the printouts indicating these discounts to Paulachak, who Aramony had put in charge of setting up the new travel agency. It made no difference. Aramony knew what was best. A United Way travel agency obviously had its benefits. I strenuously objected that the vendors we were using were not to be told of United Way's new travel agency until it was actually in business. This was very unfair to the vendor who had counted on United Way's business and rejected other customers so his agency could serve the company well. To me this approach was reprehensible, so I told the vendor, giving them several months to plan for new clientele. PTS's successor organization, *PTS International*, was also defunct by 1987.

Voluntary Initiatives America was established as the result of a contribution from Mutual of America to Aramony in the form of a "William Aramony Initiatives in Voluntarism" Fund. Aramony was to manage the interest on the fund. Its directors were Aramony, his son Robert, and Hamp Coley. Its major expenditure was the purchase of the condominium in Florida initially as an office for United Way International's Latin American program.

The purpose of the most recent spinoff, *Mobilization for America's Children*, was to develop a long-term preventive strategy to help children and their families lead self-sufficient lives. A major fund-raising effort of which Aramony was the chief salesman was undertaken.

The spinoffs were created for a variety of reasons, some good, some perhaps not so good, and others due to a lack of correct information. Henry Suhrke, editor of *The Philanthropic Monthly*, stated in his critique of the Investigative Report that:

> Protection against the adverse consequences of absolute independence is achieved by overlapping directorates and contracts. The 'appearance created' may be beneficial and proper. In the nature of things, when a limited number of officers serve one entity and nine spinoffs, there will also be overlapping among the spinoffs.[12]

Suhrke also makes the point that many organizations look to the United Way and its central position in communities to help them achieve their legitimate and socially useful goals, "just because it is there."[13] To Aramony's credit, he always maintained enormous flexibility in responding to requests which he thought would eventually help people, often bending and twisting structures to accommodate what he judged to be a good cause. "It doesn't fit or it isn't a part of our mission" were words rarely, if ever, uttered by him. This approach was taken not because he was ignoring the mission of United Way of America, but because he interpreted it very broadly; that is, anything United Way of America did was okay as long as people were helped.

It is reasonable that United Way of America would eventually set up separate organizations with separate missions with a degree of independence to deal with its increasing number of programs, while at the same time maintaining some control.

ALTHOUGH THE SPINOFFS WERE LEGAL, PERCEPTION MEANT EVERYTHING

Knowledgeable authorities began to recognize fairly early that the structures of the spinoffs were fundamentally sound and legal. It appears that one of the critical issues affecting a federal investigation will be to determine if any of the officials of United Way of America or the spinoffs violated the private inurement doctrine.

The fact remains that Aramony's salary, perks, and privileges, as well as the arrangements which established the spinoffs, were legal. In addition, the spinoffs were established for essentially sound reasons. Some may differ as to whether or not they should have been established or kept as part of United Way of America. However, the reasons for establishing them were approved by the Board. Because some didn't work, or some worked better than others, is no reason to say that they shouldn't have been created.

The lawyers retained by United Way of America were qualified to judge the legality or illegality of the spinoffs, but they were not in a position to judge whether or not the spinoffs should have been established (assuming no laws would have been violated). For example, in their report, the lawyers said, "[W]e must believe that sharing the (incentive) payment with Partnership Umbrella was an improper allocation of United Way funds." Says who? That decision was, and should have been, a Board management decision, not a legal one. The lawyers also suggested that Sales Service/America, Charities Funds Transfer, and Mobilization for America's Children should be moved back under United Way of America's control. They may have been correct. However, it was the Board's responsibility to weigh the pros and cons of doing so, based on a variety of issues—such as reducing United Way of America's overhead and bureaucracy, and allowing some of these programs more freedom to be creative in providing their services. Although the lawyers cited some of these other issues, evidently they did not consider them important. Making one-sided recommendations, such as these lawyers did, without taking into account other, sometimes larger, issues does a disservice to the organization—especially in *this* situation, because a significant part of the Board's problem had been approving many measures without knowing all of the facts and ramifications of its decisions.

Prudence should have dictated that all of the spinoffs have broad-based boards. Partnership Umbrella should not have purchased real estate and loaned money. It was clearly not a part of its mission.

Thus, the fundamental issue becomes one not of law, but of perception. Aramony was tried and convicted in the court of public opinion and not a court of law. The next chapter will deal with issues of ethics and perception. It is these issues, not the legal ones, which led to the problems of United Way of America and its president.

REFERENCES

1. *Webster's II New Riverside University Dictionary* (Boston: Houghton Mifflin Company, 1984), p. 680.
2. Verner, Liipfert, Bernhard, MacPherson and Hand. *Report to the Board of Governors of United Way of America* (April 2, 1992), pp. 27, 33.
3. Bruce R. Hopkins, *A Legal Guide to Starting and Managing a Nonprofit Organization*, Second Edition (New York: John Wiley & Sons, 1993), pp. 54–58.
4. Bruce R. Hopkins, "Republican Campaign School Held not Tax exempt; Much new law created" in *The Non Profit Counsel* (Vol. VI, No. 7, July 1989), pp. 1–3.
5. "Text of Letter in Which Former United Way Chief Replies to Same Charges," *The Chronicle of Philanthropy* (May 19, 1992), and other sources.
6. *Compensation Survey Report of Management Positions in Not-for-Profit Organizations* (Rosslyn, VA: Towers Perin, 1992).
7. "Compliance with Safety Rules: Often Grudging," *The Chronicle of Philanthropy* (March 24, 1992).
8. "Charity Chiefs Face a New Question: How Much Do You Make?" *The Chronicle of Philanthropy* (March 10, 1992).
9. Hopkins, p. 119.
10. Bruce R. Hopkins, *The Non Profit Counsel* (Vol. IX, No. 7, July, 1992), pp. 6–8.
11. Gifts In Kind America, *1991 Annual Report*.
12. Henry C. Suhrke, *The Philanthropy Monthly* (Vol. XXIV, No. 10, December 1991), p. 7.
13. *Ibid*, p. 19.

CHAPTER 7

Ethics, Lawyers, and the Press

"Those who presume to serve the public good assume a public trust."[1]

Independent Sector, Inc.

The events concerning United Way in the spring of 1992 need to be analyzed from two different points of view: legal considerations and ethical ones. The last chapter discussed the legal issues surrounding these events in general terms. But, legal issues aside, what happened to create such an outcry from the public? Clearly, there was considerable ambiguity about whether the events were illegal, unethical, or something else. To most, it just didn't "smell right." It didn't "smell right" because the violations were not so much violations of the law, but violations of commonly accepted standards of what the public perceived to be the role of charities in American society and the conduct of those who run them. Most of us intuitively know when something just doesn't seem right—and what happened didn't seem right to many different people from many different segments of the population who contributed to and benefited from the United Way. Simply stated, what was violated was the public trust.

This chapter will explore the issue of public trust, that is, the ethical issues regarding, one, public expectations of charitable organizations, two, the lawyers, and other parties who investigated United Way of America and the spinoffs, and three, the press which reported the events.

ETHICS AND THE PUBLIC TRUST

One definition of ethics is "a system or code of conduct based on universal moral duties and obligations which indicate how one should behave. It deals with the ability to distinguish good from evil, right from wrong and propriety from impropriety."[2] In the case of charitable organizations, rules or standards do not exist for the field as a whole. However, there appears to be a set of commonly held beliefs by most people based on the perception of how charitable organizations "ought" to act. Thus, how charitable organizations behave varies according to who is observing the activity. United Way of America's Standards of Excellence, cited in Chapter 2, added an ethics statement a number of years ago, although I never remember anyone ever referring to it. Defining ethics can be compared to finding a common definition of beauty, with most people agreeing that "beauty is in the eyes of the beholder." However, there may be certain individuals, or even picturesque scenes, that most people would consider "beautiful" (such as the Grand Canyon, a gorgeous sunset, a pristine mountain lake) on which there would be general agreement. In some respects, attempting to define "ethics" and "charity" is impossible. I remember the comment by a government official, who, in trying to define "pornography," said, "I can't define it, but I know it when I see it." For the purposes of our discussion, the United Way crisis will be considered within the framework of *commonly* shared beliefs about charity—beliefs which set this field of human endeavor apart from most of society's other activities.

Philanthropic gadfly Henry C. Suhrke, as well as Robert L. Payton before him, has strong reservations about the current trend of developing "codes of ethics" for voluntary organizations because of fundamental, unresolved, deeper issues related to ethics and philanthropy. Suhrke refers to the current code development efforts as an "ethical desert." Although some of his concerns could be considered hair splitting, he suggests that these codes may merely reflect the self-interests of the organizations developing them—worse, they could begin to institutionalize conformity. Words such as "distasteful," as used by the Independent Sector, in establishing ethical parameters, for example, may just be a substitution for the term "nonconformist."

Does a "specialized" voluntary organization, for example, in the arts, need to represent all of the constituencies with which it comes into contact in order to be considered open, or accountable, that is, "ethical"? Perhaps, he says, each charity, carrying out the wishes of its donors, may belie the need for diverse representation and still be "profoundly ethical." He suggests that such codes may be one other factor which can be manipulated by an arrogant leader.

He says that most codes do not address critical ethical issues such as salary (clearly an issue on the Aramony case). Any effective self-regulation in a democracy must involve elements of "due process"—hearing, testimony, etc. "The ability to meet and draw up codes and standards is a valuable privilege; however, the ability to use them to deprive others of their just powers and rights is not a part of that privilege." Ethics, he believes, have limited value unless they directly challenge "generally accepted" practices of the voluntary sector. Varying opinions on these important issues indicate that there are underlying conflicts concerning the ethical values of the sector. Fundamental issues must be resolved, he believes, if there are to be commonly accepted standards.[3]

Among the profound issues begging for review and discussion by the voluntary charitable sector as a whole, suggests Suhrke, is the question: Does present-day philanthropy reinforce class distinctions? (A strong case for this position is made by Teresa Odendahl in *Charity Begins at Home* [1990]. She mentions that most wealthy people give to services which benefit their own class such as arts and music.) What are the issues of "right" and "wrong" regarding ill-gotten wealth which may have harmed people—and then used for the public good? Alleged crime boss Meyer Lansky regularly contributed to the United Way of Dade County, and his check was gratefully accepted. Is the failure of UBIT (Unrelated Business Income Tax) reform, which effectively permits some charitable activities to compete with and therefore harm some small businessmen and women, necessarily ethical or good for charity? Are tax privileges granted by government to voluntary organizations appropriate when half the sector is supported by the government anyway? Suhrke believes that ethics and philanthropy will have meaning only if it takes on these tough, broad issues. And to some degree he's right.

More specifically, the United Way itself deals with such ethical issues as a normal part of its daily existence. For example, do the Boy Scouts have an ethical right to deny membership to gay or atheist young men and leaders? Should United Ways ethically support abortion services? Should striking workers be given services by United Way–supported charities? These and other issues face communities across the nation every day. Usually they are handled politically. Gay rights are acceptable in San Francisco, but not perhaps in a city in the

Bible Belt. Family planning is "okay" in some communities, but not others.

Our task here is not so erudite. We are dealing with the most rudimentary ethical considerations, based on perceptions. Does this make our ethics relative? Of course it does. Obviously, ethical standards applied to the voluntary sector are different from those applied to business (for example, the issue of mind-boggling salaries in the entertainment and sports field). Moreover, ethics applied to a fund-raising organization like the United Way differ from those applied to foundations. Foundations do not depend upon the public trust as a basis of acceptance and support from society as fund-raising organizations do. Virginia A. Hodgkinson of the Independent Sector says that the key difference is that donors feel that they "own" the charities to which they personally contribute. Therefore, large salaries for foundation executives are not as important to the public as are salaries for community-based fund-raising groups like the United Way.

PERCEPTIONS OF CHARITY

The attitude of the public is important for an understanding of the perceptions people have towards charitable organizations. These perceptions determine the ethical parameters within which charities need to operate in order to maintain the public trust. The public attitudes toward charity have been reviewed and summarized in a paper by Hodgkinson of the Independent Sector. In the introduction to her paper, she states that "When asked, people generally have a high regard for the work of charitable organizations and their importance to our society."

In 1973, a survey by the Commission on Private Philanthropy and Public Needs regarding how people felt about organizations soliciting money indicated the following:

> Ninety-three percent said that they agreed that charitable organizations did things they felt were worth supporting.
>
> Two-thirds of respondents were satisfied that organizations gave them enough information on how their money was being used, while one-third were not satisfied. However, two-thirds of that group said that charities to which they had contributed had *not* told them how much they spend on fund-raising. Ninety percent thought that charities ought to disclose fund-raising costs. In terms of acceptable fund-

raising costs, the most frequent reply was from "10 to 14" percent (27 percent of the respondents).*

In 1986, the Independent Sector published a survey conducted by Yankelovich, Skelly and White. In this survey, 93 percent of the respondents showed very positive public attitudes towards charity. In 1988, the National Charities Information Bureau (NCIB) sponsored a survey conducted by the Roper Organization. In response to questions about how important certain factors were in their decisions to contribute to charitable organizations, the following items were considered very important or important:

- A clear statement of mission (83 percent).
- Adequate amount spent for program, rather than management (82 percent).
- Undue pressure to give (71 percent).
- Accuracy of advertising and promotion (70 percent).
- Availability of annual report (53 percent).

Other responses relating to the survey included:

- Almost two-thirds wondered (agreed or mostly agreed) whether or not charities to which they contributed were well-managed or not.
- Nearly nine out of ten thought that more and more organizations were asking for money every year.
- Nearly three out of four of the respondents said that they sometimes wanted to know more about the organizations than what they had been told by it.
- Nearly eight out of ten said that it is increasingly more difficult to determine which organizations are responsible and legitimate.
- Nearly three-fourths of the respondents wished that another organization (such as an independent service like the NCIB) would tell them whether or not an organization was a responsible one.

---

*The authors of the study indicated that the public has an unrealistically low estimate of acceptable fund-raising costs. It should be noted that United Ways across the country average fund-raising and administrative costs are within this range (10–14%), or in some cases, lower.

- Seven out of ten thought that they knew enough about how the organizations they supported spent their money.
- Almost three out of four said that they had no trouble deciding which organizations deserved to be funded.
- Half of all the respondents said that they were not sure where to turn to for information to help them decide whether or not to contribute to an organization.
- Two out of three disagreed with the statement that they sometimes give to an organization without understanding what they do.

In general, the survey shows that contributors on the whole have a positive attitude toward the accuracy of information provided by charities.

A study completed in 1989 which targeted 350 donors in the San Francisco Bay area produced some interesting results. Ninety-five percent of the donors said that they trusted charitable organizations to put their contributions to good use. *However, 98 percent said that they would no longer support a charitable organization if they learned the organization was dishonest or engaged in unethical practice.* The same study indicated that 81 percent said that a high degree of public trust is placed in charitable organizations and that most charitable organizations are honest and ethical in their use of donated funds.

This study also concluded that disclosure statements of charities, however accurate they may be according to professional accounting standards, are generally not understood by the public. The author of the study suggested that informational materials used to report charitable information to the public be revamped to provide a more accurate understanding to the general public for which they were intended.

Hodgkinson concludes her review of the literature with the following observations:

1. The overwhelming proportion of the public believe charities are honest and ethical and use their donations for their intended purposes; but less consensus on how effectively they do their job.
2. The public would like to see more information on how charities use their money, including more laws and regulations requiring disclosure. Yet, there is little public understanding about what costs should be attributed to overhead, or administration and fund-raising, even among more educated donors. A majority feel that fund-raising costs should be kept below 20 percent.

Finally, she concludes that the public has positive attitudes about charitable organizations. However, charitable organizations are held to a higher standard than other groups. *It is clear that if charities engage in fraudulent or unethical behavior, they will lose the public trust and thus contributions.*[4]

In 1989, the Gallup Organization included some questions regarding United Way in a larger annual survey undertaken by the organization. United Way was third in the minds of people "when they think of donating money to charity" (the church was first, followed by the American Cancer Society).[5]

More recently, a Shearson Lehman Brothers survey conducted by the Roper Organization reported that a quarter of all Americans would make charity their first priority if they had "all the money in the world" to "fulfill their wildest dreams!"[6]

In 1992, a national survey conducted by the Gallup Organization for the Independent Sector, entitled *Giving and Volunteering in the United States*, asked several questions relating to public attitudes about various institutions. This survey was conducted from April 3 to May 17, 1992, thirteen weeks after the United Way crisis first broke. The respondents expressed their greatest confidence in *private education*. Federated charitable appeals (such as the United Way) ranked ninth out of a list of thirteen (federated charitable appeals had ranked third in 1990; and second in 1988 in prior surveys).[7] In the 1992 survey, only 31 percent of respondents reported a "great deal" or "a lot of confidence" in federated campaigns as compared to 51 percent who reported the same level of confidence in 1990.[8] Last were international/foreign institutions (such as cultural exchange or relief organizations). Americans expressed more confidence in all types of charitable organizations compared with other institutions in society, with the exception of the military, public education at all levels, and small business. The drop in the level of confidence in federated campaigns from second and third place to ninth place after the revelations of United Way was a significant observation.

Other conclusions related to this survey include the following points:

1. More people (88 percent) agree that charities are needed more today than five years ago than they did in 1990 (81 percent) and 1988 (71 percent); those who thought charities were more effective today than five years ago has remained about the same over a two-year period.
2. Fewer people (74 percent) agreed in 1992 that charities use

their funds more effectively than they did in 1990 (80 percent); and fewer people in 1992 (66 percent) thought that charities were more honest and ethical in the use of their funds than they did in 1990 (75 percent).[8]

3.   Although an economic downturn affects a substantial proportion of the population, only a small percentage stop giving and volunteering, but those who do contribute and volunteer less.[9]

Thus, it is clear from recent surveying following the United Way crisis that the public trust in charities has diminished in general and that within the sector, federated fund raising has dropped significantly when ranked against other sector organizations.

VOLUNTARY STANDARD-SETTING ORGANIZATIONS FOR CHARITY

In 1918, leaders of the War Chest, initiated in Ohio, established what eventually became the National Charities Information Bureau (NCIB). They were concerned about the millions of dollars people were contributing to war relief agencies. Today, its nine standards are widely circulated in pamphlet format to its members and the public. Charities are listed in several categories in the publication based on the extent to which they meet such standards.

In recent years, the advisory committee to the NCIB has developed more sub-standards related to the critical issue of governance because of the need to clearly place responsibility for oversight at the Board level. "Responsibility for ensuring sound policy guidance and governance and for meeting these basic standards rests with the governing Board, which is answerable to the public," concludes its standard on board governance.[10] Ken Albrecht, NCIB's president, believes unequivocally that when one goes into the nonprofit world, the mind-set must be different than in the for-profit world. "We're not here for profit, but to do good," says Albrecht. "If you believe in certain values, you must live those values. Nonprofits live in a fishbowl; this requires a high stewardship of ethics in order to maintain the public trust. There cannot be one set of values for stewardship and another set for management." Albrecht is an ardent defender of truth in reporting, especially in how "joint costs" are apportioned on federal reporting forms. Charities want to report a minimum amount of costs associated with "fund raising," and a maximum amount associated with education and other "program" activities. If mailings, for example, are educational, they should be used primarily to inform, *not* to raise money. To call letters, which are clearly aimed at raising funds for a charity, educational misleads the public.

The Philanthropic Advisory Service of the Council of Better Business Bureaus also maintains standards which aid its members and others in making charitable giving decisions. The Better Business Bureau movement began shortly after the turn of the century as a reaction by responsible businesses to widespread abuses of advertising claims during that period. Since 1945, one of the predecessor organizations had maintained a division which specifically reported on charitable solicitation which, at that time, reviewed the many appeals for funds related to the war effort. The Philanthropic Advisory Service continues that program for its 178 local member Better Business Bureaus.[11] Its emphasis continues to be in the area of charitable solicitation, rather than governance. Bennet Weiner, a vice president in charge of the Service, claimed that the United Way events rendered a "devastating blow in terms of the public trust." In May 1992 Weiner led a seminar exclusively devoted to the United Way issue.

ETHICS AND BIG BUSINESS

Under Aramony's tenure, United Way of America and the United Way movement gradually began to see itself as the handmaiden of business rather than of social work and social welfare. He believed that it was the business community which provided the resources which enabled the voluntary sector to serve people. Most importantly, business leaders were the elite of society by many standards and the United Way was the bridge which brought these two sectors together. It was important that top business leaders be recruited to serve the United Way of America, local United Way organizations, and the charities they support.

A popular perception is that most of American big business operates in a dog-eat-dog competitive environment where the relentless search for profits dominates the company at the expense of its employees and, ultimately, the public. And it may be true as some say that top corporate executives feel that they are somehow *entitled* to extraordinary salaries and perks.

The decade of the 1980s was a time when money and power were the measure by which one's worth was judged. This may be true of some CEOs; however, many others have recognized that corporate social responsibility is good for business. They have also recognized that ethical behavior is good for business.

I remember driving Bill Gates, the chairman of Microsoft, to the airport some years ago. He was squeezed into the back of my small Chevrolet convertible—about as far from a limousine as one could get. His mother, who at the time was chairman of United Way International, occupied the front seat. She informed me that he always flew coach class because his stockholders wouldn't have it any other way!

Jim Burke, chairman of Johnson & Johnson, exemplified great leadership by publicly admitting the problem when some Tylenol capsules had been tampered with, accepting responsibility and immediately recalling the product. In the well-deserved acclaim he received afterwards, he referred to his company's "credo" which was very clear: the customer comes first.

Since the Business Roundtable was founded in 1972, it has always included corporate social responsibility and ethics in its portfolio. In its *Corporate Ethics: A Prime Business Asset*, published in 1988, "The question of ethics in business conduct has become one of the most challenging issues confronting the corporate community in this era." It sets up guidelines for corporations in order to assist them in developing their own ethical corporate codes and standards.

In a section entitled *Lessons That Can Be Learned*, it states five ways for developing and implementing ethical standards in organizations.

1. The Role of Top Management—Commitment, Leadership, Example
It states that:

... the Chief Executive Officer and those around the CEO need to be openly and strongly committed to ethical conduct, and give constant leadership in tending and renewing the values of the organization. ... Companies find it necessary to communicate that commitment in a wide variety of ways—in directives, policy statements, speeches, company publications, and especially in actions. ...

There is deep conviction that a good reputation for fair and honest business is a prime corporate asset that all employees should nurture with the greatest care.

Among those managers there is also widespread recognition that corporate obligations extend to a variety of constituencies or stakeholders and that these responsibilities are central to the ethics of a corporation. Customers, shareholders, employees, suppliers, local communities and the larger society are basic constituencies that are considered in planning and evaluating corporate policy and action. ...

2. Importance of a "Code"—Clarity of Expectations
The importance of a "code" is two-fold: First, it clarifies company

expectations of employee conduct in various situations; and, second, it makes clear that the company intends and expects its personnel to recognize the ethical dimensions of corporate policy and actions.

3. The Process of Implementation—Making Ethics Work
. . . the value of "openness" as being critical to building an atmosphere of trust along with the involvement of personnel at all levels.

4. Involvement and Commitment of Personnel at all levels
No ethics program can be successful without the strong leadership of the CEO, and no CEO can ensure high standards of conduct in the organization without the strong personal contribution of each manager.

5. Measuring Results
Various means are used to measure the results of ethics programs by corporations—surveys, audits—and by more subjective observations and assessments.

Executives who participated in the development of the document, over 100 of them, believed that "a culture in which ethical concerns permeates the whole organization is necessary to the self-interest of the company." None saw a conflict between ethical practices and acceptable profits.[12]

John J. Phelan, Jr., former chairman of the New York Stock Exchange and a member of the Board of Governors of United Way of America, has had to deal directly or indirectly with his member companies, many of whose employees have gone to jail. Each year, every employee at the New York Stock Exchange must read and sign an ethics statement (that is, those individuals who buy and trade on the floor and who must be true to their word for the business to work). There is "the need," he says, "for all of us to convince our people that values and ethics are not antithetical to making a profit."

"People behave the way they are expected to behave. If we don't expect ethical behavior from the people of our organizations, they won't behave that way. But if we do expect it and let them know that anything else won't be tolerated, then people will behave the way we want them to."[13] Thus, there is a very strong sensitivity among many leading corporate executives for a corporate ethical behavior that is consistent with profit making.

ETHICS AND THE VOLUNTARY SECTOR

The concept of ethics and its relationship to the United Way is clearly *relative*, depending upon where you stand. The major ethical issue concerns how one perceives the United Way. If you define the United Way as a social welfare organization, certain ethical standards come into play. But if you view the United Way as being closer to business, then different ethical standards come into play.

Leaders of social welfare organizations are not expected to have high salaries, fly the Concorde, ride in limousines, or hire their children to head major activities related to the organization. This would be the standard if you perceive the United Way as a social welfare organization.

However, if you perceive the United Way as a business, then these perquisites become more acceptable. Corporations have plush offices and many of their executives command huge salaries. At the time Aramony's salary was divulged in *The Washington Post*, Roberto Goizieta's salary and stock options as president of Coca Cola exceeded $80 million. There was not a whisper from the public about that. People still bought Coca Cola. And overall, most corporate executives regularly hire limousines and fly first class. The public thinks nothing of this. So why was there such an outcry when Aramony did the same?

Perhaps, as some say, contributors felt that they owned the United Way and that it was their company because they supported it. They felt betrayed.

There is a special set of ethics which relates to nonprofit organizations. Hank Rubin, associate director of public administration at Roosevelt University in Chicago, states that the basic perception of the voluntary sector is predicated on altruism; and altruism, like ethics, is considered an "ultimate good." People are drawn to the voluntary sector in order to act out their altruistic motives. They are linked by bonds of "shared goodness." He says that "bad actions" can be attributed to three reasons:

1. The presence of people drawn to the sector by nonaltruistic motives;
2. The acquiescence of deluded altruists to self-serving temptations; and
3. The presumption of some in the sector that unethical means may be justified by altruistic ends.

The irony, he states, is that in the sector, which is essentially altruistic, ethics is a significant issue because we expect "more good" and we'll accept "less bad."

What he calls "legal ethics" transcend *all* sectors and are based on federal, state, and local laws. What he calls "normative ethics" vary from sector to sector. Each sector has its own culture because its ends are manifestly different. In my experience, this cultural difference between the sectors is so strong that it is very difficult for individuals to transcend these sectors in one lifetime. How many people do we know who have been able to effectively bridge these sectors in their work life? Not many. Two examples I can think of are Ken Albrecht, who worked for Equitable Life, and Bert Knauft, who worked for Aetna and later became vice president of the Independent Sector. Both served two of the largest insurance companies in America and had been active in the area of corporate philanthropy for their respective companies.

Standards of legal and normative ethics prescribe the behavior of people within organizations. They do not describe the organizations themselves. Administrators and technicians are the two types of individuals within organizations that are constrained by such legal and normative ethics. Administrators (those who have planning, management, and supervisory responsibilities) are expected not only to act ethically, but to "establish climates that insure legal and normative ethical behavior throughout their institutions. Presumptively, they are guarantors and weather vanes of ethical conduct. Their managerial practices and ethos are the fibers that transfer and weave legal and normative ethics into the fabrics of their institutions."

"Technical" experts are bound not only to the specific laws regulating their profession (legal ethics), but to their own set of professional codes of conduct (normative ethics). These codes of conduct, that is, for the lawyers, accountants, and others who work in the sector, influence the normative ethics of the institution they serve. To the extent that these so-called technical people participate in management activities, their legal and normative ethics are woven into the fabric of the organizations they serve as well.

Thus, both legal and normative ethics, says Rubin, combine to set the standards for acceptable accountability. Under this construct, boards of directors are responsible for all of the legal requirements of the organization they serve within the ethical context of the sector, while the administrators and technicians are expected to adhere to the normative standards embodied in the mission of their organization as they seek to achieve its goals.

The complexity of the accountability issue for the voluntary sector rests in two areas:

1. The infinite variety of purposes and, therefore, their relativity to normative ethics; and

2.   The higher standards of normative ethics that society imposes on the sector.[14]

These issues bear a direct relationship to Aramony's "extravagant lifestyle" and his controversial management practices. Many observers of the charitable scene recognize a fundamental difference between how the public perceives charitable, voluntary organizations as compared to their perception of private companies or the sports and entertainment field. Aramony perceived his own role as that of surrogate for the corporate community. He interpreted this role as an endorsement from his high-level Board, entitling him to the corporate lifestyle as well. In responding to a question by *The New York Times* regarding the reason for this lifestyle, he replied, "You don't find these people [donors] . . . in McDonald's; you rarely find them in the New York subway.[15]

Perhaps his greatest ethical lapse is the one cited by a management consultant, the late Robert K. Greenleaf:

> The failure (or refusal) of a leader to foresee may be viewed as an *ethical* failure; because a serious ethical compromise today (when the usual judgement on ethical inadequacy is made) is sometimes the result of a failure to make the effort at an earlier date to foresee today's events and take the right actions when there was freedom for initiative to act.[16]

In *Ethics and the Nation's Voluntary and Philanthropic Community—Obedience to the Unenforceable*, a watershed statement by the Independent Sector, the authors of the report recognized the extremely fragile nature of the public trust. The report identifies three levels of ethical behavior: The *first level* is concerned with obeying the law. The *second level* is composed of those behaviors where one knows the right action, but is tempted to take a different course. The *third level* is one which recognizes that ethical decisions are not necessarily based on what is right or wrong, but among competing options.

The document recognizes that there are essential ethics and values which *all* voluntary organizations share:

> *Commitment beyond self* is at the core of a civil society. Example of unethical behavior: "High, dishonest, or inappropriate expenses submitted for travel and meetings."
> *Obedience of the laws* including those governing tax-exempt philanthropic and voluntary organizations is a fundamental responsibility of stewardship. Example of unethical behavior: ". . . trustees are paid inflated annual fees for very few meetings and decisions."

Commitment to the public good requires those who presume to serve the public good to assume a public trust.

Example of unethical behavior: Foundation guidelines are broad and its procedures complicated, with most of the money going to a few institutions with contacts with the trustees.

Respect for the value and dignity of individuals is a special leadership responsibility of philanthropic and voluntary organizations.

Example of unethical behavior: "A small executive committee of insiders makes all of the decisions for the board on the grounds that the issues are too sensitive or complex to bring to the Board."

Tolerance, diversity, and social justice reflect the independent sector's rich heritage and the essential protections afforded it.

Example of unethical behavior: "No minority persons are on a social service board serving minority neighborhoods."

Openness and honesty in reporting, fund-raising and relationships with all constituencies are essential behaviors for organizations which seek and use public or private funds and which purport to serve public purposes.

Example of unethical behavior: "The combination of four grants given to the organization by different donors covers 200 percent of the education director's time, salary, and space."

Accountability to the public is a fundamental responsibility of public benefit organizations.

Example of unethical behavior: "For the fifth year in a row the fund-raising appeal talks only about plans and not about what's been done to date."

Prudent application of resources is a concomitant of public trust.

Example of unethical behavior: "In lieu of salary, the staff director prefers a percentage of all funds raised."[17]

As the Independent Sector committee debated the complex area of ethical practices, it stated that "It is the gray domain of ethical choices that creates tensions and dilemmas for those entrusted with the leadership as well as the day-to-day operations of voluntary and philanthropic institutions," and "[I]n the independent sector, public trust stems from our willingness to go beyond the law or even the spirit of the law. We act ethically because we have determined that it is the right thing to do." And, "[T]he ethical behavior of an institution is the ultimate responsibility of its trustees."[18]

Charitable organizations depend upon donations for their survival; this is money that people are *not* obliged to give. People give voluntarily, expecting that the volunteers and professionals entrusted with their funds will spend them in the most judicious way to achieve the results for which the contribution was solicited. Voluntary organizations do not face elections as in the government sector; nor do they have a bottom line of profit or loss as in the corporate sector. People's faith in the voluntary sector is simply the expectation that its activities are charitable and that as much money as possible will be used for the public good. The report correctly points out that concern regarding ethical behavior of charities is part of the bigger picture of general skepticism of the public towards all social institutions. It calls for high standards of openness, honesty, and public service. If public support is eroded, so is the sector's capacity for public service.

It is very clear that the public perceived United Way of America and, by extension, those identified with the name "United Way" as having violated the public trust, *even though no laws may have been broken.* Whether they were legal or not, flights on the Concorde, cars and drivers, the perception of an extraordinary high salary, and pension benefits for a chief professional officer of a charitable organization did not wash with the bulk of United Way contributors who are mostly working people.

The question that begs to be answered is how could it all have happened? What was the environment which allowed the events to transpire, events which brought down the largest voluntary organization in the world?

THE VIEW FROM THE BOARD

The Board of Governors of United Way of America is considered one of the most prestigious in the nation. Top corporate people vie to serve on it. It was rarely difficult to recruit members from the top echelons of corporate America, even if some were unwilling. Reportedly, Jim Robinson, chairman of the American Express Company, initially had strong negative feelings about the United Way. It did not take Aramony long to convince Robinson of the error of his ways. He eventually became one its most active and influential members. The introduction of the Investigative Report stated: "Because he [Aramony] led a not-for-profit institution to record contributions and worldwide renown, Board members placed a significant degree of trust in him."[19]

I attended many Board meetings over the years. They were structured in such a way as to direct and control the flow of discussion almost exclusively toward *program* goals rather than operational ones. This means that a great deal of staff attention was devoted to educating volunteers so that they could adequately explain the program they had been asked to present to the Board. The origin of the program was almost always an Aramony initiative. Programs deemed particularly important were sold directly by him to the volunteers. Although Board members made suggestions about refining or enhancing a program in various ways, these changes were usually cosmetic. The basic program always remained intact. The more controversial the program was expected to be, the more prestigious the volunteer who presented it. If Aramony could not get the backing of his top volunteers for a program, he would modify it in such a way as to gain its acceptance. Other than the person who happened to be the current chairman, Robinson was Aramony's primary sounding board for new program initiatives.

This approach to Board meetings left very little time to consider other matters such as those related to procedures, management policies, salaries, and various internal control issues. Aramony always dismissed these areas as inappropriate activity for such high-level Board members. He had virtually no patience for management per se, or those who practiced it. Staff with a so-called "management mind" were considered by him to be a necessary evil. He had always refused to allow his chairmen to send subordinate staff to work with him. Robinson and Akers both, not having the time themselves, attempted to assign some of their company staff to find out what was going on at United Way of America. Aramony would have none of this. He would deal with his chairmen *directly*. No one was to come between him and his chairmen. Robinson and Akers gave in and withdrew their staff, except those who dealt in the program areas. If the company staffs of the chairmen had been allowed to monitor at least some internal functions, they might have been able to sound some alarms. In any case, Aramony felt that management of the organization at all levels was *his* responsibility; and if the Board didn't like it, they could fire him—a thought which turned out to be unusually prophetic.

Therefore, a clear distinction must be made between an active Board and one that assumed its proper oversight responsibility for the organization. Aramony was justly proud of the fact that he was able to recruit these top corporate leaders to donate enormous amounts of time. And no one questions the fact that the Board members were extremely active, albeit in the program area only.

Thus, motions related to the establishment of spinoffs were passed in a perfunctory matter. These decisions were considered "administrative" and, therefore, less important. There were no Board committees which looked at the feasibility of the various spinoffs and their arrangements. In fact, you could say that the Board members knew nothing about them other than that they existed. Many probably never remembered voting for their establishment in the first place.

There were virtually no committees devoted to internal controls and management practices. The only functioning internal committee was the Audit Committee. This committee approved the auditing firm and reviewed the completed annual audit prior to its presentation before the Board for approval. Aramony's *modus operandi* was to treat the Executive Committee as a surrogate Board. It was the Executive Committee which dealt with issues of salary for the president and ranges for other categories of staff. The Executive Committee also dealt with his pensions and other more sensitive matters. This group, always headed by a minority or a female, dealt with these matters the same way as the Board itself dealt with program issues—perfunctorily. Key matters were decided beforehand and any difficulties ironed out well in advance of the meeting. Salary and other items were dealt with in closed sessions attended only by trusted advisors and/or the company legal counsel. All other staff, including Aramony, left the room during these closed sessions of the Executive Committee. This provided the appearance of "arm's length" distancing from the discussion.

Now that you understand how Aramony managed the Board meetings and that the Board had complete faith in him, it is easier to believe that none of them knew what was really happening and were not in a position to defend the corporation against the allegations.

When the bullets started flying in the spring of 1992, the Board members deserted Aramony *en masse*, as though he had utterly betrayed them, *even though* they in essence had approved everything. The only practical option when the crisis occurred was for the Board to run for cover, because there was no one who knew enough to explain to the public what had happened. It was sad to see such a respected figure like Dr. LaSalle Lefall, one of the most charismatic and articulate of leaders, trying to respond to questions from the field and the press during the first difficult days of the crisis about issues with which he, like so many of his colleagues on the Board, were, at best, only vaguely familiar.

In regard to Aramony's extravagant lifestyle, it is my opinion that his salary and pension benefits, flying the Concorde, having a car and driver, and buying condominiums in New York and Florida would not have been given even superficial condemnation by the Board had they thoroughly discussed these matters beforehand! This was what was expected of a well-managed enterprise *like their own.*

THE VIEW FROM UNITED WAY OF AMERICA STAFF

The professional staff at United Way of America was, for the most part, aware of the unequal application of management policies by Aramony. This awareness created most of the morale problems, particularly in the area of salary determination. The staff was highly differentiated in terms of titles and positions. There was a time, for example, when the staff was located in the previous headquarters, that a change in position automatically produced a change in the configuration of the individual's office. In one case, when a staff person was promoted to a higher position, the office had to be made two feet wider to be the same size as others at his or her level, a policy which was soon dropped due to a lack of appropriate space and the increasing changes in titles and positions. Although Aramony generally avoided chain of command directives, on paper and in the distribution of perks, the staff was highly structured with senior vice presidents, vice presidents, directors, etc. Major morale problems resulted when his personal staff, those who worked with him most closely, were perceived as having received salary increases and benefits which were not reflective of their position. In order to make a "silk purse out of a sow's ear," he would send an aide to buy clothes for a new secretary if he didn't like the way she dressed.

The extravagant travel and other lifestyle issues were of somewhat less concern because no one, other than Aramony, could use a car and driver (unless, as I have said, they happened to be with him on a trip), fly first class, or assume many of the perks to which only he was entitled. It was always clear to staff who supported him that he was a special, unique, and gifted person who had every right to set his own rules and standards. When the organization began to unravel, the senior staff mostly assumed a very low profile.

THE VIEW FROM THE FIELD

United Way organizations were fully aware of Aramony's "imperial" lifestyle. Many of them, where possible, sought to emulate it. One thing most United Way professionals are grateful for is that Aramony made it seem "OK" to ask for big salaries, nice company cars, and club memberships. At last, they were receiving the status and hence the respect that had been denied them for so long. So they believed. He had, by improving his own standard of living, improved theirs as well. After all, the greatest leaders in America who served on his Board seemed to say it was all right.

Deep down, many recognized that when the crisis occurred they weren't surrogate businessmen after all. They were (once again) merely social "do-gooders" who had been put in their place for assuming the prerogatives of a lifestyle to which they had no right to aspire. The respect they sought had been denied them. I view this as the major tragedy of the whole affair. People in social service deserve to earn a decent wage and respect from the community. They are working to make communities better places for people to live and work. As much could be said about teachers as well.

What Aramony failed to do was bring the rest of the public along with this perception of the value to society of its "caretakers"—a value important enough to be well remunerated. He may be correct, but the public isn't ready to buy this vision.

There were very few voices that ever objected to the Aramony lifestyle they sought to emulate. But, there was substantial criticism of Aramony's son, Robert, heading Sales Service/America without any competitive search, even though he was considered well qualified for the job.

Most local United Way volunteers and professionals in the field were never aware of the rationale for the establishment of the spinoffs. They deserted Aramony because of issues completely unrelated to the events of the crisis. Indeed, their concerns had to do much more with his almost total lack of interest in meeting their needs, his penchant for pushing his programs down their throats, his disinterest in seeking their advice on most matters, but mainly for staying too long at the job. They, too, abandoned him *en masse*.

There were, of course, the other constituencies—the charities supported by United Way and the public. These constituencies also deserted him for many of the previously discussed reasons.

DISPARITY OF ETHICAL PERCEPTIONS

The effects of the events at United Way were so extensive from the viewpoint of violating normative ethics that it transcended virtually every organization in this sector. Thus, the public perception of the United Way was transferred to other organizations whose Boards suddenly came to life and belatedly exercised their responsibilities.

However, as the public reaction demonstrated, United Way was clearly an organization that was considered a charity and not a business corporation. United Way clearly had violated the normative ethics of not only its own organizational environment, but the entire nonprofit sector.

So powerful was the public outrage that the Board initially made no attempt to justify or explain the perquisites to the press or the public. Any explanation would have only made things worse, its leaders reasoned. So colossal was this misjudgment and gap in understanding between how the corporate community viewed the United Way and how it was viewed by the general public that the Board members were soon forced to deal with the issues. The public outcry was overwhelming. What then is the issue? The issue is that the Board never attempted to bridge the gap between the negative public perception and an explanation of the decisions they had made and approved over the years (decisions which related to Aramony's salary and perks and the establishment of the spinoffs). Not once did the Board take the high ground and publicly state the justifications for their decisions which were certainly not only legal, but in many ways, quite sound.

Ample explanatory material was available. Numerous materials had been sent to United Ways and the press by United Way of America. Yet, the provision of this information would have had a much greater impact if it had been stated publicly and by members of the Board. There were considerable opportunities to do so. In the earliest stages of the crisis, no member of the Board was made available as a public spokesperson. By doing nothing, the Board aggravated the crisis. A number of people faulted IBM, and particularly James G. Parkel, IBM director, corporate support programs, and his sidekick, Jack Sabater, for their less than adequate management of the events. This lack of response and indecision by IBM redounded negatively on United Way of America and substantially aggravated the crisis as it was unfolding. This nonavailability was no more pronounced than the failure to provide a national spokesperson for the first "Nightline" broadcast of February 27. In fact, Charles Shepard, a guest on the show and *The Washington Post* reporter who broke the story, gave a more cogent explanation of United Way than any of the other participants! Berl Bernhard stated during the first teleconference that Aramony apparently had not committed any crime, but that they were going to persist with the investigation on behalf of the Board anyway. The implication was made that something was amiss and that they, the lawyers and investigators, would get to the bottom of it. This brings us to questions of law and ethics as it relates to the crisis.

THE LAW, ETHICS, AND THE UNITED WAY

The investigation itself was carried out by the same law firm in which Lisle C. Carter, Jr., United Way of America's legal counsel, was a former member (namely, Verner, Liipfert, Bernhard, McPherson, and Hand). He recommended his old law firm to United Way of America. In fact, the firm had previously done other legal work for United Way of America. It was this same law firm that Aramony agreed to hire to investigate the allegations when they first surfaced late in 1991. It was this firm which suggested hiring the Investigative Group, Inc., run by former Watergate prosecutor Terry Lenzner. During the first teleconference, Aramony was defended by Berl Bernhard the senior partner responsible for the investigation; during the second, following disclosures to the press, Bernhard's firm had been retained by the Board to investigate him.

There are several issues which arise from this scenario:

1. *Does the fact that Verner, Liipfert represented Aramony at one time, the Board of Governors at another time, and were employed as investigators constitute a conflict of interest?*

Probably not, because it could be argued that Aramony worked for the Board when the firm was retained in the first place. But it does raise questions about the firm exercising proper judgment. It is a question of ethics and perception, which is what this affair is all about. There are numerous investigative law firms in Washington. It would have been prudent for the Board to have hired another law firm and a different investigative company which had had no previous contact with United Way of America at the time of the press reports and no affiliation to its in-house legal counsel. Verner, Liipfert had a letter inserted in the Investigative Report, obviously to avoid this specific criticism, composed by Wilmer, Cutler & Pickering, another law firm, which stated, "Based on the participation described above, we are satisfied with the methodology, objectivity, and integrity of the investigation and concur generally with the findings and recommendations of the report."

2. *Where was United Way of America's legal counsel?* Lisle Carter worked for United Way of America as in-house counsel from January 1988 to the end of 1991. He resigned just over a month before these events broke. Carter had always intended to leave at that time due to ill health and other personal reasons anyway. There was clearly no connection between his leaving and the events which transpired. How-

ever, Carter was never made available, as he should have been, to explain the rationale for the establishment of the spinoffs. He was also an officer of the corporation (United Way of America) and secretary to the board. This meant that he had the legal authorization to sign official papers for the corporation and that he was responsible for drafting the minutes of board meetings, both positions of great responsibility. By virtue of his role with the organization, he was in an excellent position to explain and defend the legality of the spinoff arrangements. In addition, his reputation as former chancellor of the University of the District of Columbia, as well as the fact that he is extremely bright and articulate, would have added to the credibility of the explanations.

3. *Was there a presumption of "guilt by association"?*

What occurred is best called a "clash of cultures."—the adversarial nature of the legal profession versus the accommodating nature of social service personnel. In the social service profession, we are trained to work with people, to negotiate, to compromise, and to problem solve in order to achieve mutually agreed-upon ends. Our own success depends on how well we are able to help one party see the viewpoint of the other. One of Aramony's primary responsibilities was to educate the board on the human service needs facing communities so that people could be helped.

Many staff were interrogated by lawyers and investigators as though they were already guilty. I can only suppose that the presumption is that inquisition-type procedures are the best way to reach the truth, denying what the layman believes is "due process." At least, this was the case during the early stages of the investigation in the spring of 1992. There were only three organizations which had broad-based boards: United Way of America, Gifts In Kind America, and United Way International. Although Gifts In Kind America was never subject to serious inquiry regarding wrongdoing (Aramony had virtually no interest in the organizations after its founding), the other two organizations were intensely investigated by teams of high-priced, uncompromising lawyers and investigators which cost hundreds of thousands of dollars. Most if not all of the spinoffs retained counsel. These lawyers would meet periodically. Reportedly some were unhappy when they found out the high hourly rates being charged by some of their colleagues.

The boards of both United Way of America and United Way International had abdicated their responsibility once again—this time to lawyers. When credibility was of the essence, the Board of Governors:

1. Inappropriately retained the same lawyers and investigators originally hired by Aramony, which had cleared him to the extent that the board voted him a "resounding vote of confidence." Perceptions at the time were important.

2. Approved publication of the Investigative Report on April 2, which had numerous errors, innuendo, and conclusions which the investigators lacked the competence to make. Dam was under considerable pressure to produce a final report by April 2 because of a Board meeting scheduled at that time. The quality of the report clearly indicates that it was a rush job. Verner, Liipfert, supposedly a vaunted law firm in Washington, had produced a document that was both carelessly written and laced with numerous inaccuracies. In addition, many questions were left open leaving the impression that something was "not quite right." Should lawyers or investigators be making recommendations on personnel and financial matters, as Bernhard indicated at the teleconferences? Should they be making decisions on whether or not there was justification for establishing spinoffs? The Board had approved Aramony's budget as well as the spinoffs, *then* it hired lawyers to make other decisions and recommendations because the "public" through the press had expressed concern about them! Yet its members took no responsibility.

3. Hired high-powered lawyers who interrogated staff as though they were already guilty of covering up and/or not telling the truth.

4. Asked the lawyers to serve as principal spokespersons for United Way of America during two televised conferences to the United Way constituency (something much more pronounced at the first conference at which Akers was not present).

A VIEW FROM UNITED WAY INTERNATIONAL

United Way International was one of the spinoffs subject to intense legal investigation because of alleged abuses by Aramony in his overseas travels and the related issue of the discarding of files. Although I recognize that what follows could be construed as self-serving, it is an example I was very familiar with and demonstrates again an abdication of Board responsibility. I'm told that similar situations occurred at United Way of America and at some of the other spinoffs as well.

From the very beginning, there was a presumption of guilt. I was totally truthful with my chairman, James F. Mulvaney, a lawyer from San Diego, about exactly how the events transpired regarding how the files were discarded at Aramony's request. He retained the Washington, D.C. law firm of Cadwalader, Wickersham and Taft.

Raymond Banoun and Martha Rogers from the firm were assigned to investigate the matter. It was clear from the beginning that the nature of the exercise was to find me "guilty by association" with Aramony. When Rogers was told that I would be represented at my hearing by Seymour Glanzer, a former Watergate prosecutor and very experienced in inquiries of this kind, she expressed considerable consternation.

Banoun's officious attitude was evident in the way my staff, who wasn't represented by lawyers, was dealt with. At one point during an interview with one of them, he asked about my professional reputation. When she began to describe it in a positive way he reportedly threw down his pencil, saying, "I don't want to hear *that!*" and immediately changed the line of questioning.

Over a quarter of a million dollars were charged by Cadwalader, Wickersham and Taft (at supposedly discounted prices) and, after reviewing virtually every single United Way financial item and program activity over the past five years, nothing incriminating was found. In addition, a comprehensive and expensive audit of the files by Arthur Andersen turned up no wrongdoing. This last exercise was done despite the fact that my accounting was thoroughly reviewed on a regular basis by United Way International board member Thomas M. Hallin, himself a retired partner with Arthur Andersen! Ultimately, nothing for which I was responsible as chief operating officer of United Way International (reporting to Aramony, its president) was found to be out of line. Nevertheless, I was asked to resign after 23 years of service, albeit with a very positive letter of recommendation from the chairman. My out-of-pocket costs for legal fees in order to defend myself against the lawyers hired by the chairman far exceeded my severance package. I also lost 40 percent of my pension benefits because I had to leave two years short of early retirement.

In January 1992, Aramony, who was the unpaid president of United Way International, had requested that I discard *all* files from previous years which had been audited. Even with repeated questioning, he assured me it was okay. When he asked where they were, I said that some were still in the United Way of America building. He ordered the five-drawer filing cabinet with these old files brought over. Despite my protestation, he demanded that they be discarded. Since these particular files were old and duplicate records, I had them discarded. All other files remained intact. Therefore, when asked by Aramony if the files had been discarded, I suggested that his request had been complied with, even though I had not complied with it. A few days after the *Washington Post* reported the destruction of files, investigators from United Way of America requested and received reports from the files which I had been told to discard, but hadn't. A list of the discarded files, which we had kept, was also turned over to them. Discarding these old files was not even an illegal act; it was a mundane task. Shepard's account of the disposal of files on my part was incorrect. He reported that "[f]ederal law requires that financial records be preserved at least three years past the filing date for the return for a particular year." Technically this is not true. The report advanced by Shepard was based on an erroneous premise, that is, that files had to be maintained for three years. The fact is that the rule to which he was referring (although in a distorted way) requires, as does common sense, that only those records need to be maintained which support the tax-exempt purpose of the organization, in this case, United Way International. However, since the Internal Revenue Service can audit tax-exempt organizations for their most current three years, it would obviously be prudent for the organizations to keep all their tax records for a three-year period. As an independent audit later confirmed, there were ample records, duplicates and otherwise, available to support the filing of the return for the years in question. However, under the circumstances, it created a perception of wrongdoing, which is what this book is all about, and caused an irreversible personal crisis for myself.

Over the years, Mulvaney had been one of Aramony's major boosters and true believers. Aramony had elevated him to various prestigious positions at United Way, as a Western regional chairman for United Way of America, and chairman of United Way International. When the press reports hit, he, as did so many others, joined the throng and sought to distance himself from Aramony. Like the trustees of United Way of America, he had failed his ongoing oversight of responsibility as well. He himself had been a close associate of C. Arnholt Smith who appointed him president of the U.S. National Bank in San Diego in 1973. Smith was eventually tried for grand theft, tax evasion, and fraud. Mulvaney himself was cleared of any wrongdoing. But his own very difficult association with an unpleasant event evidently did not transfer into any empathy for me.

WHERE WERE THE ACCOUNTANTS?

I have interviewed numerous individuals involved in accounting procedures at United Way of America and it appears that proper procedures were conducted and proper reports presented to the Audit Committee of the Board for review, prior to being approved by the full Board.

However, accounting firms have vested interests in continuing to do business with clients. Certainly, United Way of America would be considered a prestigious client by Arthur Andersen. Customarily, to save expenses and ensure greater profits, accounting firms will generally send young, inexperienced auditors to perform the fieldwork which is then reviewed by a senior partner at the firm. Managers, who report to partners, are generally under great pressure to "cross-sell" additional services to clients. These services might include a review of internal controls, computer consulting, management advisory, and tax assistance, etc. Success in this area is one way managers become partners.

Loren Kellogg, publisher of *Financial Statement Alert*, a research publication which scrutinizes the accounting practices of public companies, says that auditors, especially inexperienced ones, sometimes don't know the difference between form and substance. Managers see only work papers which are summaries of transactions. They often are unaware of their substance. When transactions take place year after year, they tend to be glossed over, especially when staff turnovers can place different people in the job every year. I never saw the same auditor two years in a row at United Way of America.

Auditors are charged under generally accepted auditing standards for making suggestions on how to improve the system of internal control of the organization they are serving. This is usually done by means of a "management letter." If the auditors fairly report on the position of the organization, whatever it is, and follow up with suggestions made in the letter, they have done their job. If the Audit Committee then does not act after receiving repeated management letters, then it, and not the auditors, is at fault.

United Way of America followed these procedures. Yet, we still have a problem of perception. Should nonprofit organizations periodically change their accountants? Governments frequently do. Most experts say that this may not be wise for a couple of reasons. One, the costs of starting with a new firm which does not have a history with the charity could be very costly. Two, if the managing partner in charge of supervising the audit is changed every few years, it is not necessary to change the firm. Maybe. At best, it is a fuzzy area which pits accounting firms who want to continue doing business with the charity against the charity's own accountants to make sure that an unqualified or "clean audit" is released to the public. As long as there is at least some reasonable justification for an action, a clean audit can usually be delivered.

The Accounting Issues Committee of the National Association of State Charities Officials stated that:

> We have witnessed an increase in the number of CPA practitioners willing to pander to the wishes of their nonprofit client at the expense of their professional and ethics responsibility to the public which is to present financial statements which *best represent the true performance* of the nonprofit.[20]

THE PRESS, ETHICS, AND THE UNITED WAY

Displayed just opposite the elevators on the ground floor of *The Washington Post* building in Washington are the "Seven Principles for the Conduct of a Newspaper" written by Eugene Meyer, the first president of the Washington Post Company. He had bought the newspaper in 1933 for $12,500,000. It begins with:

> "The first mission of this newspaper is to tell the truth as the truth can be ascertained."

The press was the major force in "exposing" Aramony's lifestyle and the spinoffs. As is customary with the press, only the worst aspects of Aramony's lifestyle were discussed as well as criticisms of the spinoffs as being a repository for Aramony's friends, colleagues, and relatives. It is these negative features which sell papers. Was it the truth?

According to some experts, generally accepted standards for journalistic competence include the following abilities:

- To recognize a story (the intrinsic importance of an event, its inherent human interest, its novelty, its consequences, etc.);
- To use language well enough to convey the story adequately to readers;
- To organize and edit copy so that a story can fit into a limited space; and
- To check facts quickly and accurately and to weigh the various elements of a story so that they are fairly represented in the final product.[21]

The reporter, Charles Shepard, has been widely hailed as meeting these criteria. I heard only positive comments from United Way of

America staff and from those who were impressed with his understanding of United Way on the "Nightline" show on February 27.

It is unlikely that the ramifications of these events would have been so vast were it not for the massive, front-page treatment it received. The previously published Jack Anderson article created virtually no stir, and the *Regardies* article which hit the stands between the two Shepard articles did not have the same impact because of its limited distribution and because it served a local market. *The Washington Post* made deliberate decisions to take the high road and not deal with the seamier allegations regarding Aramony's personal lifestyle, which had been provided to them from apparently numerous sources. Shepard had pulled it all together in a few months, although I was told he was not even sure he had a good story until a short time before the first article was published.

CONCLUSION

This chapter has demonstrated the crucial importance of public trust. This trust is based on how people expect charities and those who run them to behave. When these perceptions do not meet expectations, the public trust is violated. The United Way, more than any other charity, is considered to be a national charity and, until recently, possibly the most sacrosanct and respected in the nation. It violated that trust, not because it broke laws, but because it violated commonly accepted ethical standards which have their origins in the twilight years of the republic.

REFERENCES

1. A statement by The Independent Sector. "Ethics and the Nation's Voluntary and Philanthropic Community." (Washington, D.C.: Independent Sector, 1991), p. 5.
2. *Ibid*, p. 22. A definition provided by the Josephson Institute for Ethics.
3. Henry C. Suhrke, "An Ethical Desert," *Philanthropic Monthly*, Vol. 24, No. 7 (September 1991), pp. 5–15. See also Robert L. Payton's *Philanthropy, Voluntary Action for the Public Good* (MacMillan, 1988).
4. *Independent Sector*, pp. 136–143.
5. "Summary and Graphs of December 1989 Gallup Survey," (United Way of America, 1990), unpublished.
6. "Charity is Top Priority for Americans, Poll Finds," *Chronicle of Philanthropy* (July 14, 1992).
7. Giving and Volunteering 1992. Findings from a National Survey. (Washington, D.C.: Independent Sector, 1992), p. 192.

8. *Ibid*, p. 267.

9. *Ibid*, p. 6.

10. National Charities Information Bureau, Standards in Philanthropy Pamphlet (New York: National Charities Information Bureau, 1991), p. 2.

11. Candace Van Salsen, "CBBB Standards for Charitable Solicitations: Their History, Purpose and Application," *Insight* (Issue 1), (Arlington, VA: Council of Better Business Bureaus, 1987).

12. *Independent Sector*, pp. 162–170.

13. *Ibid*, pp. 178–181.

14. Hank Rubin, "Dimensions of Institutional Ethics: A Framework for Interpreting the Ethical Context of the Nonprofit Sector," *Nonprofit Organization* (Pacific Grove, CA: Brooks/Cole 1990), pp. 211–216.

15. "Ex-Chief of United Way Vows to Fight Accusations," *New York Times* (April 10, 1992).

16. Robert K. Greenleaf, *The Servant as Leader* (Indianapolis: The Robert K. Greenleaf Center, 1991), p. 18.

17. The Independent Sector, pp. 12–16.

18. *Ibid*, p. 7.

19. Verner, Liipfert, Bernhard, McPherson and Hand, *Report to the Board of Governors of United Way of America* (April 2, 1992).

20. From unpublished report of the Accounting Issues Committee of the National Association of State Charity Officials (September 10, 1992), revised.

21. Stephen Klaidman and Tom L. Beauchamp, "The Virtuous Journalist: Morality in Journalism," *Philosophical Issues in Journalism*, Elliot D. Cohen, ed. (New York: Oxford University, 1992), pp. 46–47.

CHAPTER 8

Issues Facing the New United Way

> "The individual can hardly feel he has a unique role in our society unless in fact he has one. He can hardly be expected to feel that what he personally does can make a difference in this world unless it does. This is a lesson—the uniqueness of every human being—that we in our business have learned that we neglect only at our peril."[1]
>
> John D. deButts, Former Chairman of the Board
> of America Telephone & Telegraph Company

This chapter will discuss some key issues facing United Way of America and the United Way movement now and in the future: board governance and responsibility, competition and donor choice, unrelated business income tax, and tax reform. The heart and soul of the organization came to be embodied in the vision of one person who operated in an environment which created few if any checks and balances on his lifestyle and behavior. For the United Way, the country's foremost charity, this complete centralization of power was particularly disastrous. The success of the charitable cause itself depends upon the standards of its leaders more than any other institution in our society— on the same level as religion. Helping people is the *only* reason for the existence of the United Way. Through the unchecked management policies of its leader, it created an egregious violation of the public trust.

Blame for what went wrong and why does not lie with Aramony alone. The entire United Way movement simply failed to recognize and deal with the problems of its professional leadership until it was too late. Placing blame and fault is far easier than determining the causes of the crisis. In essence, it was the fault of everyone who knew what was happening and could see the handwriting on the wall. The senior executives on the national staff failed to confront Aramony, the professionals in the field failed to provide the organizational leadership themselves and exercise their power to withhold their support until it was too late, and, lastly, the Board failed to understand the different perceptions people have of organizations which make profit their measure of success as opposed to those whose bottom line is serving people.

But it's more than that. It is an issue of means and ends. Great things were accomplished under the leadership of Bill Aramony; no one denies that. What caused the crisis were numerous missteps during the journey, not the destination itself. The previous chapters have attempted to describe this journey, a journey which lasted for over two decades. As it progressed, the baggage became too heavy, the road increasingly cloudy, and the compass didn't work any more. Our leader had lost his way. Failure was inevitable.

The journey can now continue because the vitality of the United Way does not depend upon one person. Its friends and supporters are legion. They number among the tens of thousands of contributors in every community in the nation and among the millions of beneficiaries. The United Way system is fundamentally a democratic system. Its constituencies have spoken. Democratic systems eventually replace their wayward leaders. That's why the United Way will last as long as our system of democracy lasts.

Under the interim leadership of Kenneth Dam and the new president, Elaine Chao, efforts have been undertaken to correct the inadequacies of board governance—some even would call it overcorrection. Appropriate board governance is the most critical issue facing the United Way, not just on the national level, but in communities as well. Other charitable organizations of the sector have also been affected. Once this governance issue is settled, the United Way will face other challenges concerning its relationship with its environment.

BOARDS OF DIRECTORS—THEIR ORIGINS AND RESPONSIBILITIES

Trusteeship is the holding of a charter of public trust *for* an institution.[2]

The Board of Governors of United Way of America must bear a major brunt of the responsibility for the tragic events that befell United Way of America, and by extension, all voluntary organizations in America in the spring of 1992. As agents of the public trust, it was their responsibility and theirs alone to exercise the proper oversight. Nowhere in this country is this responsibility more important than at United Way of America. United Way was the paramount, and until February 1992, one of the most respected charitable organizations in the nation. Although lesser charities might fall as a result of what happened, the United Way, which held up so many charities with its broad shoulders, was considered one of the most sacrosanct charities of all.

One of the most widely used definitions of a "board" is the one put forward by Cyril O. Houle, author of *Governing Boards* and considered one of the nation's leading experts on the subject:

> "A *board* is an organized group of people with the authority collectively to control and foster an institution that is usually administered by a qualified executive and staff."[3]

In early days of our republic, when some form of government became necessary, most decisions were made by everyone in the village or town. These became known as town meetings. This was democracy in its most pure form. At the same time as governments began to organize themselves into more manageable oversight entities, public boards developed for school systems, libraries, roads, welfare problems, museums, and so on. Citizens interested in these activities represented the will of the people—the larger community, as it were. As our society became more complex, the decision-making process had to change. Obviously all of the people could not make all of the decisions all of the time; small groups of people began to represent the common good in areas other than the government sector.

Thus, the same specialization and decentralization of authority began in the voluntary sector as well as with the government. As voluntary organizations grew, it was necessary for a group of people, smaller than the entire membership, to provide the requisite oversight. Frequently, voluntary organizations represent the inspiration of great leaders who want to make a change. A board of citizens would then come into being to help him or her accomplish the socially useful goal. Thus, in 1636, Harvard University created what was probably the first of such boards recognizable in form and function as similar to those seen on the American business landscape today.[4] Leaders like Ben Franklin created the junta of community members and friends to help him carry out his dreams for the betterment of his hometown of Philadelphia. Modern-day examples include political gadfly John Gardner, chairman of the Urban Coalition and founder of Common Cause; consumer advocate Ralph Nader, founder of "Nader's Raiders" and numerous other consumer rights groups; and labor organizers, such as Cesar Chavez, founder of La Causa.

Corporate boards evolved in similar fashion in order to manufacture goods and promote their sales or to create services and deliver them effectively at a profit. Should this "bottom line" not be reached or some management failure occur which is not in the interests of the shareholders, the board members can be voted out.

Most individuals recognize that it is very difficult to assess the impact of community services, that is, identify a measurable bottom line against which achievement can be measured. Kenneth N. Dayton, former chief executive officer of Dayton Hudson, has served on many corporate, foundation, and charitable boards. He wrote that, in his experience, "a board's role in the governance of nonprofit organizations—both philanthropic and voluntary—is exactly the same as it is in for-profit corporations." He goes on to say that this includes moral and legal responsibility, strategy determination, allocation of resources, goal setting, making the tough decisions on top personnel, and the like. On a corporate Board, an individual will usually be paid for his or her expertise and also assumes some legal liability. However, when an individual serves on a voluntary board, the responsibility is actually *much greater*. The individual is expected to inspire and lead, and to lend his or her time and expertise by serving on various committees which carry out the mission of the organization.[5]

Brian O'Connell, president of Independent Sector, cites the most important quality of a good board member: "doing what is right." This may mean bucking the tide and not voting with the majority—just to go along and be accommodating. Other important qualities are *fairness* (balancing what is right with a sensitivity and concern for others), *controlled ambition* (that is, the ability to recognize and give credit to the contributions of others), and *flexibility* (being able to see another point of view). Lastly, he considers the quality of *enthusiasm*. "Nothing was ever accomplished," said Ralph Waldo Emerson, "without enthusiasm."[6]

After observing several dozen meetings, I hasten to add that in the strictest sense they followed the forms and procedures as presented to them by the president, Bill Aramony. However, the goal was almost always to achieve a consensus. This was considered the "gentlemanly" thing to do, that is, to be a "team player." I can remember very few, if any, who voted against anything, and almost never were internal procedures discussed.

However, material presented to the Board had already been reviewed and massaged, either by the officers or by the committee chairmen so as to eliminate any dissension at meetings. Board members who often disagreed or asked embarrassing questions were not given committee assignments and eventually left the board. I never heard any comment about a board meeting other than "Great meeting, wasn't it?"

A board of directors has many different levels of responsibility. Among the first and foremost is its legal responsibility, determined largely by the laws of the state in which it is incorporated. The National Center for Nonprofit Boards has published a guidebook for board members, which I have briefly summarized here because of its importance and relevance to several aspects of the United Way situation.

State Laws

The American Bar Association Model Nonprofit Act delineates most of the federal and state codes relating to nonprofit organizations. There are two basic documents which establish the internal law on nonprofit organizations.

The organization's corporate charter, or articles of incorporation, typically contains the organization's purpose and an enumeration of its legal powers and authority, as well as limitations of that power. Once its articles are approved by the state, the nonprofit must work within this framework.

The bylaws enumerate in greater detail the provisions of the articles of incorporation. They can be amended at any time. Most of us are familiar with these provisions, which include how board members are selected, duties of corporate officers, committee structures, and the like. The bylaws of an organization usually do not have to be filed with the state or otherwise approved by government officials.

Before major new activities are undertaken, legal counsel should be consulted to make sure that they are consistent with state nonprofit corporation law. State nonprofit corporation laws contain minimal requirements for an organization to be legally incorporated as a nonprofit in that state. For example, in the case of United Way of America, this means the laws of the State of New York. Among such common requirements of the state is the filing of annual reports. As previously stated in Chapter 6, some New York State laws may have been violated.[7] Also, although some nonprofits (like United Way of America) are incorporated in one state, but operate in another one, the requirements of the host state must also be considered, something not mentioned in the Investigative Report.

State laws may also include charitable solicitation statutes to prevent fraud and abuse in fund-raising activities. It is this area in which state attorneys general devote much of their time because the activity directly engages the consumer. Certain registration requirements for fund raising may be required under these statutes. Other state laws may relate to granting tax-exempt status and issuing licenses, for example, for day care facilities, health clinics, etc. State laws also enforce health and safety codes and could leave the organization liable to personal injury suits. They also regulate the extent to which a nonprofit and individual board member may be held liable for damage to a third party's person or property (known as the *law of tort liability*). Recently, states have enacted laws which make volunteers working with charitable organizations immune from tort liability. Board members need to understand and assess their potential exposure to personal liability in their state.

In summary, board members must be very familiar with all of these organizing documents and act in accordance with their requirements.

Board members need to establish internal policies and procedures and follow them. If they became outmoded, they should be changed. Nonprofit organizations should have internal policies and procedures regarding such operations as personnel, financial management, and travel. These policies are usually as binding as the articles and bylaws, and are so interpreted by the courts.

Although the number of third-party contracts which a nonprofit can engage in are virtually without limit, directors must adhere to contracts approved by their predecessors and recognize that third parties can enforce contractual obligations.

Federal Tax Requirements

The philosophy of nonprofit tax law has already been discussed in Chapter 6. Most board members are aware of the value of tax-exempt status, that is, the nonprofit organization is not required to pay taxes, and contributions to it are often tax-deductible. A significant requirement, which is worth mentioning again, is that the nonprofit must meet the "operational test" to maintain its tax-exempt status. This means that any significant change in direction, such as setting up profit-making operations, should be carefully considered to determine whether or not it might jeopardize the organization's tax-exempt status.

To maintain a tax-exempt status, a nonprofit with gross receipts exceeding $25,000 must file Form 990. In fact, it's a good idea to do it even if the gross receipts are less than that amount. In the Cumulative List of Organizations Described in Section 170(c) of the Internal Revenue Code (Publication 78), all organizations eligible to receive tax-deductible contributions are listed. Other forms need to be filed, for example, if organizations have any profit-making activities.

A board committee should review these documents to determine if the financial operations clearly reflect the board's policies. This is also an opportunity to make sure that the organization does not violate the doctrine of private inurement, that is, that the organization's funds do not "inure" to the personal benefit of individuals connected with it. In addition a nonprofit must comply with income tax withholding requirements and pay social security taxes and federal unemployment insurance taxes (your organization also may be required to contribute to state unemployment insurance programs).

Board members and administrators can be held personally liable for taxes and penalties up to 100 percent of taxes due for failure to comply with employment tax obligations. Nonprofits need to make sure that they properly determine their employment tax liability in the first place. This issue relates as well to whether or not an employee is termed an independent consultant (no tax liability), or an employee. The IRS uses a "right-of-control test," that is, if the organization has the right to control not only what the worker does, but also how the work is to be accomplished, that person is an employee, not a consultant.

Boards should have their employment practices reviewed by a knowledgeable attorney or tax accountant. The Fair Labor Standards Act regulates the minimum wage for clerical and support staff when an organization is involved in interstate commerce. Employers who violate this law are liable for any back wages owed, a penalty of an equal amount, as well as interest and attorneys' fees.

The Employment Retirement Income Security Act (ERISA) regulates pension and health benefit plans maintained by employers for their employees, should a nonprofit elect to provide such benefits. ERISA requires disclosure of terms of the plans to employees and ensures that highly compensated employees don't receive benefits out of proportion to those lower paid. Most nonprofits retain outside pension plan "fiduciaries" who exercise authority concerning the management of the plan and disposition of its assets. The board will be considered fiduciaries if they retain any authority for managing the plan. If a board member is a fiduciary, he or she must clearly separate that role from that of a board member. This individual is also personally liable if the fiduciary responsibility to plan participants is violated. United Way of America did not have such a person, although Steve Paulachak handled most matters related to pension information as well as the negotiations on behalf of United Way of America with the pension insurer.

And the board of a nonprofit must not discriminate against individuals on the basis of race, sex, age, religion, and nationality. As of July 1992, if your organization had more than 25 employees and received federal grants and contracts, you cannot discriminate against the handicapped or deny them program benefits and services; as of July 1993, the same provisions went into effect for organizations with 15 or more employees. Public accommodation provisions for the handicapped went into effect in 1992.

Liability. There are basically two separate types of liability: one, by those who have suffered personal injury or financial loss because of their dealings with the organization (third-party actions), and two, suits brought against board members by other board members, members of the organization, or the state attorney general seeking to hold board members liable for breaches of duty (derivative actions). *It is a general rule that as long as a board member exercises diligence and reasonable care, the member will not be held liable even for actions made in poor judgment that cause damage or injury.*[8]

To avoid any possibility of personal liability, a board member should fulfill all of the legal obligations discussed above and other obligations of the organization. Board members should attend board meetings and committee meetings and make sure that the minutes reflect their negative vote (I cannot recall any negative votes in United Way of America Board meetings.) Also, if a board member questions an action which is not voted on, he or she should submit the objection in writing. In a landmark decision in 1974 in what is commonly referred to as the *Sibley Hospital* case adjudicated by Judge Gerhard Gesell of the federal district in Washington, D.C., he ruled for the first time that there may be some cases in which directors could be personally held financially responsible for the actions of the organization they serve. Since there was no legislation on the role of boards of voluntary organizations, Gesell took the first steps in outlining the circumstances under which trustees of nonprofit organizations could be found liable for certain acts and how to avoid them.[9]

Some protection against personal liability can be achieved through indemnification by the organization (subject to state law), and/or by purchase of directors and officers (D & O) liability insurance. These policies generally have two parts: payments to the organization for indemnification paid to directors; and direct payments to them when not reimbursed by the organization. Since state statutes vary considerably, an understanding of the relevant statutes is essential. Where indemnification is allowed, its provisions are spelled out in the organization's bylaws.[10]

WHAT ARE A BOARD MEMBER'S RESPONSIBILITIES?

Houle suggests that all modern boards which have been around for a while are differentiated according to a *tripartite system*: the work to be done, the administration of that work, and the establishment of policies which guide it.[11]

Robert K. Greenleaf has a very expansive definition of the role of a trustee:

> Trustees delegate the operational use of power to administrators and staffs, but with acountability for its use that is at least as strict as now obtains with the use of property and money. Furthermore, trustees will insist that the outcome will be that people in, and affected by, the institution will grow healthier, wiser, freer, more autonomous, and more likely to become servants of society.[12]

United Way of America's Board consisted of top corporate and labor leaders, a smattering of ethnic representatives, and a requisite number of women. Although many of these Board members had had local United Way experience, they were not generally selected by their local United Way. If a Board member from a particular community was wanted on the Board, the chief United Way professional officer from that community, of course, would be consulted. Until recently, a local organization might recommend one of its Board members to serve on the national Board, but there was no expectation that the request would necessarily be granted.

One of the major criticisms leveled at the national Board was its failure to include a predetermined number of representatives from local United Way organizations. If such representatives were present, it is reasoned, controls would have been put in place, and many of the alleged abuses of the national association would not have occurred. However, if the Board is to be truly representative, it might consider having representatives of contributors, that is, on-line workers who provide most of the money to the United Way through payroll deduction, as well as heavy contributors, such as Walter Annenberg, who was among those most critical of the "excesses." Without broadened representation, accountability to the public and important constituencies cannot occur.

Well-established principles of nonprofit corporation law have determined that board members must meet certain standards in order to carry out their responsibilities. Until I did research for this book, I had never heard of these principles. I trust most readers have not either.

First is the *Duty of Care* standard. A board member is obligated to take "the care that an ordinary prudent person would exercise in a like position and under similar circumstances." This standard applies regardless of why the board member was asked to serve, for example, because he or she was an accountant, lawyer, or donor. Board members must attend meetings on a regular basis, read the reports presented to them, and ask questions if they do not fully understand the information on which they must act.

Second is the *Duty of Loyalty*. Faithfulness to the nonprofit organization must take precedence above any opportunity for personal gain. (This standard is often called the *doctrine of corporate opportunity* under corporate law.) Business dealings between the charity and its board members are subject to the highest scrutiny under this standard. Generally, these arrangements are acceptable if there is full disclosure and there is a fair, open process that results in a contract with competitive prices. However, recent events tend to indicate that *any* arrangements between board members and vendors are inappropriate because they do not meet the "smell test." It has not been reported that there were any business dealings between board members and vendors, and I cannot recall this subject ever being discussed.

Third is the *Duty of Obedience* standard. This standard requires that board members remain faithful to the mission of the organization. It is reasoned that nonprofits must carry out their stated activities which are not inconsistent with the central goals of the organization in order not to violate the public trust.

Michael R. Ostrowski, a charity executive, also points out that what emerges from an understanding of nonprofit law is that there is a higher standard of behavior for nonprofit board members than for corporate ones. With corporations, shareholders have a direct financial interest and can remove board members by proxy votes at annual meetings. The "bottom line" of profit and loss is a direct yardstick.[13] Local United Way members could also exercise similar power at their annual meetings by not voting for prospective board members or nominating others. However, these events have always been rubber-stamp affairs.

FUNCTIONS OF THE BOARD

Virtually every book on boards of directors lists the functions which a board should be performing. Several of these manuals mention the 12 functions of a board put forward by John W. Nason in 1982 and published by the Association of Governing Boards of Universities and Colleges:[14]

1. Appointing the chief staff officer.
2. Supporting the chief staff officer.
3. Monitoring the chief staff officer's performance.
4. Clarifying the institution's mission.
5. Approving the long-range plans.
6. Overseeing the program of the organization.
7. Ensuring financial solvency.
8. Preserving institutional independence.
9. Enhancing the public image.
10. Interpreting the community to the organization.
11. Serving as a court of appeal.
12. Assessing board performance.

Most of these functions were carried out by United Way of America's Board of Governors to a greater or lesser degree. As we have said many times, the Board totally supported Aramony. Generally there were no long-range plans; however, program goals were reviewed yearly by the senior staff. Some programs, such as the Program for the Future, were extended in various forms over a period of several years. There were no effective appeal procedures.

LOBBYING FOR SOCIAL CHANGE

One role for voluntary organizations which has been clarified in recent years relates to lobbying, which is the carrying out of activities to influence legislation. Lobbying by tax-exempt charitable organizations was restricted in 1934. In 1976, Congress passed a public charity lobbying law which permits most charitable organizations to elect to have their lobbying activities measured by an *expenditure test*. Lobbying may be "direct" as when an agent of the charity directly contacts a legislator (or his or her staff) or through grass-roots lobbying. Charities may elect to have their lobbying measured by the expenditure test, that is, they may expend money for lobbying up to certain financial limits.

If a charity does not elect to fall under this test, it is subject to the *substantial part test*. However, what constitutes "substantial" has never been appropriately defined. Bruce Hopkins, by applying the definition of the word *substantial* taken from other tax situations, suggests that it is about 15 percent; others consider it to be only 5 percent (based on a 1955 federal court opinion which suggested that legislative activities amounting to 5 percent of an organization's total activities were not substantial).[15]

In August 1990, after 14 years of lobbying by the Independent Sector and other groups, the Treasury and the IRS issued final regulations on lobbying by public charities which elect to have their legislative activities governed by the expenditure test. According to Walter B. Slocombe of the Washington, D.C. law firm of Caplan and Drysdale, "The terms of the regulations reflect—in every critical area—responsiveness to (though not complete acceptance of) the criticisms and suggestions offered by nonprofits during the long process of developing guidance under these special provisions."[16]

The Independent Sector has encouraged charities to elect to come under the 1976 law, which it believes offers ample room for lobbying by charities and avoids the ambiguity of the "substantial part test."

The Nonprofit Lobbying Guide by Bob Smucker of Independent Sector provides a valuable layman's guide to this often complicated area.

A WEAKENED UNITED WAY FACES A HARSH ENVIRONMENT

Once procedures which can ensure against abuse are established, the United Way will still have the more difficult task of determining a role for itself and how it will relate to its external environment.

The United Way of the future will have to address certain key issues which will impact the future of the movement in the years ahead. A primary issue has to do with the number-one reason for the United Way in the first place: control of the fund-raising franchise at the place of work. Over the years, this franchise has been eroded. In part, this erosion reflects the tenor of the times over the past three decades and the desire of people to take charge of their own destiny.

Eleanor Brilliant, possibly the most thoughtful independent chronicler of United Way events in these times, says it well in her recent book, *The United Way: Dilemmas of Organized Charity:*

> But the United Way . . . is now facing pragmatic and philosophical strains which are deeper and broader perhaps than any it has faced in recent years. It is being forced to respond in many directions at once: to be a universal collection agency, to provide extensive donor designation opportunities, to develop public-private partnerships with government, and to market its own services, as well as to help communities solve problems—but not to give up its hegemony of the one workplace campaign.[17]

A single campaign, once a year, at the workplace has been the central fund-raising vehicle for the United Way since its founding over a hundred years ago. The value of this approach is obvious. Even prior to extensive corporate involvement in the United Way, even before payroll deduction at the workplace, there was an historic effort to make fund-raising more efficient by reducing multiple solicitation of donors and by developing a rational way to distribute funds based on need. The United Way became the natural vehicle to pursue that goal. It received its greatest impetus during the two World Wars when the top government and private sector leaders demanded that fund-raising for the war effort be organized and well managed. The modern United Way was the fallout of this process.

An Age of Entitlements

The 1960s and its War on Poverty (established by the Economic Opportunity Act of 1964) witnessed the enfranchisement of minority groups and organizations. At the time, government largess to support these new organizations was relatively plentiful, so the organizations grew and prospered, making dramatic changes on the American landscape. As a result of this era in America, minorities achieved the right to vote without artificial restrictions, access was granted to public facilities not based on race, and housing and integration laws helped to produce a more open society.

This process resulted in a gradual change in the collective American psyche. People began to believe that they were *entitled* to other rights and prerogatives which emerged during this era in the area of hiring and college admissions. This is not that much different than the belief of corporate executives cited in the last chapter who believe that they too are entitled to certain preferential treatment when it comes to salaries and perks. And governments at all levels "set aside" certain contracts for minority groups, including women.

As a result of these developments, people began to want a greater voice in all areas of life. Many women demanded control over their own bodies and refused to remain passive victims of sexual harassment and victims of the "glass ceiling" which prevented their promotion where they worked. Company executives no longer would automatically uproot their families to move to a new location just to get a promotion. Minorities such as Hispanics, African-Americans, and Native Americans developed their own programs for self-sufficiency. Working people demanded more flexible work hours and benefits.

So when it came to their charitable contributions, the donors also became more sensitive and more interested in not only where their money would go, but whether or not it would even get there. This phenomenon was aggravated when the Reagan and Bush administrations, faced with an enormous budget deficit and politically unable to significantly raise taxes, had to cut off funds to institutions and governments which supported many organizations born decades earlier as the result of battles fought during the War on Poverty. Increased voluntary funding was the only recourse.

United Way's Consensus Versus Dissension Dilemma

The United Way was the premier voluntary organization in America. It had affiliates in virtually every community in the country. It had survived over the years because it worked and it had the support of big business and big labor. Yet, it had built-in incompatible elements. Its purpose was to address the most important community needs. In order to accomplish this, it had to achieve a broad consensus of community givers. The result was the only charities which met commonly accepted community standards received funding. The "virtue" of United Way, namely, being a product of the local community it served, had usually been able to reach such a consensus. However, in recent years, United Way members have been faced with increasing criticism and cancellation of pledges on such issues as abortion services provided by United Way–supported charities and, more recently, the unwillingness of the Boy Scouts to accept atheists and gays as members or leaders into their troops. Local priorities began to clash with national institutional concerns.

United Way members have been dominated by corporate and labor leaders who primarily wanted the United Way to support charities which provided services to people and helped build character. Corporate leaders perceived that the United Way could help keep the community healthy and happy, and that a healthy and happy community could create a climate which was good for business. Labor leaders were interested in ensuring that their members received such services.

Long ago, the labor movement had decided not to establish a separate organization to meet the needs of its constituency and decided instead to rely on the United Way–supported services to meet those needs. The labor movement itself was at the forefront of social change. Yet, social harmony, not social change, was the overriding concern for most supporters of the United Way. The agencies for social change which had arisen from the movements in the 1960s who needed private funding were told that they need not apply, or if they did, they would stand a good chance of being rejected. Thus, gay rights organizations, advocates for legal rights of minorities, and environmental causes were inherently not acceptable to the broad community leadership. They were too disruptive to corporate self-interest (for example, the environment) or community harmony (for example, gay rights).

United Ways have always been proud of their community problem-solving ability. Aside from distributing funds to worthy organizations, local United Ways and their leaders would often serve as chairmen of various ad hoc committees of interested parties to help solve special community problems. Often non–United Way supported groups would participate in these meetings.

United Ways are products of their pasts when funding of charities meant support for the principle of "least offensive to most people." In recent years, United Way members have established special funds to support "new initiatives." This is an attempt by United Ways to have it both ways. These special funding mechanisms usually circumvent the normal allocations process, while at the same time provide the local United Ways with the ability to support organizations which did not strictly meet their established criteria, but which were supporting a constituency the United Way wanted to serve for one reason or another.

Over the years, there has been an historic antifederation position of health groups such as the American Cancer Society, and the American Heart Association, as well as various arts and educational organizations. Health appeals have always been popular because it has been very easy for donors to identify with one disease or another. All people have had friends and/or relatives who have had either cancer or heart disease and, as one United Way of America Board member said, "No one ever died of the United Way." One of Aramony's most significant contributions has been to encourage the development of local United Way partnerships with these organizations.

The Trends—Are Clear—Increased Competition

Other trends which have made the United Way environment more competitive were cited in an unpublished paper by George Wilkinson and Linda Forbes of the United Way Strategic Institute. They include:

1. The number of nonprofit organizations continues to increase. In 1982, there were 124,000 active nonprofit organizations; by 1988, there were 400,000.

2. The changing economy resulted in declining home ownership and greater inequalities in income, as well as the two-wage-earner family, higher taxes, and a decline in disposable income.

3. Corporations have moved from their historic focus in the local community to a national and international perspective. Companies have also increased their focus in the areas of their special interest, for example, on education or on programs which provide high visibility for the corporation. Another shift has had to do with restructuring through corporate mergers, acquisitions, downsizing, and relocation—all resulting in the more frequent shifting of CEOs to new communities resulting in a lessened concern for local needs. Corporations have also taken a tip from the Japanese and increased the amount of in-house services they are providing their employees, most notably day care and fitness programs. It is critical to United Way positioning that the services it supports be available to everyone in the community. If companies begin to provide numerous services to their employees, there may be less interest in both groups in supporting the United Way.

4. Giving opportunities have proliferated through the use of direct mail, affinity cards (where a percentage of funds would go to a particular charity), promotional marketing (buy a hamburger and part of the money will go to charity) and special events. Electronic transfers of money make it easier for people to have funds deducted from their bank accounts or charged to their credit cards. They also mention that the computer technology will enable companies to operate multiple fund-raising campaigns with much greater ease.

5. Some charities have exploited telemarketing with great success, decreasing their dependency on direct mail with its rising costs. They also cite the greater sophistication by charities in the application of marketing, public relations, and business strategies.

6. The growing access to information has increased public awareness of alternatives for charitable donations.

7. Tax law changes have made charitable giving less attractive for the small giver or for the wealthy to set up family foundations.[18]

David Wase, a former United Way of America vice president, pointed out other concerns such as the unwillingness of the judiciary to tolerate monopolies or single providers of services, the increasing emphasis by companies on personalizing goods and services to retail customers (resulting in higher expectations of similar attention by donors regarding the charities to which they contribute), and negative advertising campaigns which directly seek to discredit a competitor's product.[19]

As early as 1975, Professor Stanley Wenocur, a widely respected social worker activist, articulated the political nature of the United Way. He was referring to its control over scarce charitable resources, recognizing that "past methods of managing environmental contingencies have brought about organizational rigidity and conservatism, which, perhaps, is an even more serious consequence for the viability of the United Way in an increasingly public-oriented welfare system," and that "local United Ways will in the future have to interact with their environments more 'pro-actively.' " He also suggests various "power balancing strategies" for charities within the United Way as well as those who want to be.[20]

The Competition Organizer

In the mid-1970s, the grass-roots, community-based organizations which had emerged during the 1960s eventually galvanized under the umbrella of the Committee on Responsive Philanthropy. The Committee grew out of "The Donee Group Report & Recommendations," a loosely knit coalition of public interest, social action, and volunteer organizations initially pulled together on March 6, 1975 by Pablo Eisenberg. He and his colleagues severely criticized the Filer Commission for concentrating on the problems of donors at the expense of the needs of beneficiaries of charitable largess. Although it made multiple recommendations concerning the entire voluntary sector, those specifically referring to the United Way are as follows:

> We, therefore, recommend national legislation to require businesses to provide equal access to workplace charitable solicitation and payroll deduction programs for all federated charitable campaigns if access is provided to any such campaign.

> We recommend legislation to prevent conflicts of interest between the governing boards and allocation committees of federated fund-raising organizations on the one hand and the governing boards of recipient agencies on the other.

> We, therefore, recommend that the governing boards of all United Ways, United Funds and similar, ostensibly representative federated fund-raising organizations should be discouraged from having more than minimal (preferably 25 percent or less) control by effective donors.[21]

In a 1978 article in *Society*, David Horton Smith of Boston College criticized a wide range of United Way principles and practices. He called for businesses to terminate the United Way monopoly at the place of work and to recognize multiple campaigns and for laws requiring equal access for other federations to the Combined Federal Campaign. He also said that designations are generally not encouraged because they go to highly visible agencies to the detriment of other pressing, but less visible, services. He even suggested that United Way of America be more representative of its own constituency, and that United Ways at all levels be more open, collaborative, and participatory.

The same issue of *Society* included a response by me which stressed the local nature and contributions of the United Way system. I indicated that payroll deduction is "a privilege made available by employers in the interest of the community. United Ways have earned this privilege by being efficient, accountable, open, and responsive in helping meet community needs." Edmund M. Burke, a professor of social work also at Boston College and a United Way consultant, also criticized the Smith article by citing several fallacies and Smith's lack of historic and substantive knowledge of the United Way.[22]

The National Committee for Responsive Philanthropy (NCRP) has become a permanent gadfly to the philanthropic sector since it was organized in 1976 under the leadership of former Urban Coalition and former Office of Economic Opportunity staffer Robert O. Bothwell. Although Bothwell has been a persistent critic of the United Way for a decade and a half, he is also one of the strongest supporters of federated fund-raising and payroll deduction at the workplace, and has expressed admiration for United Way's overall management capabilities in effectively running these campaigns. His major concern is that the United Way has a monopoly in the workplace, which he attributes to the interests of corporations to fund only those services which are "safe" and noncontroversial.

In her study of the United Way, Brilliant said that "the philanthropic community was now forced to recognize openly a concern that had long smoldered under the surface. The fact was that the United Way has historically tied to a group of large, established agencies, with affiliates located across our country, and generally with strong national organizations."[23]

She describes the "citizen review process," the hallmark of the United Way allocations system, as a rational process undertaken by community volunteers drawn from all walks of life managed by United

Way professionals. Volunteers are divided into various "panels" typically representing family service, character building and recreation, health, etc. It is assumed that this consensus-building process results in good decisions in the public interest.

Bothwell and his constituencies recognized that the allocations process of United Way was not a viable option for supporting the alternative funds which consisted of advocacy, minority, environmental, and social justice organizations. He knew that it was not possible for the government or corporations to open up their workplace solicitation to *all* charities who wanted to participate, but he firmly believed that employees should have the right to choose among other federations supporting these so-called "controversial causes." He indicated that Aramony and the United Way could have easily co-opted the "alternative movement" 10 years ago when it was just coming into its own. Now, it is much too late.

DONOR CHOICE—BECOMING MORE INCLUSIVE

For the fund distribution system, donor option is the camel's nose pushing under the tent flap, threatening to push out the occupants and take over . . . to say we are perplexed and confused about donor option is to understate our situation.[24]

James W. Greene, former United Way
Chief Professional Officer, San Diego, California

It was in the early 1970s when the threat to United Way's monopoly of workplace giving was challenged by the emergence of the Black United Funds and Combined Health Agency Drives (CHAD). The latter received little support from the private sector outside of colleges and universities and, in some cases, from the governmental sector. During the 1970s, as we have seen, the American Cancer Society and the American Heart Association had come back to the United Way movement, *not* as member agencies, but as partners with contractual obligations. Competition to the United Way franchise found its greatest expression on the West Coast. San Francisco was the first to permit the distribution of designated gifts to any bona fide charity. Philadelphia opened its doors next.[25]

Recognizing the inevitable, and sensitive to the new trends, local United Way members began to institute what were then called "Donor Option" programs. The initial intent was to accommodate donors in communities by making choices available, but not to emphasize them as the best way to give. At the same time, the virtues of the citizen's review process were emphasized. The citizen's review process tends to provide funding to organizations that are meeting a valuable community need but may not have much popular appeal, or be able to promote themselves enough to attract the public's attention, or may feel it would be inappropriate to do so. For example, it might be thought inappropriate to promote homes for unwed mothers.

In 1978, United Way of America's Long-range Planning Committee on "inclusiveness" (one of the five critical issues confronting the United Way as cited in Chapter 2), recommended Donor Option programs as an opportunity to "include" more groups under the United Way community umbrella. United Way of America had for some time been carefully monitoring donor-type option programs in Baltimore, Los Angeles, Philadelphia, and San Francisco. In 1982, the Board of Governors passed a Donor Option resolution which concluded that:

> ... United Way organizations ... consider ways to provide Donor Option programs in a manner appropriate to their community which can be integrated with the on-going citizen's review and allocations process.[25]

Aramony used to say that when he was a child growing up in Worcester, Massachusetts, the Community Chest banner which stretched across the main street would invariably be blown down in a strong wind. Eventually, holes were placed in it. Behold, the wind would blow through it and it would not be blown down. Thus, he would say, donor option, whether desirable or not, was necessary to prevent the United Way from coming apart.

A 1984 study by the National Committee on Responsive Philanthropy by Dick Cook of the Neighborhoods Institute of Baltimore of 12 of the most active Donor Option programs showed that in all but two cases, less than 5 percent of the total dollars raised went to non–United Way charities. Where agencies have direct access to the workplace, donations increase substantially, according to the NCRP.[27] There was little information provided on how to donate to other organizations, and generally the donor had to request a separate pledge card and the charity had to be written in rather than just checked off—all very inconvenient. A survey conducted in 1989 by United Way of America's Research Services indicated that 78% of local United Way respondents indicated some form of "choice" for the donor.[28]

Yet, the growth of the Alternative Fund movement has been dramatic. It has grown from 88 funds in 1987 to 164 plus in 1992, from fund-raising income of $56 million in 1982 to an estimated $310 million in 1992 a sixfold increase.[29]

The Alternative Fund movement achieved its greatest success in obtaining access to the Combined Federal Campaign, which raises money from four million federal workers, including those in the military. United Ways have managed most of these drives in local communities for many years (ever since 1931 when Herbert Hoover allowed the Community Chest in Washington, D.C. and the local Red Cross chapter to solicit funds from federal workers). Organizations which raise those funds from federal workers in communities are called *Principal Combined Fund-raising Organizations* (PCFOs). Today there are almost 500 PCFOs which solicit funds from federal workers. Most of the campaign PCFOs are still managed by local United Ways.

In 1956, the White House agreed to the solicitation of federal employees at their place of work. These campaigns permitted contributions to the United Way, the Red Cross, national health agencies, and an international consortium of organizations. Undesignated funds were given to the United Way for distribution. The next year, President Eisenhower, through an executive order, limited solicitation to three campaigns yearly (the United Way, the combined health campaigns, and the Red Cross). A sealed envelope system for contributions actually succeeded in reducing the amount of funds raised, a system which was not eliminated until three years later.

In 1961, President Kennedy, through executive order 10927, limited campaigns among federal workers to one yearly, involving three different federations, and transferred responsibility for fund-raising in the federal establishment to the U.S. Civil Service Commission (now called the Office of Personnel Management).

It was not until 1977 that a change occurred in the nature of the Combined Federal Campaign, when the Sickle Cell Anemia Association joined the CFC. Sickle Cell Anemia is a genetic disorder primarily affecting African-Americans.

"The purpose of the CFC should be to permit federal workers to use the convenience of payroll deduction to give to the charitable organization of their choice," said congresswoman Pat Schroeder.[30]

In the fall of 1979, precipitated by the NCRP, her Subcommittee on Civil Service held hearings concerning restrictive eligibility requirements of the CFC which denied access to less established charities. The subcommittee recommended "opening up" the CFC to such charities. By 1980, the U.S. Civil Service Commission changed the CFC regulations so that local charities which were not members of the United Way were allowed to participate in the CFC.

In July 1980, a federal judge ruled *(National Black United Fund v. Campbell)* that the National Black United Fund had been illegally excluded from the CFC, thereby striking down its rules which said that eligible charities must have chapters in every state and not spend more than a quarter of their income on fund-raising and administration. In part, the Court relied on an earlier landmark decision by the U.S. Supreme Court *(Village of Schaumberg v. Citizens for Better Environment)* that upheld the principle that charitable solicitation is a form of free speech. A year later, a federal court also struck down a requirement stating that eligible charities provide direct services *(NAACP Legal Defense and Education Fund v. Campbell)*. In 1983, a federal court held that charities could not be excluded from the CFC because they attempt to influence public policy through advocacy, lobbying, or litigation (although some provisions were overturned by the Supreme Court two years later).[31] A report issued by the General Accounting Office in 1984 criticized United Ways' control of undesignated money which "creates the appearance of, if not an actual conflict of interest."[32] Under the Reagan administration, multiple attempts were made to restrict access to the federal campaign by advocacy groups, but to little avail.

In 1980, only 33 national charities had been admitted into the CFC; five years later, there were 120, including minority, environmental, women, consumer, and public interest groups.[33] Seven hundred and eighty-five charities participated in the 1992 campaign. From 1981 to 1991, the CFC campaign more than doubled from $95 million to $204 million, while the United Ways' share moved over the same period from $65.3 million to $71.8 million. Its market share, however, has decreased from 68.7 percent in 1981 to 35.2 percent in 1991.[34]

In 1992, United Ways no longer received most of the undesignated funds which were divided, more or less, among all the participating charities based on their percentage of designated gifts. Experts estimate that this is likely to reduce the amount of money which would be allocated by community-wide fund-raising campaigns to local charities, while providing more money to non–United Way organizations.[35]

Although many in the charitable sector hail these developments, they also recognize that the system can become too open and unwieldy. Bothwell has said the system will become workable only if the charities who participate eventually form into federations themselves.

On July 25, 1991, the long-awaited Donor Choice Committee Report was submitted to the Board of Governors of United Way of America by its chairman, John J. Phelan, former chairman of the New York Stock Exchange and member of the Board of Governors. The charge of the committee was:

> . . . [T]o undertake a critical analysis of the advantages and disadvantages of donor choice and propose a plan to the United Way of America Board of Governors to help the United Way system in dealing with donor choice in a wide variety of operating environments.[36]

Unlike Donor Option, which was essentially a passive program which permitted but did not necessarily encourage donor designation, Donor Choice gives United Ways an opportunity to be more aggressive. Its single pledge card might include the United Way itself, various issues, or an "area of service," for example, day care, United Ways in other locales, specific member agencies, or nonmember alternative funds.[37] The report basically concluded that the nature and form of a donor choice program rests with each local United Way. In 1989, over 220 United Ways offered donor choice on a pledge card or on a separate designation form. These United Ways represent 63.6 percent of all the funds raised.[38]

As late as March 1992, the *Atlanta Journal and Constitution* reported on a meeting of federations competing with the United Way. One of the participants called the "donor choice" program of United Way "a smokescreen for restricting entry" into the $2 billion payroll deduction market.[39]

Donor choice is a critical issue facing the United Way movement in the years ahead. It has been studied and subsequently recommended to United Ways as a necessary evil to open up the monopolistic nature of the current system. Students of the subject recognize that if United Ways do not provide more flexibility in providing funds to organizations outside of its membership, they will eventually cease to be a major charitable force in the nation. Taken to the extreme, if donors increase designations to particular charities of their choice, then the United Way becomes basically just a neutral accounting service for channeling funds from the donor to the recipient. It is the citizen's review process and the availability of undesignated funds that gives the United Way much of its power. Without discretionary funds at its disposal, the United Way will lose much of its reason for being, and its staff and board will become little more than glorified accountants.

There are a series of other issues which bear mentioning because of the possibility that they could have a potential impact on United Way and the voluntary sector.

UNRELATED BUSINESS INCOME—A TOUCHY SUBJECT WHICH COULD BECOME TOUCHIER

Another issue facing the United Way and other charities is the issue of unrelated business income. Unrelated business income derives from activities conducted by a charity which are not related to its tax-exempt purpose (for example, a day care center renting out its social hall for weddings). However, the laws are complex, and situations can be structured in which the income is considered to be related. Recently, the seriousness of the issue has decreased; however, its potential impact on income to the voluntary sector at a time of scarcity could be an important factor in the future. In these days of increased government cutbacks and possible tax reform adversely affecting the United Way, voluntary organizations are increasingly conducting activities which might be unrelated to their exempt activities. Since the 1970s, this area has become one of increasing public debate. The purpose of the unrelated business income tax is to place unrelated business activities conducted by a charity on the same basis as commercial businesses with which it might compete, resulting in unfair competition. It may be useful to the reader to understand the underlying legal basis for evaluating unrelated business income since it was raised in connection to some of the spinoffs (particularly Sales Service/America and Partnership Umbrella) and since it affects many of the charities supported by United Ways.

Since 1950, the activities of tax-exempt organizations have been divided into two categories: those that are related to the tax-exempt functions of the organization and those that are not. The latter are called *unrelated activities* and are subject to taxation.

In order to determine which activities of a tax-exempt organization are subject to taxation and which are not, it is necessary to determine which activities are related to the exempt functions of the organization. In 1969, Congress began to look at activities not only conducted outside of charitable organizations, but those conducted within the organizations.

In order to qualify for tax-exempt status, the charity must meet the *operational test* to see whether or not the organization is being operated principally for exempt purposes and an *organizational test* to determine if its corporate documents allow it carry out more than an insubstantial part of its activities which are not in furtherance of its exempt purposes.

The operational test may be satisfied even if a charitable organization operates a trade or business as a substantial part of its activities if these activities are in furtherance of its tax-exempt purpose, and if an organization's primary purpose is not to carry out an activity not related to its exempt purpose.

Feeder organizations are those whose profits are put back into the business or given to charity. They are treated like any other business organization.

The United Way for-profit spinoffs, that is, Partnership Umbrella and Sales Service/America, are set up as feeder organizations. They are nonstock state corporations, which means that their profits do not rebound to stockholders, because there are none. The profits go to operating costs and for charitable purposes. They can legally be termed nonprofit, but not charitable.

The Revenue Act of 1950 added rules regarding feeder organizations. These rules denied tax-exempt status based on the *destination of income theory,* which held that the destination of income was more important than the source of its funds. These provisions thus prevented trade or businesses from achieving tax-exempt status simply because their proceeds were being used for charitable purposes.[39]

In 1986, the Supreme Court struck a balance between the two objectives of encouraging charity and preventing unfair competition. Thus, before a tax-exempt organization is subject to federal income tax, it must now meet three tests:

1. The activity must be a "trade or business."
2. The activity must be "regularly carried on."
3. The activity must *not* be "substantially related" to the tax-exempt purposes of the organization.

Many fund-raising activities are exempt from tax simply because they are not defined as "businesses" that are "regularly carried on" or are "businesses" conducted by volunteers or using donated materials. Unrelated business income rules are not clear since the courts are developing additional and sometimes conflicting opinions on what constitutes the presence of an unrelated business.[40]

In 1988, Congressman J.J. Pickle, chairman of the House Committee on Oversight, held a series of hearings related to the issue of unrelated business income. Proposals were advanced to modify or eliminate the "substantially related" test as well as numerous other proposals which would restrict nonprofit activities from competing with business.[41] However, the committee soon backed away from the proposals, and they were never submitted to Congress.

During the 1990 United Way annual campaign, the Business Coalition for Fair Competition (BCFA), a group of trade and professional associations, state organizations, and individual small businesses, distributed letters encouraging a boycott of the campaign because they claimed the United Way supported organizations, such as the YMCA and its fitness programs, which competed unjustly with small business. In 1991, the BCFA proposed a model state law whose provisions severely restrict the ability of charities to engage in activities which create forms of unfair competition.

It doesn't appear that the activities of the sales department or discount purchasing by United Way of America would have jeopardized its tax-exempt status. Neither of these services was likely to become United Way's primary activity or unrelated to its original purpose of serving its constituencies. At the time these spinoffs were created, there was concern that laws would be changed which would make the location of these activities at the United Way of America less desirable. However, there were other valid reasons for establishing spinoffs (such as freeing them from bureaucratic restraints of the parent organization). When funds are transferred from a taxable subsidiary to a tax-exempt parent, the income is taxable as unrelated income to the parent if it is in the form of interest, rents, royalties, or capital gains where the parent organization has a direct or indirect control of more than 80 percent of the subsidiary. On paper, at least, this is not true of the spinoffs, which were legally independent.

This issue won't go away. The following are some excerpts from an open letter to Congress by Barbara O'Hara (June 9, 1992), chair of BCFC, commenting on the United Way scandal:

> Or, did [Aramony] just take advantage of this existing Federal rules which allow tax-exempt organizations to syphon off funds into for-profit business ventures?
>
> For example, in May 1991 United Way of America was operating a video production facility service in competition with the many other commercial production facilities in the Washington area.
>
> With no changes enacted by Congress or by Federal rules, United Way set up a variety of businesses, as outlined in the news media. They were losing the feeling of being a charity and were gaining the feeling of being in business, with an incidental benefit accruing to their charities.
>
> The UBIT has not been reformed in 23 years. The flaws revealed by the United Way of America scandal may be repeated in tomorrow's news.[42]

THE TAX LAWS AND CHARITABLE CONTRIBUTIONS

> With individuals in voluntary organizations . . . there are varied ex-
> periments and endless diversity of experience. What the State can use-
> fully do is to make itself a central depository, an active circulator and
> difusor, of the experience resulting from many trials. Its business is
> to enable each experimentalist to benefit by the experiments of others;
> instead of tolerating no experiments but its own.
>
> John Stewart Mill, 1859

Among the most important external factors affecting gifts to the
United Way and its charities is favorable tax law and its interpretation
by the Internal Revenue Service and the federal courts. The Revenue
Act of 1913 was the first (constitutional) piece of federal legislation
which defined entities which would be subject to taxation. To do so, it
also had to define organizations *not* subject to taxation, that is, tax-
exempt organizations. The act defined tax-exempt organizations as
nonprofit charitable, religious, and educational organizations, fraternal
beneficiary societies, certain mutual savings banks, and mutual insurance companies.

These types of organizations are essentially those that have come
down through our British heritage and common law as it relates to
philanthropic organizations. These definitions, which were basically
maintained in subsequent legislation, had their foundations in court
opinions. For example, an 1877 Supreme Court decision stated that: "A
charitable use, where neither law nor public policy forbids may be applied to almost anything that tends to promote the well-being of social
man." The charitable contribution deduction was enacted about two
decades later.

The Sixteenth Amendment to the Constitution, which authorized
an income tax, was ratified in 1910, and the Revenue Act of 1913 not
only permanently established tax exemption for certain organizations,
but defined them better. This Act also added scientific purposes as tax-
exempt activities, as well as the doctrine of personal inurement of net
income to private persons. Also recognized in the tax-exempt sections
of the Act were activities related to the prevention of cruelty to animals
and children. In 1921, community chests, foundations, and literary
groups were made tax-exempt. The Revenue Act of 1934 prevented
charities from substantial lobbying activities, and the Revenue Act of
1936 made charitable deductions available to business corporations. In
1938, the Revenue Act stated that exemption from taxation of money
and property for charitable purposes was justified because government

is compensated for the loss of revenue by being relieved from a measure of the financial burdens of providing for the general welfare. The Revenue Act of 1950, in addition to restrictions on feeder organizations, added rules for unrelated business income which were seen as being effective in determining whether or not an organization should receive tax-exempt status.

In 1954, in a reorganization of the Internal Revenue Code, the section of the Code affecting charitable organizations was labeled as "501(c)(3)," the name by which the generic class would be known in the future.

The regulations explaining the 1950 law greatly expanded the definition of charity, bringing it closer to its British common law origins:

> . . . relief of the poor and distressed or of the underprivileged; advancement of religion; advancement of education or science; erection or maintenance of public buildings, monuments or works; lessening of the burdens of Government; and promotion of social welfare by organizations designed to accomplish any of the above purposes, or (i) to lessen neighborhood tensions; (ii) to eliminate prejudice and discrimination; (iii) to defend human and civil rights secured by law; or (iv) to combat community deterioration and juvenile delinquency.

The Tax Reform Act of 1969, whose oppressive provisions eventually gave rise to what was to become the Independent Sector, dramatically revised the federal tax law by imposing extensive changes affecting tax policy, particularly regarding private foundations. For the first time, private foundations were clearly distinguished from public charities. A *public charity*, in connection with carrying out its exempt duties, receives a substantial amount of its support from the general public or supports another charitable organization that does. Private foundations, of course, do not meet these standards. The Act also redefined the percentage limitations for deductions of charitable contributions providing a 50 percent limit for gifts of cash, among other changes.

In 1981, with the passage of the Economic Recovery Act, taxpayers could avail themselves of the so-called *above the line charitable contribution deduction*.[43] Jack Moskowitz, director of Government Relations for United Way of America, fought long and hard for this provision. It meant that for those who do not itemize, the charitable contribution deduction can be subtracted from an individual's gross income before the tax rate is applied. This was very significant for United Way because it also covered most of its donors, that is, taxpayers who do not itemize because they fill out the short form. They could now deduct charitable deductions in addition to taking the standard deduction. Unfortunately, this provision was eliminated in 1986. The advantages, however, were largely offset by President Reagan's budget cuts, which cost charities an estimated $110.4 billion between 1981 and 1984.

In 1990, a 3 percent floor was approved for itemizers making over $105,000 per year. It expires in 1995. Floors tend to go up and, therefore, decrease the incentive to give by not providing any special advantage to the donor of a reduced tax liability.

CONCLUSIONS

Of the issues discussed above, *donor choice* is the one principle affecting the United Way movement. It is by far the most significant external issue which will determine the direction of the movement in the future. The major purpose of the United Way is to meet community needs. How it balances this important purpose with the desire of people to give to the charity of their choice is a fundamental management and marketing challenge which must be met.

This issue of *unrelated business income* in an age when charities must look to other sources of income is an area which must be carefully monitored by the United Way and its affiliated organizations. Clearly, the creation of spinoffs, despite the brouhaha, is a viable means to achieve this end. Most would agree that the ability to generate income is much greater when these functions can be performed independently of a bureaucracy. Tax issues and lobbying concerns are important because they impact donations and the ability of the United Way and other charities to serve people.

REFERENCES

1. "Not Less Trust in Freedom . . .," a Tanglewood Lecture (Center for Human Values: Clemmons, NC, May 1, 1975).
2. Robert K. Greenleaf, *Trustees as Servants* (Indianapolis: Robert K. Greenleaf Center, 1991), p. 4.
3. Cyril O. Houle, *Governing Boards* (San Francisco: Jossey Bass, 1990), p. 6.
4. *Ibid*, pp. 3–5.
5. Brian O'Connell, *The Board Member's Book* (New York: The Foundation Center, 1985), p. 24.
6. *Ibid*, pp. 24–27.
7. Verner, Liipfert, Bernhardt, McPherson and Hand, *Report to the Board of United Way of America* (April 2, 1992), pp. 27, 33.

8. *The Legal Obligations of Nonprofit Boards—A Guidebook for Board Members,* © 1992, The National Center for Nonprofit Boards, 2000 L Street, N.W., Suite 411, Washington, D.C. 20036 (202) 452-6262. Used with permission by Jacqueline Leifer and Michael B. Glomb, pp. 3–41.

9. Houle, pp. 141–142.

10. *The Legal Obligations of Nonprofit Boards,* pp. 42–44. Suhrke strongly recommends *Board Liability—Guide for Nonprofit Directors* by Daniel L. Kurtz (New York: Association of the Bar, 1988) on that issue.

11. Houle, pp. 2–3.

12. Greenleaf. Michael R. Ostrowski, "Nonprofit Boards of Directors," pp. 12–13.

13. *Legal Obligations of Nonprofit Boards,* pp. 31–33. Also see: *The Nonprofit Organization* (Pacific Grove, CA: Brooks/Cole Publishing, 1990), pp. 182–183.

14. Ostrowski, p. 184.

15. Leifer, Jacqueline Covey and Michael B. Glomb, p. 18.

16. Walter B. Slocombe, Walter B. "Public Charity Lobbying: An Overview," p. 265, unpublished.

17. Eleanor L. Brilliant, *The United Way: Dilemmas of Organized Charity* (New York: Columbia University, September 11, 1990).

18. George Wilkinson and Linda Forbes, "Competitive Challenges to United Way" (United Way of America, United Way Strategic Institute: Alexandria, VA, July 1990), unpublished.

19. David E. Wase, "Strategies for Competitive Environment at the Workplace" (Alexandria, VA: United Way of America, March 1989), unpublished.

20. Stanley Wenocur, "A Political View of the United Way," *Social Work,* Vol. 20, No. 3 (May 1975), p. 228.

21. *The Donee Group Report and Recommendations,* pp. 24–26.

22. See "Commentaries: The United Way of America" in *Society,* Vol. 15, No. 2 (January/February 1978), pp. 8–21.

23. Brilliant, p. 77.

24. Robert X. Chandler, "Reconciling Donor Choice with Community Needs and Priorities in United Way Fund Distribution Processes," George A. Shea Memorial Fellowship Lecture, 1988–1989 (Alexandria, VA: United Way of America, 1990), from a statement by James W. Greene, previous year's recipient, pp. 1–2.

25. Chandler, pp. 9–12.

26. *Donor Option—A Consideration* (Alexandria, VA: United Way of America, 1982), pp. 3–4.

27. *Charity Begins at Work.* National Committee for Responsive Philanthropy (Washington, D.C.: 1986), p. 35.

28. *Donor Choice Committee.* Report to United Way of America Board of Governors by John J. Phelan, Jr. (July 25, 1991), p. 29.

29. *Charity in the Workplace* National Committee for Responsive Philanthropy (Washington, D.C., Fall 1992), p. 3.

30. *Charity Begins at Work,* pp. 13–44.

31. *Ibid,* pp. 24–25.

32. *Ibid,* p. 16.

33. "Government Charity Drive Begins," *The Washington Post* (September 23 and June 30, 1992).

34. "Rise in Gifts to United Way Fails to Keep Pace with Inflation Rates" (June 16, 1992).

35. "United Way Charities Fear a Funding Drop," *The Washington Post* (May 18, 1992).

36. Donor Choice Committee, p. 1.

37. Gary N. Scrivner, "100 Years of Tax Policy Changes Affecting Charitable Organizations," *The Nonprofit Organization* (Belmont, CA: Brooks/Cole Publishing, 1990), p. 128.

38. Donor Choice Committee, p. 31.
39. "Charities Want to Break United Way's Monopoly," *The Atlantic Journal and Constitution* (March 12, 1992).
40. Bruce R. Hopkins, *A Legal Guide to Starting and Managing a Nonprofit Organization* (New York: John Wiley & Sons, 1993), pp. 164–177.
41. Scrivner, pp. 133–134; also see Bruce R. Hopkins, "Unrelated Income Proposals Unveiled: Would Have Big Impact," *The Nonprofit Counsel* (May 1988).
42. Open letter to Congress from Barbara O'Hara (June 9, 1992).
43. Scrivner, pp. 126–137.

CHAPTER 9

Lessons Learned

Our responsibility is not discharged by the announcement of virtuous ends.[1]

John F. Kennedy

The story of what happened to the United Way movement in 1992
is a tragedy of immense proportions. Its failures were not so much
in the excesses of recent years, but on the abdication of moral leadership
and responsibility. Its anguish was not so much in fund-raising losses,
but in the despair felt by the legions of caretakers from across the country who must daily try to make a difference in the lives of the people
in the communities they serve against enormous odds.

This chapter will highlight a number of suggestions for ways to heal
the wounds, culled from my own experience and numerous interviews
with academics, experts, and long-term associates at the United Way
and throughout the voluntary sector.

The crisis in 1990 that affected Covenant House, a home for troubled
youth in New York City, took a similar path when its president, Father
Bruce Ritter, resigned after allegations of sexual misconduct. A top-
level committee (including William Ellinghaus as chairman and Rev.
Theodore M. Hesburgh, Rabbi Marc Tannenbaum, Cyrus Vance, and
Paul Volcker as its members) was established to rescue the organiza-
tion. It, too, immediately hired lawyers, investigators, and accountants.
In this case, Father Ritter was the sole "member" of the organization.
He appointed all of the directors and officers, and he had complete
legal and operational control! The Covenant House board eventually

asserted its proper oversight role and established appropriate bylaws. Now, allegations of "serious misconduct" are to be reported directly to the board. Relationships between directors and vendors are strictly regulated to avoid potential conflicts of interest. Competitive bidding policies were developed as well as those involving the employment of relatives. A new audit committee was established and the finance committee reinvigorated.[2]

The suggestions which follow will hopefully serve as a guide to those who work in and serve the sector to help prevent similar tragedies from happening again. Such social devices as laws, regulations, policies, procedures, and guidelines are, of course, only as good as the devotion and commitment of those who carry them out. In addition, there are certain conundrums which arise and trade-offs which are inevitable in arriving at an optimal set of recommendations for such a complex issue as governance in the voluntary sector. Its enormous diversity suggests that common themes and similar conclusions may be totally inappropriate to certain segments of the sector. Surely the reader will have other additions and suggestions.

13 LESSONS LEARNED

Lesson 1: Public Expectations of Charities

A charity is a charity. It is part of the voluntary sector, not the business sector, and must abide by the constraints imposed by the history, ethics, and public perceptions of the sector.

This book has pointed out that the problems of the United Way resulted from the huge abyss that separates public perception about what's "right" from what the United Way leaders "thought was right." Freud said that "the child is the father of the man." So, too, are the traditions of our nation when determining factors on how its citizens view their institutions. The past *is* prologue to the future. If these events demonstrated anything, they demonstrated one central fact: Voluntary organizations are viewed much differently than business organizations. And government is viewed differently still.

What is considered excess in the voluntary sector is often not even considered inappropriate in the business sector. Could one ever imagine a large company criticized by the public for forming a spinoff? And although salaries of CEOs of major companies are coming under greater public scrutiny, its negative consequences pale in insignificance compared to the public outcry towards the United Way.

Leaders of the voluntary sector have failed to demonstrate the worth and value of its contributions to American society. Social workers, like teachers, are for the most part poorly compensated. They clearly do not command the respect accorded most other professions. A major challenge to the sector is to elevate public appreciation and, hence, its perception of the valuable contributions performed by these individuals.

Lesson 2: Charitable Activities Must Be Defensible in the Court of Public Opinion

All actions of the nonprofit organization and its officers must be not only legal but defensible in the court of public opinion.

Clearly blame is not easy to levy. If Aramony were a different kind of person, the calamity may not have occurred. If the board understood popular perceptions of charity, the events may not have taken place. If United Way professionals had been able to organize themselves to pressure Aramony to resign prior to the public exposure, outcomes may have been different. And finally, if the national staff had had recourse to parties other than the press, this book wouldn't have been necessary. But these are all "ifs." The fact is that it happened, and history demands an accounting.

Every action taken by a charity or its leaders must meet what many have called the "smell test." If it doesn't smell right, don't do it! Another way of putting it was told to me by Washington lawyer Ed Sheppard. He said that no one should do anything that would be embarrassing if it appeared on the front page of *The Washington Post*. I've since heard this from others. Amen. Does this mean that charities need to weigh every decision in terms of what the public might think about it? Of course not, but they need to be able to defend themselves in public if such actions are ever questioned. Maintaining the public trust is the most pressing concern for every charitable organization, especially those which raise public funds. Most participants and observers of the sector believe that Aramony's salary was not out of line considering his almost four decades of service, his prodigious contributions during that period, and his immense responsibility associated with "managing" so vast a movement as the United Way. It alone might have been defensible. After all, the Board set the salary, and it was up to the board to defend it aggressively as it was to assume its responsibility by defending all of the other benefits, perquisites, programs, and spinoffs which it had voted for, a point made by Barry Nickelsberg, president of the Funding Center. He concludes that it is the United

Way directors who should be stepping down.[3] Aramony or any other nonprofit executive should not have to stand alone and defend decisions of its board, which is what happened in this case.

It would be trite to say that there are no easy answers. It is more a question of weighing options and making trade-offs . . . at best a very complex undertaking. In 1970, the Board could have selected a less flamboyant individual. It could have chosen a negotiator and compromiser. It could have hired someone who would serve its constituency rather than lead it. If the Board had followed this approach, it is unlikely that the same enormous number of accomplishments which took place during the Aramony years could have happened, simply because it takes a great leader with vision to do great things. What, then, went wrong?

Somewhere along the way something happened. For whatever reason, Aramony began to see the United Way as an extension of himself. This has been pointed out by several observers, such as Tanya Glazebrook, a former chief professional officer in Miami, Florida: "He seemed to believe he *was* the United Way," she wrote.[4] Only Aramony knew what was "best" and *no one* could tell him otherwise. He always believed that the most powerful voluntary board in the nation (which he had personally selected) would protect and defend him against all comers. As a last resort, he could use corporate leverage to lean on local volunteers to bring wayward executives back in line. As far as the national staff was concerned, he believed he was truly beloved by most everyone, and if he wasn't, well, the hell with 'em. Anyone he truly needed could be persuaded with more money and/or more perks.

THE BOARD AND THE ORGANIZATION

Students and observers of the sector have cavalierly stated that the fault lies with the board for not exercising proper oversight. Those who believe that statement may be correct, but such a position greatly oversimplifies the problem and, therefore, presupposes a prosaic but at best an incomplete assessment. There are two reasons why the issue is not so simple. One, the effectiveness of voluntary sector boards often depends upon recruiting board members from outside its own sector, that is, the business sector. Voluntary organizations strive for people with money, position, and clout. However, business sector boards recruit primarily, if not exclusively, from within their own sector. Public boards are often a mixture of people from all three sectors. Two, it follows that for a voluntary board to be successful, the cultural differences must be bridged.

Thus, we have a situation where the cultural differences between the two sectors can be compared to living in a foreign country. It is not that different when businessmen serve on voluntary boards . . . it is a different culture. Jonathan Powers, the retired IBM executive who assisted the interim president, Kenneth Dam, told it to me this way: "To the businessman, the product is not as important as the management process." This is why top business executives like John G. Smale can sell soap one day (Procter and Gamble) and then make cars the next day (General Motors). In the voluntary sector, it is more often the cause that is the product that makes the difference; the means is taken for granted. Volunteers and professionals generally affiliate with charitable organizations whose cause they like—saving stray cats, curing cancer, or serving food to the homeless.

The Board at United Way of America recognized that they didn't know anything about health and social services. Aramony told them that he was really running a big business just like they were. He talked their language. He was a great salesman. He implemented many of the ideas that were suggested to him by businessmen with whom he worked: Jack Hanley of the Monsanto Company for long-range planning, John Akers for marketing and the *nouveau* idea of "quality." In effect, Aramony convinced them that the voluntary culture was, or at least should be, just like their own business culture! This made them comfortable. This comfort was supported by the many accoutrements which Aramony made available to them: limousine pickups at the airport, the beautiful surroundings of the national office, and mostly, helping them think they had become good and caring community leaders after a day of cut-throat competition in their own world.

Board members believed that Aramony was the expert and knew what was best, and it certainly appeared that way. He correctly understood that these volunteers were busy people, and to gain maximum effectiveness from them, he would involve them primarily in the program areas, that is, the National Corporate Leadership program, National Academy for Voluntarism (the training program), and the Hispanic Development program (to bring more Hispanics into the field), and exciting new initiatives concerning illiteracy, children, and so on. The volunteers assumed that internal controls, which they weren't particularly interested in and didn't have the time for anyway, were taken care of. He would rarely recruit businesspeople to his board who were not chairmen or presidents of their companies (unless they were women and/or minorities), the bigger the better.

The volunteers had every reason not to doubt Aramony. He had risen to the top of his field in large measure due to his success within his profession and because his own peers had held him in the highest regard. Why shouldn't they as volunteers also feel the same way? It wasn't as if they had *really* selected him; his own peer group had largely done so years ago by putting him out front as one of their best and brightest. This is essentially what happened during the selection process when he was first chosen for the job in 1970.

Lesson 3: Charities Must Represent Constituents

A voluntary board must be widely representative of its constituencies, particularly those elements which provide support and receive services, as well as those who are influential enough to produce results; and there should be a limit to the number of nonprofit boards on which a volunteer can serve.

From Aramony's point of view, he believed that his success would be measured to the extent that he could mobilize the corporate leadership of America to influence government and the society at large for the social good. Twenty-two years ago, he had inherited a mixed board of charity executives, local professionals, and mid-level business executives. He knew that the top executives he desired would soon tire of endless debate and discussion about relatively mundane issues. Since he fundamentally believed he knew what the country needed, other feedback was unnecessary; he would simply explain to the top guys what he wanted and motivate them to do it. Therefore, he began an exclusive club and it worked well for over 20 years. Obviously, what he lost was someone who could tell him to slow down, pay attention to details (which he admitted in many interviews he had neglected to do because he was "a mover and a shaker" and not a "bean counter"), service those who pay his salary, and remember that he was running a charity and *not* a business.

Therefore, the challenge becomes one of finding a balance, a trade-off. According to Jane Kornblut of the National Center for Nonprofit Boards, some programs mandate representation from different groups, for example, government-sponsored "affordable housing" legislation. This act puts subsidized housing residents on boards with business leaders and politicians, similar to the "maximum feasible participation" programs in the 1960s. They are held together by a sense of mission—everyone working together for the common good. It is not easy to do this. Yet, those who do recognize that a balanced board, in some ways less powerful perhaps, nevertheless reflects the community and constituency from which it came and which it is pledged to serve.

Nonprofit executives must be able to establish a sense of common mission and purpose so that they are able to work with a representative board to achieve greatness. Aramony easily had the capacity to do this, but he chose not to. Diversity threatened him. He wanted a powerful board but also one that he could control, a board that would trust him. He would not be surrounded by people who would question his decisions.

In addition, it is important that volunteers have sufficient time to devote to voluntary board work. Most of the volunteers with whom I worked served on many voluntary boards. Proper oversight is an important public responsibility. There is no free ride towards status and recognition. It means more that just doing the "fun things" in the program areas. It means studying and asking questions about the less interesting areas of finance and personnel policies and practices (accountants and auditors, please don't take offense!).

The Volunteer Consulting Group, Inc., founded over 20 years ago by the Harvard Business School Club of New York, is a good resource for top-level volunteers.

Lesson 4: Character Is More Important than Administrative Ability

Always select character and commitment over managerial ability when selecting executive and program staff.

A major fallacy perpetuated by corporate executives and well-paid managers in the voluntary sector (and their friends and associates) is that the community must pay top dollar to get a good manager. How about paying top dollar to get a good person? The voluntary sector *cannot ever* afford to sacrifice character to management. The impression has often been that high character and commitment somehow are less valuable and antithetical to the possession of sound management skills. Unfortunately, good management in our society is often equated with toughness as in, "He's tough, he's a good manager!" How often do you hear, "She cares about people, she's a good manager?" Not as often, I bet. This attitude is frequently found among businessmen as well who believe that their managerial abilities are the best society has to offer— better than the government's, certainly better than that of charitable organizations, and infinitely better than that of their competition. However, this country's vaunted management expertise has been losing worldwide market share in most industries mainly because its management is top-down, nonparticipatory, and geared toward short-term success.

The British may have the answer. They specifically train people to be administrators. The charismatic leader takes the top job.

Pablo Eisenberg put it well: "Better management has clearly been a need for nonprofits ... [but] for too many, management became an end in itself, overshadowing the services to be delivered and the human factor that characterizes public service ... good management boils down to people—how to care for and get the best out of employees."[5]

Lesson 5: Boards Must *Really* Evaluate Staff

Board members must set a clear mission and goals for their nonprofit organization and evaluate its top staff and program based on them.

The mission is central to everything an organization does. It not only informs the public of the organization's purpose, but sets the parameters within which it defines and carries out its goals. How effectively an organization performs these tasks in serving people is the basis upon which it should be judged, including the performance of its staff. Aramony interpreted the mission of United Way very broadly, basically, anything he decided it should be, and within which anything he wanted to do could be done.

John Carver, a consultant in nonprofit governance, says that voluntary boards must set clear, precise, and unambiguous goals for staff, and concentrate on mission, ethics, and long-term ends. It must govern, not just advise. With clear parameters, it will be easy to judge the performance of executives of nonprofits.[6]

Lesson 6: Boards Must Know Their Legal Responsibilities

All board members of nonprofit organizations must be knowledgeable of their legal responsibilities under state and federal law and regularly review them.

Although it may be obvious, boards must be aware of their legal responsibilities as outlined in Chapter 8. They cannot, and should not, depend exclusively on the staff for informing them of these responsibilities. In fact, they should obtain an understanding of these responsibilities from independent sources. The federal government and each state should prepare primers for board members outlining their legal and fiduciary responsibilities. *Independent* legal counsel should review any major initiatives such as setting up spinoffs. In fact, board orientations on basic legal responsibilities should be mandated by law. General obligations of board members are well described and summarized by such organizations as the National Center for Nonprofit Boards of Washington, D.C. The Center was established by the Independent Sector in part to serve this purpose.

Lesson 7: Boards Should Have Conflict of Interest Statements

Conflict of interest statements should clearly define all relationships between members, the charity, and its subsidiaries, as well as establish clear procedures for overlapping directorates.

Conflicts of interest, actual or perceived, were a significant part of the negative reaction by the public toward the United Way. Voluntary regulatory organizations for charities have long recognized the importance of this issue.

Under its first standard, "Board Governance," the National Charities Information Bureau states that a board should have "policy guidelines to avoid material conflicts of interest" and "no material conflicts of interest involving board and staff."[A]

In its "Governance" section, the Council of Better Business Bureau Standards for Charitable Solicitations states that "In situations where there may be a potential for conflict of interest, charities should take appropriate steps to avert an actual conflict. Many charities develop formal conflict of interest policies for board and staff members to address such possibilities. These policies can include such factors as competitive bids, full involvement of the entire board in the decision-making process and the affected board member abstaining from voting on the issue in question."[B]

Under its section on "Standards of Conduct for Nonprofit Board Members" in *The Legal Obligations of Nonprofit Boards: A Guidebook for Board Members* (cited extensively in the last chapter), the National Center for Nonprofit Boards says that a nonprofit board may wish to adopt a formal statement of conduct for its members. Such a statement could include the "circumstances under which board members must disclose business and family relationships that create a potential conflict of interest; the extent to which a board member may participate in board decisions in which the member has a personal financial or other inter-

---

[A]National Charities Information Bureau, *Standards in Philanthropy* (pamphlet), (New York: National Charities Information Bureau, 1991), p. 2.
[B]Candace Von Salsen, "CBBB Standards for Charitable Solicitations: Their History, Purpose, and Application," *Insight* (Issue 1), (Arlington, VA: Council of Better Business Bureaus, 1987), p. 5.

est; and policy for retaining board members to provide services to the organizations, such as accounting or legal services."[c] In its preface, the statement also says that grants or contracts may require certain standards of conduct in their administration, *such as antinepotism rules* (italics are mine).

The message is clear. Conflict of interest statements are a must for today's board.

Lesson 8: Boards Should Have Viable Internal Standing Committees

All boards should have a certain number of standing committees with outside special consultants reviewing work on a periodic basis. At a minimum, these committees should include personnel practices, audit, finance, and nominating.

There are a certain number of minimal standing committees which should be a part of most boards. Many have been adopted by the new United Way of America. They include committees on finance, personnel practices, and nominating. An ethics committee might be valuable in the beginning, although it should be only temporary. Ethics is a board responsibility and should be reviewed periodically by the board as a whole. Outside auditors representing different types of expertise should be consulted to review the work of these types of committees on a regular basis. United Way of America will probably ask for auditors from its board member companies to review the financial systems. Boards might consider something like an operations oversight committee proposed by the Institute for Community Leadership and Nonprofit Management in Virginia. The committee would:

1. Establish policies which define "executive latitude," that is, those values and perspectives of the board which would define the prudent and ethical parameters for the organization's management.
2. Provide ongoing oversight over internal management practices and programs.[7]

Lesson 9: Boards Should Have a Risk Management Plan

Boards must have a risk management plan in times of crisis which includes press, financial, and legal experts at the board level.

The National Center for Nonprofit Boards produces an excellent publication, *Board Members and Risk—A Primer on Protection From Liability*. It begins with the caveats, "Avoid it; reduce it, retain it, transfer it."[8]

Jennifer Moore in *The Chronicle of Philanthropy* outlines several steps an organization can take to manage an emergency situation based upon information from administrators and board members who have gone through such crises:

1. Develop a management crisis plan.
2. Set up special funds to cover unexpected costs.
3. Know the missions and values of the organization.
4. Gain support from key constituencies.
5. Respond quickly.
6. Be prepared to work long hours.
7. Be honest.
8. Expect a period of major transition.
9. Set new policies to help deal with an internal crisis.
10. Look for positive side effects from the crisis.[9]

Those United Way organizations who were aggressive in dealing with the crisis within their community did much better than those which hunkered down and hoped the problem would go away. The active United Ways went out to their various constituencies and offered opportunities for them to ask any questions and respond to them about the problems of United Way of America and in their local communities.

PERSONNEL AND THE NONPROFIT

If Aramony had been a different kind of leader, a different person with a more conventional management style, a strong case could be made that everything would have been fine. If he had properly structured the Board to include constituencies representing local communities, perhaps the excesses would not have been tolerated. If he had established more operational committees, internal financial, expenditure and personnel practices might have been more evenly enforced (a source of great consternation among the staff).

Lesson 10: Boards Should Set Acceptable Salaries and Ranges

Top salaries for chief professional officers of nonprofits who raise funds from the public cannot effectively exceed $200,000 at this time; and the disparity *between the top executive and the next highest paid person must be reasonable as must the ratio between the highest and lowest paid worker.*

A major issue has been one of salary. Although Aramony's salary might be justifiable, it could not meet the "smell test."

An argument that a nonprofit must be able to compete with business to attract qualified people is fallacious for anyone but businesspeople. The reasons people go into nonprofit work are entirely different than those which motivate people to go into the commercial sector. I firmly believe that after three decades in social service, very qualified people can be found who would work for a quarter of Aramony's salary and do as good a job. Ideally, human care professionals should be paid more for the work they do. However, in a free enterprise economy, market forces determine worth. As a result of the controversy, it appears that there is now a ceiling on top salaries for nonprofit executives (about $200,000). It's what Towers Perrin calls the "minimizing the noise factor." Anything much beyond that will not be acceptable to the public.

One argument voiced by businesspeople is that Aramony could have made a fortune in business. That may be, but it is totally beside the point. He chose the nonprofit field and, therefore, must be bound by its constraints imposed by the public.

Another issue related to salary is the disparity in compensation between Aramony and the rest of the staff, which was about two to one (that is, Aramony's salary was twice as much as the next highest paid person on the staff). It was also 30 times higher than the lowest paid staff person. In fact, his compensation was measured against other United Way executives in the large cities. The argument was made that Aramony should be paid more than the highest-paid local United Way chief professional officer. When the salary of Elaine Chao, the new president, was set, there was general agreement that it could not exceed $200,000. It was set at $195,000. Many of America's corporate executives in America make 85 times what the average blue-collar worker makes. In Japan, the ratio is closer to ten to one.[10]

Lesson 11: Boards Should Enforce Equal Application of Policy

All staff-related practices which include perquisites and benefits, including pensions, must be strictly and fairly determined and enforced for all staff, with regular review and appropriate appeal procedures.

For the voluntary sector, the democratic and fair administration of policies and practices is essential. Violations of these important functions at United Way of America was a major part of the problem. Any perks accorded some staff and not others must be justifiable and necessary to carrying out organizational tasks. There can be no perks without a bona fide business purpose. Flights on the Concorde should never be routine; however, a car and driver might be justified at times, for example. I believe most people think that a retirement package of $4.4 million is excessive by any standard, but especially for an executive of a charitable organization. Most of Aramony's pension money came from nonqualified plans; although perfectly legal, they depended upon the ability of the nonprofit organization to fund them. Outside consultants should report directly to the board on many of these matters. Nonqualified plans mean less money for services. In this case, a *lot* less money.

It is essential that appeal procedures be established at all levels. This is not to say that staff has a right to appeal to the board in personnel disputes, but the board should review procedures and practices to determine whether or not people are being or were treated fairly. Some organizations have a paid ombudsman who acts as an intermediary and reports directly to the president.

Lesson 12: Boards Should Set Terms of Office

Set a "reasonable" term of office for the chief professional officer with a mandatory retirement age.

In Chapter 3, Aramony's operating style was analyzed in some detail. It was important to point out that his leadership created a stressed-out organization and many unhappy people. The issue became one of recognizing this and doing something about it. However, the solution was not simple. Clearly, if the Board had reviewed Aramony's performance at any given time in his career, he would have come out with flying colors. It approved virtually everything he had ever suggested. One answer is to enforce Lesson 4. Boards need to recognize there is a time in the life of an organization for certain people at certain times. Most observers of the United Way would agree that Bill Aramony may have been the right kind of person for the United Way in the 1970s and the early 1980s. Yet, no one is indispensable. Aramony told me that he wouldn't leave because there was no one in the country who was good enough to succeed him. It is truly unfortunate. He could have left the United Way a hero, an *eminence grise* of philanthropy as suggested by Linda Grant in the *Los Angeles Times Magazine*.[11] Many feel that he should have left no later than the time of United Way's Bicentennial. Therefore, it is necessary to set a strict limitation on tenure, just like we do with our country's president, regardless of the excellent work of a chief executive.

Lesson 13: Boards Should Bring In Outside Evaluators

Boards should periodically conduct evaluations to determine staff attitudes and issues related to intraorganizational relationships.

One central issue remains. Would all of the knowledge on what went wrong and why, as well, as the lessons learned, prevent what happened from happening again? Armed with this book and other materials, would a board be able to spot organizational problems and take corrective action? At best it's a stretch; that's why board members must take their oversight responsibility seriously. It has been found many times that the public trust is a scared trust. Every board should consider bringing in a top-notch management consultant who reports directly to the board. The management consultant should conduct interviews and attitudinal surveys which would determine the problems, if any, of the organization. This is probably something most boards could never conceive of doing. Yet, boards must take charge. The failure to do so could be, as we have seen, disastrous.[12]

This book closes with 13 lessons learned. It began with Aramony's 13-Point Program, which revolutionized and revitalized the United Way movement. In some small measure, I hope this book will contribute to a stronger and healthier voluntary sector.

REFERENCES

1. *Asterick* (American Red Cross/904 April 1966).
2. A Report to the Board of Directors and the Oversight Committee of Covenant House (August 3, 1990).
3. Letter to the Editor (*Wall Street Journal,* April 14, 1992).
4. Tanya J. Glazebrook, "At United Way, the Easy Way Out Wasn't Easy," *Chronicle of Philanthropy* (February 27, 1992).
5. Pablo Eisenberg, "Corporate Values Could Poison Non-Profits," *Chronicle of Philanthropy* (March 10, 1992).
6. John Carver, "Time to Junk the Old Formula for Boards," *Chronicle of Philanthropy* (September 8, 1992).
7. "Operation Oversight Committee for United Way of America" (Virginia Tech: Institute for Community Leadership and Nonprofit Management).
8. *Boards Members and Risk—A Primer on Protection from Liability* (Washington, D.C.: National Center for Nonprofit Boards, October–November, 1992), p. 6.
9. "Crises Test Trustees," *Chronicle of Philanthropy* (January 29, 1991).
10. "CEO Disease—Egotism Can Breed Corporate Disaster—And the Malady is Spreading," *Business Week* (April 1, 1991).
11. Linda Grant, "Acts of Charity," *Los Angeles Times Magazine* (September 13, 1992).
12. I'm grateful to management consultant George Wilkinson for this particular construct.

E P I L O G U E

A year and a half has passed since the February 28, 1992, resignation of Bill Aramony, the president of United Way of America for 22 years. John Akers, chairman of IBM, and James D. Robinson III, chairman of the American Express Company, both former Chairmen of the Board of United Way of America, are gone, resigning under fire from their positions at the top of corporate America—Akers because he failed to lead his company into the future, Robinson for expanding too far too fast and in the wrong direction. An unsurmountable competitive environment for their products and services was a key factor in contributing to the difficulties they faced. In many ways, their problems were similar to those which have confronted the United Way movement during the later Aramony years and before.

Following Aramony's resignation, the United Way movement undertook the most intensive self-evaluation in its 100-year plus history. The Board and staff, under the leadership of Kenneth W. Dam (and later under the new president, Elaine Chao), immediately began to restore credibility by launching an intensive investigation by high-powered lawyers and investigators. The perquisites which Aramony had retained for himself were summarily eliminated in order to quell the public outrage, strict accounting and cost-control procedures were put into place, the staff was reduced by offering various incentives to leave in order to reduce overhead, and the involvement of local United Way offering various volunteers and professionals in the governance of the organization increased dramatically.

Almost from the very beginning of the events, United Way of America began to sort out its relationship with the spinoff organizations established by Aramony and approved by the Board. The spinoffs came under particular heavy criticism because of allegations regarding cronyism and nepotism concerning their governance and management.

Possibly more important is the intensive soul-searching done by each one of us whose hopes were dashed and self-confidence shattered. United Way professionals throughout the country, although many were uncomfortable with Aramony's lifestyle, failed to do anything about it. It was they who held the ultimate weapon—withholding of the dues which would have forced changes. Others, like myself, who had been one of Aramony's associates for many, many years, who were more aware of what was going on, also failed to act in any significant way.

Most important was the neglect by the Board, which had failed to recognize that they were entrusted with the oversight of a charitable organization and not a business organization. Whose fault was it? The board members of United Way of America believed that they were performing a vital contribution to their country. They reasoned that Aramony, the social welfare expert, knew what he was doing so all they had to do was "leave it to Bill." Aramony, on the other hand, recruited essentially powerful leaders, but social welfare novices. He set himself up as the new breed of "social worker businessman" who knew what was best for society. Board members would not have to involve themselves in the nitty-gritty of procedures and processes and internal accountability. These tasks would be left to the "clerks" among us. United Way of America volunteers would be involved in important program thrusts and initiatives of great benefit to the country. He, along with like-minded colleagues in corporate America, knew what the country needed. Under this scenario, the synergy between big business and big charity would eventually become a volatile mix. It didn't take much to ignite it.

The year 1993 is a transitional year for United Way of America as it responds to the events of 1992 and develops new methods of participation for its constituency. Regional councils consisting of both volunteers and professionals are being formed to advise the Board on policies and programs and to reduce the necessity of other special meetings throughout the year. A new Professional Member Council consisting of five people from each of five regions and 25 others appointed by the president will advise that person on issues, trends, and concerns.

At its meeting in January 1993, the Board of United Way of America reaffirmed its desire for leadership of certain national program initiatives—but only if they meet certain agreed-upon criteria.

For the first time since 1946 (the year following the end of World War II), campaign results had declined lower than the year before. This was attributed mainly to the economy and only secondarily to the crisis. As of this writing, just over half of United Way of America's members have agreed to pay their dues.

During the 1992 community-wide fund-raising campaigns following the public revelations of abuse, United Way organizations and many charities confronted an outraged public. "How could you!" was a response reported by a top United Way executive in New York City when he visited a workplace to seek donations. Others had a unique view of the United Way problem. They saw the United Way as one of the final bastions of nonregulation left in the country. Charities in America were the last setting where corporate executives could work out their own deals outside of an increasingly regulated corporate environment. Whatever the reasons, whatever the impact, things would never be the same.

Among the continuing issues regarding Aramony are concerns over the settlement of his pension benefits exceeding $4.4 million. Any settlement even close to this amount could have a devastating public relations impact. This possible scenario has prompted some United Way professionals to suggest that the courts be required to decide the matter in order to take the burden off the movement.

Another critical issue is how to balance a powerful and very busy board of corporate and labor executives with the need to perform the careful monitoring necessary to secure and maintain the public trust. This task was made more difficult because there was no *prima facie* evidence of significant illegality, only clear evidence of highly negative public perception—it was simply "not right."

A vibrant voluntary sector is critical to the well-being of the nation. Our serious social problems will require leadership and vision if they are to be resolved. There is room for *all* in this effort. The eventual success of the United Way will depend upon its eagerness and ability to reach out to its critics and work with them to mobilize the public in addressing these problems. No other organization exists which has the potential to build those bridges.

In the last decade of this century, the United Way movement risks being brushed aside, one step at a time or one city at a time, by those seeking greater participation and control over the community-wide fund-raising process. Overcorrections in the direction of "too much" representation is expected. United Way of America Board members, accustomed to dealing in broad policy areas, are finding themselves pressed by the new regional representatives to become more involved in process and procedures.

The most important issue may be the most subtle one. It has to do with what Aramony himself used to call the "soul" of the United Way. Clearly, the purveyors of the new regime have done the "politically correct" things. They have emphasized accountability, ethics, and participation—all very important issues considering the circumstances of the crisis.

Yet, these politically correct steps will ultimately be of minimum value, very minimum value. Rules and regulations do not inspire, they do not motivate, they do not stir the heart to care, to give, and to serve. Eventually, I believe the United Way will have to come full circle by demonstrating leadership and aggressive commitment to serve people and solve community problems—similar in many ways to Aramony minus the lifestyle and self-absorption he epitomized. This rationale may sound strange considering the foregoing.

Ultimately, the United Way will not be able to restore its previous levels of influence and prestige without a leader at the top who can articulate a vision of a more hopeful future, inspire volunteers and professionals with an abiding sense of purpose to achieve that vision, and embrace other charities which have for far too long been left out of the remarkable invention we call the United Way.

Time is not a friend of the United Way at this point in its history.

Having read this book, you are now rather knowledgeable about the management of charities in this country, private inurement and private benefit, spinoffs, and more. And you now know a lot about the United Way of America and Bill Aramony.

You have read a book about a talented, energetic, and in many ways a selfless man, who built one of this nation's finest charitable organizations. Bill Aramony did what few others could have done.

You have also read a book about a man who often misused the power he accumulated, who too frequently allowed his perception of his rank in society to cloud his judgment and cause him to make foolish decisions, and who became insensitive to the treatment of fellow human beings and to the appearances he was creating that would come to severely damage the United Way of America.

What Is This Book About?

It may strike you as odd that I would presume to tell you what this book is about, now that you have read it. But let me emphasize some points. This book, as its title states, is about a "scandal." It is also about a tragedy. It is about one of the biggest and finest charitable organizations in the United States, which was nearly destroyed by the doings of one man.

There is much irony here. The United Way in 1992 was not the United Way that existed when Bill Aramony assumed its presidency in 1970. The United Way in 1992 was a massive, complex, sophisticated, and highly effective organization. This is due in large part to Bill Aramony's leadership, drive, and vision. So, the man who built the United Way is the same man who nearly wrecked it.

John Glaser's book is a book of lessons.

The true import of this book is not the telling of a good story (which John has done). Its real value is in the telling of the tale so that it won't be repeated. There are valuable lessons here for everyone involved in the management of a nonprofit organization. This book should be read by every individual who is a director, trustee, officer, or employee of a nonprofit organization. This is because what happened at the United Way could happen anywhere. Everything that these individuals do should be tested against the standard of whether they would like their acts (or failures to act) detailed in a book of this nature.

There are three aspects of these lessons that warrant some additional attention. They are the role of the board of directors of a charitable organization, the proper uses of money for compensation and like ends, and the use of subsidiaries.

The Board of Directors

Charitable organizations and other nonprofit entities in the United States are managed by a board of directors. Sometimes this group is termed the board of trustees. (There are some instances where the organization will have only one or two directors or trustees, but they are rare.) In this sense, the structure is not much different from that of the for-profit counterparts.

A board of directors is a policy-making body. This is where the objectives of the organization are envisioned and the major programs are formulated. This is the "big picture" role of the board.

The board also has an oversight function. (I have never ceased to be awed by the wry oxymoron built into that word.) It should not micro-manage the organization, but its members should have a fair idea of its programs and how they are working, its fund-raising practices, its investments, and its compliance with the applicable laws. It should hear, from time to time, from the organization's lawyer, accountant, fund-raiser, money manager, and the like, to determine independently (that is, not filtered through the staff) what and how the organization is doing.

The law of charitable organizations in the United States came from the English common law of charitable trusts. There (as today), these trusts were administered by trustees. These trustees were (and are) expected to treat the resources of the organization in the same prudent manner that they would follow in managing their personal resources. The trust's assets are to be carefully managed and properly used; they are not to be wasted or frittered away. These trustees became known as "fiduciaries"and they were said to have a "fiduciary responsibility" with respect to the income and assets of the trust. Some today say that these individuals are "stewards" of these charitable resources. Trustees in this sense are more than caretakers of money and investable assets; they are stewards of the charitable organization's total resources, both tangible and intangible. This includes the organization's reputation—its image, if you will.

In carrying out these fiduciary duties, the board of directors is supposed to be proactive. While fiduciary responsibility can be breached by acting, it can also be breached by not acting. The days are gone when an individual sits on a charity's board to look good in the community, to be rewarded for something done in the past, or to fatten a resume. Being a director or trustee these days is important business to be taken seriously. One who is not prepared to assume these burdens should resign—or not take the position in the first instance.

What, then, should the director do? He or she should know the organization's programs, investment policies, and fund-raising practices. He or she should know at least a little about applicable laws, accounting principles, investment practices, and techniques of management, public relations, and fund-raising. He or she should read, from time to time, the organization's corporate documents (such as the articles of incorporation and bylaws); see to the accuracy of the minutes of board meetings, financial reports, program brochures and reports, and fund-raising material; ask questions (there is no such thing as a "dumb question" in this setting); and read materials and attend seminars about the contemporary role and liabilities of directors of charitable and other nonprofit organizations.

He or she should think. What is the organization doing? Can programs be done better? How is the staff functioning? Is everything of consequence being reported to the board? And here is the pertinent question: Is the organization doing anything that wouldn't "look good" if made public? This test, sometimes known as the "smell test," is a critical standard for a fiduciary to meet. It is not enough to avoid lawbreaking; appearances are all-important.

This is the standard that the members of the board of directors of the United Way of America failed. They knew (or should have known) about Bill Aramony's extravagances. They should have reined him in, curbed some of the excesses. But they did not. (As discussed below, by merely not being lawbreakers, they may well end up being lawmakers.)

The United Way scandal is a tale of abdicated responsibility by a board of directors. This is the most important element of this tragedy. Here was a governing board comprised of some of the most talented people in the business world; it was a "dream" board, a collection of corporate heavy-hitters that nearly any other organization could only wish for. With this wealth of talent, how could anything go wrong? Well, it did, as John has explained.

I have a friend and colleague, who I will not identify and thus not embarrass, who has worked as a fund-raiser for charities for over 20 years. He once observed that when corporate executives become directors of nonprofit organizations and arrive at meetings of these organizations, they "check their brains at the door." While that may strike some as rather harsh, at least in the instance of the United Way board, it does give the reader a perspective on what happened—or, more accurately, didn't happen.

Private Inurement and Private Benefit

The book is also about money—how a charitable organization should spend the money it receives, including gifts. It is about appropriate levels of compensation. How much money can an employee of a nonprofit organization be paid? How much money should be paid? Should employees also be officers and/or directors? What about travel expenses, retirement programs, and other perquisites ("perks")? What about employment of members of a director's, officer's, or employee's family?

The time has come to focus more intently on this funny-looking and sounding phrase, "private inurement" and its cousin, "private benefit."

To fully understand the difference between a nonprofit organization and a for-profit organization, you need to know about private inurement. These two words embody the fundamental distinction between the two types of organizations.

This distinction is best described by first looking at the purpose of a for-profit organization. Superficially, its purpose is to operate a business for a profit. But the real purpose of a for-profit organization is to make a profit for those who own the business. In the case of a corporation, for example, these owners are the stockholders. Thus, there is profit at the "entity level" and profit at the "ownership level." The true meaning of the term "for-profit" is the generation of profits at the ownership level. This means a passing of the profits from the entity to the owners.

In a business corporation, for example, this transfer of profits is accomplished through the payment of dividends. The net profit of the organization is passed along to the stockholders. This transfer of profits from an organization to its owners is termed "inurement"; the phrase becomes "private inurement" because the money is transferred to these owners to be used by them to advance their "private" (personal) ends. Thus, private inurement is the essential purpose and function of a for-profit organization.

However, charitable and many other types of nonprofit organizations are not supposed to engage in practices that constitute private inurement. It is inconsistent with the very concept of "nonprofit." That is, it is appropriate for a "nonprofit" organization to make a profit at the entity level, but it is inappropriate for a nonprofit organization to cause profit to flow to the ownership level. Actually, few nonprofit organizations are "owned"; they are usually "controlled." So, the word "nonprofit" does not mean that the organization cannot enjoy a profit; rather, it means that the profits may not be passed along (inure) to those who control it. These individuals are primarily the directors, officers, and key employees (insiders) of an organization. Thus, a nonprofit organization may not be operated in a manner as to cause its net earnings to inure to those who control it. If the organization is tax-exempt, as most charities are, private inurement is a basis for loss of the tax exemption.

It is rare for the board of directors of a charitable organization to sit around the board table and divide the organization's profits among themselves. While this would clearly be private inurement, in real life private inurement occurs in more subtle ways. It may mean unreasonable compensation, excessive retirement benefits and other perquisites, questionable loans or rental arrangements, and other business practices that trigger inappropriate benefits or other forms of self-dealing.

Private benefit is somewhat different. It means operation of a charitable organization in such a way that somehow, someone (it does not have to be an insider) is receiving an unwarranted gain. Unlike the law surrounding private inurement, the law will tolerate an insubstantial amount of private benefit. Consequently, while all forms of private inurement are forms of private benefit, not all forms of private benefit rise (or fall) to the level of private inurement.

(By the way, John makes reference in the book, from time to time, to "conflicts of interest." These "conflicts," while frequently troublesome, are not illegal and in most instances do not constitute private inurement or private benefit.)

Did the board of directors of United Way of America allow Bill Aramony to run it in a way that caused private inurement or private benefit to either Aramony or anyone else? Personally, I think the answer to that question is no. I hasten to add that the law is very general—mostly vague—on these points. Thus, in part, this state of affairs makes it easy to answer the question no. I do think that the United Way edged very close to the line and I fault the board for allowing that. The resulting practices resulted in a media field day and career enhancements for reporters.

This book forces a look at these difficult topics—a look that every nonprofit organization can no longer avoid. As discussed at the close, the book is timely, if only because the U.S. Congress is starting to look very closely at contemporary compensation and like practices of the nation's public charities.

The Spinoffs

This book is, as noted at the outset, also about what the media and the United Way crowd (including John Glaser) choose to call "spinoffs." These organizations were briefly discussed in the Foreword; I would like to add some details here.

This term "spinoff," loved not just by corporate lawyers, is used to describe the creation of an organization to take on a function previously performed by, or to be more effectively performed by, another organization. The function is said to be "spun off" from the first organization and placed in the second organization. In the language of for-profit organizations, a "spinoff" is a "subsidiary."

In the world of for-profit organizations, one corporation is a subsidiary of another (the other being termed a "parent") when the parent owns all of the stock of, and thus controls, the subsidiary. However, in the world of nonprofit organizations, stock is rarely used, so nonprofit parents control nonprofit subsidiaries by means of the indiduals who sit on the board of directors of the nonprofit subsidiaries; these individuals either also sit on the board of the parent or are handpicked by those who are on the board of the parent. Related boards of directors of this type are called "overlapping" or "interlocking" directorates.

There are many reasons why a nonprofit organization may want to spin off one or more functions and place them in a subsidiary. Management of a nonprofit organization may decide that the activity would thrive in a separate organization with a separate board. Sometimes the activity is deemed inappropriate for the parent and thus suitable for another organization. Sometimes the function is transferred to another corporation in the hope of avoiding liability that would endanger the resources of the parent. Sometimes an activity is spun off for tax reasons, particularly when the activity may generate income that is or may be taxable.

This matter of spinoffs is very common in the world of nonprofit organizations. A close look at churches, universities, hospitals, trade associations, and many similar nonprofit organizations will reveal numerous spinoffs, some tax-exempt and some taxable. Federal and state tax and corporate law amply support the use of spinoffs in this manner.

It is, therefore, a matter of judgment by the management of a nonprofit organization as to whether to spin one or more activities off into one or more separate organizations. As I said, it is a common practice and the law permits it—in many instances, encourages it. Thus, John is quite correct when he writes: "The establishment of so-called spinoffs is perfectly legal, and in fact may be an appropriate management decision, depending on whether or not its purpose is consistent with the parent organization's mission and goals" (p. 142). And "When the hysteria died down and the experts were able to provide a sober analysis of the situation, virtually everything that was done to create the spinoffs was, in fact, deemed perfectly legal" (p. 158).

This book squarely addresses these three very important elements—the role of board members, the proper use of money for compensation and like purposes, and the utilization of spinoffs—and does so in a way that will benefit every charitable and other nonprofit organization.

What This Book Is Not About

This book is not about lawbreaking. Readers may find this statement hard to believe, but I will repeat it: Bill Aramony did not break a single federal law. Neither did the United Way of America.

The "scandal" is about a set of facts that *look* bad; it is not about facts that *are* bad. In many respects, then, the public has been duped, defrauded, and misled. Despite the media hype and the many newspaper stories, magazine articles, and radio and television reports, no one did anything wrong in the eyes of the federal law. (I will admit that facts as yet undisclosed to the public could change this view, but I doubt if those facts exist.)

This scandal took on the proportions that it did because the media scooped up a batch of facts and presented them in such a way as to make it seem like wrongdoing took place. Television, radio, magazines, and newspapers were full of stories (and that is what they literally were—stories) suggesting evil doings, dark and somber tales of "high" salaries, employment of relatives and friends, rides on the Concorde, spinoffs and other corporate mysteries, and more. Reporters, television talking heads, commentators, and cartoonists took these facts and deliberately misled the public into thinking that laws were broken.

I will not claim I saw every television report, heard every radio broadcast, and read every magazine and newspaper article on the United Way scandal. But I saw, heard, and read a lot of them—and not one ever mentioned that no laws were violated. This scandal was, in too many ways, a media hoax.

In this book, John Glaser tells the truth. On page after page, he says it flatly: Bill Aramony and United Way did not break a single federal law. (Again, I concede he has some concerns about state law.) Despite many investigations, some by governments, no one has been charged with lawbreaking.

The only "law" that Bill Aramony and United Way broke was the "law" of "appearances." Bill did a lot of things he should not have done—not because they were wrong as a matter of law but because he as a custodian of charitable dollars should have known better. John chronicles the characteristics of the man that brought him down and that nearly took the organization with him.

Thus, the lesson to be learned from this book is this: There is a difference between running a nonprofit organization and running a for-profit organization. If one attempts the former using the rules of behavior of the latter, he or she is destined for trouble. In many ways, this is unfair, but it is the way things are—and the nonprofit executive and board member who fail to heed this distinction will, sooner or later, pay a price. And so too, tragically, will the organization they are serving.

There is nothing inherently wrong, as a matter of law, when the chief executive officer of a charitable organization flies the Concorde (or even flies first class), provides jobs for friends and relatives at the organization or at one related to it, earns a healthy salary or is provided a fine retirement package, times trips to coincide with personal interests (such as dates), or contracts for cars with drivers (instead of hailing cabs). But, before that chief executive officer does one of those things, he or she better think twice about the propriety of doing it, rather than the legality of doing it. He or she is the steward of the organization's assets and other resources; the test is not whether the counterparts in the business world do these things—the test is what will be the repercussions if the doing of these things is detailed on the front page of the *Washington Post*.

Bill Aramony's adventures were embarked upon at an awkward time for the nation's charities and other nonprofit organizations. Many policymakers in and out of government are seriously considering, right this minute, the factors that properly distinguish a nonprofit organization from a for-profit one. They are also focusing on potential new definitions of private inurement and private benefit involving amounts of compensation, the size of retirement and other benefits, and the placement of family members and personal friends on the payroll.

Today, the management of nonprofit organizations is more sophisticated and aggressive than ever before. This is due in part to the pressures of demand for more services at a time when government funding for them is declining. Traditional ways of raising money are proving to be insufficient, forcing nonprofit organizations into more creative ways of generating financial support. They are becoming more "efficient," "entrepreneurial," and "businesslike."

In many ways, this is good. Usually, society benefits when a segment of it becomes more efficient, sophisticated, and productive. Nonprofit organizations that have these characteristics can more effectively provide their services to those who need them. Managers of these nonprofit organizations bring expertise and an approach to leadership that enables the organizations to improve performance. Thus, this was a milieu in which a Bill Aramony could thrive and succeed. It was a context in which a United Way could soar to the top.

This development is also not good. As charities and other nonprofit organizations become more "businesslike," they minimize the differences between them and commercial businesses. The public becomes confused. Legislators and regulation-writers become concerned about forms of competition between these two types of entities. Courts become uncomfortable when they see charities engaging in commercial practices. Attitudes begin to change, as do laws and regulations—and, from the standpoint of nonprofit organizations, none of this is positive.

The public today wants it both ways. They want their charities to not "make money"; the year-in and year-out deficits reassure them that their favorite charities are truly "nonprofit." They want lots of volunteers, not business school–trained, highly competent, and forward-looking executive types. They want their organizations supported by gifts, not by commercial business ventures.

They get confused when they see sophistication, efficiency, and state-of-the-art management techniques deployed in the nonprofit setting. Subconsciously, they wonder if all of this is "appropriate." Deep down, they think it isn't. Confusion leads to suspicion. It is in this context that a major newspaper story playing up high salaries, luxury travel, nepotism, and corporate spinoffs triggers nationwide anger and revulsion. Suddenly, the public feels cheated by a United Way, they feel ripped off by a Bill Aramony. Few stop to think that no laws were broken—the whole "mess" just "looks bad."

The sensationalism has its intended effects. Newspaper and magazine sales increase. The broadcast media attracts more watchers and listeners. Reporters win journalism awards. Public anger evolves into complaints, which are passed along to legislators and others in government. Investigations start. Congressional hearings are held. There is talk of new law. The cry becomes: "If it's not illegal, it oughta be!"

Thus, John perceptively writes that:

The general impression of the public, and indeed virtually every constituency from United Way of America board members to online
workers, was that the excesses of Aramony regarding his salary and
perks described by the press were possibly illegal. If not illegal, they,
in some sense, should be—since they appeared to have violated acceptable social norms (p. 157).

Congress is starting to get into this act. For example, the House
Subcommittee on Oversight has begun a series of hearings to review
the activities of public charities, such as colleges, hospitals, and universities. The first of these hearings by the subcommittee, a unit of the
House Ways and Means Committee, was held on June 15, 1993. The
focus of the hearings, at least at the outset, is on the adequacy of existing
law in relation to instances of private inurement and private benefit.

The motivation underlying these hearings is twofold. One is the
view that the tax-exempt sector is growing significantly in size and
complexity, and the IRS has not been able to keep pace with these
developments. The other is that some charitable organizations are allowing their insiders to derive private benefit from them. These two
views are the essence of the opening statement by the chairman of the
subcommittee, Rep. J.J. Pickle (D-Tex.).

As to the first of these motivations, Chairman Pickle observed that
"[i]n recent years, tax-exempt organizations have been the fastest growing sector in the U.S. economy." He noted that:

- There are more than 1.2 million organizations that are exempt
  from the federal income tax, not including an estimated 340,000
  churches.
- These organizations annually generate $500 billion in revenues,
  have assets of approximately $1 trillion, and employ about 7
  million people.
- As of 1991, about one-half of all tax-exempt organizations were
  public charities (other than private foundations); there were
  519,000 of them.
- There are 30,000 charitable organizations created each year.
- The IRS has fewer employees today monitoring tax-exempt organizations than in 1980, funding for the Employee Plans/Ex-
  empt Organizations Division continues to decline, and the
  number of audits of tax-exempt organizations performed by
  the IRS has dropped sharply.

As to the second of these motivations, Chairman Pickle said that "some charitable organizations have abused the public trust and have allowed tax-deductible contributions to inure to the benefit of select privileged insiders." He said that staff review of the annual information returns for the 250 largest tax-exempt organizations found that, of the top 2,000 executives at these organizations, 15 percent were paid more than $200,000 per year and 38 percent of them were paid more than $400,000. He asked:

- "Is it appropriate for a charitable organization to shift $5 million, tax-deductible dollars to its for-profit subsidiary"?
- "[S]hould a medical school vice president be allowed to borrow $1 million, interest free, to buy and renovate his house"?
- "[S]hould charitable contributions be used to pay a $1 million salary to the chairman of an educational organization"?
- "[S]hould the administrator of a small pension plan be paid $500,000 in salary"?

He also noted the use of "tax-deductible donations" to provide "charity officials" with "extravagant perks, like luxury cars, servants, chauffeurs, country-club memberships, and extremely lucrative severance packages."

Chairman Pickle said that the purpose of the hearings is to learn "what the IRS knows about these activities, or possible abuses, and whether they should be allowed or stopped," "if federal law is adequate to ensure compliance by public charities and to appropriately punish wrongdoing," and "if the public is currently being provided access to the information necessary for them to make informed judgments about charitable giving." He added that these hearings "are not an attempt to attack the character and good work of public charities in our cities and neighborhoods."

Chairman Pickle signaled two areas of possible law revision. One is to speed up the IRS audits of tax-exempt organizations. The other is the imposition of a penalty, in cases of private inurement or private benefit, other than revocation of tax exemption. As to the latter, the concept is that of an "intermediate sanction," such as the imposition of one or more excise taxes as is now done in the case of excessive lobbying or political campaign activity by charitable organizations.

The first witness at this hearing was the new commissioner of Internal Revenue, making her first appearance before a House committee,

Margaret Milner Richardson. She summarized the law on private inurement and private benefit, and said that these rules "present difficulties for effective tax administration." Endorsing the idea of intermediate sanctions, she added that having as the sole sanction the revocation of tax exemption "makes enforcement of the charitable organization provisions difficult" and that "it would be useful to provide the Service with a sanction short of revocation to address violations of these [private inurement/benefit] standards."

As to abuse in the private inurement/benefit field, Commissioner Richardson said that "in particular, we are concerned about potentially excessive compensation." In general, she observed that "in considering any new sanctions, consideration should also be given to the possibility of clarifying the standards for tax exemption." She added, "Changes to Form 990 [the annual information return filed by nearly all charities] to enable the public to have greater knowledge of a public charity's operations may be appropriate."

She concluded her testimony with this thought: "Because public charities play a valuable role in our society, any new sanctions applicable to public charities should be carefully tailored so that they do not interfere with the charities' legitimate philanthropic activities."

It seems clear that the subcommittee will be making recommendations for some form of intermediate sanction. At least it seems clear that Chairman Pickle wants to do so. In a final statement, he said that he would be willing to support a freeze on the issuance of rulings by the IRS to new charitable organizations if the problems of private inurement and benefit are not resolved.

A Suggestion

This is not a law book and I am not trying to make it one. Nor is a writing of laws the real answer to preventing other United Way "scandals." The real answer is educating individuals who serve as directors, trustees, and officers of nonprofit organizations as to their duties, responsibilities, and (yes) liabilities. If an individual pays attention to what is going on at the nonprofit organization, thinks, is not afraid to ask questions, and otherwise follows the standard of prudence expected of fiduciaries, he or she is not likely to get himself, herself, and the organization into trouble.

Alas, it is too late. This "real answer" is not the only answer. The policymakers, the statute-writers, and the regulation-writers are and will be insisting on some revision of the law to prevent forms of private inurement and private benefit from occurring. This is most likely to take place at the federal level and, as noted, as part of a revision of the federal tax laws.

Assume, as I do, that law revision is inevitable. This assumption is necessarily based on the view that existing law is inadequate. There are two basic flaws in today's law on private inurement: The rules are too vague and the sanction is misplaced.

I am nervous about remedying the vagueness problem by statute. It will prove very difficult to legislate what is "reasonable" compensation, for example. There are those who advocate extension of the self-dealing rules that are applicable to private foundations to all charitable organizations. I oppose this approach. Private foundations are unique entities and the self-dealing rules as designed for them (as complex as they are) are working fairly well. But havoc and unjust results would be the consequence if the self-dealing rules were summarily extended to public charities. Besides, even the self-dealing rules, when the focus is on compensation, simply state that there is no self-dealing where the compensation is "reasonable," which is further defined as not "excessive." So, there is little help there anyway.

The rules on private inurement and private benefit are being worked out by the courts and the IRS on a case-by-case basis, and that process is working quite well. If there is any criticism, it is that the process is moving too slowly.

I think it is more productive to focus on the sanction. The only true sanction for engaging in acts of private inurement today is to take away the tax-exempt status of the organization. In most instances, the IRS and the courts are reluctant to do this. It is a harsh result, and also a harmful and counterproductive one. Revocation of the tax exemption of a charitable organization in most instances only hurts the beneficiaries of the charitable organization's programs.

Assume, as an illustration, that Bill Aramony's salary was in fact excessive (unreasonable), so that the payment of it in a particular year was private inurement. (This would be the result because Bill was the consummate insider.) Society would not gain if the IRS revoked the tax exemption of United Way. The losers would be the thousands of individuals who are helped daily by virtue of the many services provided by the United Way of America and the many local United Way organizations.

Moreover, lest we forget, organizations are legal fictions. They are operated by human beings. Whatever an organization does, it does it because one or more human beings made it do it. So, why "punish" the organization—and its program beneficiaries? Why not instead "punish" the human being or beings that directly caused the inappropriate conduct?

Technically, this approach is termed the use of "intermediate sanctions." This means that the penalty for some type of wrongdoing falls on the individuals involved rather than the organization they manipulated. At the federal level, this intermediate sanction is likely to be one or more taxes.

Here is my proposal—and I submit that the United Way "scandal" is Exhibit Number One for its adoption: Congress should enact one or more excise taxes that would fall on the individual or individuals who caused the nonprofit organization to commit private inurement. The term "private inurement" would not be differently or more expansively defined. An initial tax would be, say, 10 percent.

This tax would operate as follows. Suppose a domineering chief executive like Bill Aramony caused the board of directors of a charitable organization to agree to pay him or her a salary for a year in the amount of $500,000. Assume that the IRS is able to show that a reasonable salary under the prevailing facts and circumstances is no more than $400,000. Thus, the payment of the excess of $100,000 was an act of private inurement. Under today's law, the only sanction would be to revoke the tax exemption of the employer organization. But the employee still was paid and has (or has the benefits of) the full salary. However, suppose the sanction was that the recipient of the salary had to pay a 10 percent tax on the excess amount; that is a $10,000 tax.

You are probably thinking: That's not much of a penalty—the employee still gets to keep the remaining $90,000.

But suppose this initial tax also fell on each member of the board of directors who did not act reasonably in deciding that the amount of salary to be paid was an appropriate sum? (This form of reasonableness could be defined, such as by setting some threshold before the rules kicked in and allowing the directors to rely on an outside, professional analysis of what the compensation should be.) The $10,000 would have to be paid by every director who, acting unreasonably, voted for the compensation amount.

Suppose also that the individual who was paid the excess amount was required to pay the excess amount back to the charitable organization in a timely manner. Now this individual would have to both pay a $10,000 tax *and* return $100,000 to the charitable organization— and see to it that his or her salary for future years was adjusted to a reasonable amount.

Suppose further that if this individual did not return the excess compensation to the employer organization in a timely manner, he or she would be subject to an additional excise tax of 100 percent. At this point, the individual would be facing the requirement to pay $100,000 to the charitable organization and $100,000 to the IRS. And each board member who did not take reasonable steps to see to it that the initial tax was paid and the excess salary returned would also be subject to a $100,000 tax.

If all of this didn't work, the IRS could revoke the organization's tax exemption and still pursue collection of the various taxes.

There is precedent in the federal tax law for this very approach. The private foundation self-dealing rules are structured in this fashion, and there are like rules that apply when a public charitable organization engages in too much lobbying or political campaign activity.

The fact of the matter is that very little, if any, of these taxes would actually be paid. This would not be due to tax avoidance but to behavior on the part of insiders and the organizations to prevent the abuses from arising in the first instance. The law terms these rules "prophylactic" ones, and the experience under the three existing sanctions noted shows that that is the case. Individuals facing sanctions that apply to them personally will modify their behavior rather than be exposed to these taxes.

Would this book exist if these sanctions had been in place as the United Way of America and Bill Aramony were evolving to the climactic experience in 1992? No, because there would not have been a "scandal" to begin with.

I will close as I opened. John Glaser is to be congratulated for producing this book; some courage is to be recognized as well, since it pained him to so quickly review the details of this unhappy phase of his life.

My hope is John's hope: that this book will lead to the changing of practices (and perhaps law) by those who oversee and administer charitable organizations in this country, for the betterment of the charitable sector in general and enhancement of the programs that serve so many needy beneficiaries.

Bruce R. Hopkins
Washington, D.C.
August 1993

I N D E X

SOC.